6/11/17

COLONIAL CHURCHES
of VIRGINIA

COLONIAL CHURCHES
of VIRGINIA

BY DON W. AND SUE MASSEY

Howell Press
Charlottesville, Virginia

Designed by Lisa Wayand
Edited by Dara Powers Parker

Library of Congress Cataloging-in-Publication Data

Massey, Don W.
    Colonial churches of Virginia / Don W. and Sue Massey.
        p. cm.
Includes bibliographical references and index.
    ISBN 1-57427-136-9 (alk. Paper)
  1. Historic buildings—Virginia. 2. Church buildings—Virginia. 3.
Historic buildings—Virginia—Pictorial works. 4. Church
Buildings—Virginia—Pictorial works. 5. Architecture,
Colonial—Virginia. 6. Church architecture—Virginia. 7.
Virginia—History—Colonial period, ca. 1600-1775. 8.
Virginia—History—Colonial period, ca. 1600-1775—Biography. 9.
Virginia—Church history. I. Massey, Sue. II. Title.
    F227.M35 2003
    277.55`07—dc21

                                        2003007496

ISBN 1-57427-136-9

Printed in China

12 11 10 09 08 07 06 05 04 03   10 9 8 7 6 5 4 3 2 1

Published by Howell Press, Inc.
1713-2D Allied Lane
Charlottesville, VA 22903
(434) 977-4006
www.howellpress.com

DEDICATION

This book is dedicated to the Right Reverend Robert Poland Atkinson, fifth bishop of West Virginia, 1973 to 1989, and retired assistant bishop of Virginia, 1989 to 1993 (ordained deacon and priest, 1953 to 1954).

Thank you for being my friend and sharing your talent and knowledge of the ministry. Your support of my own ministry for Christ has been an inspiration in my life. I honor you for what you have been to countless numbers of parishioners—"A People's Bishop."

And to my loving and faithful wife and very best friend, Sue:

You once again have shared in a new project and made it worthwhile. We both felt the impact that God's people left at Fort Story (the site of the first landing); Jamestown, and the early church tower that still remains; and all of the colonial churches, which still stand as monuments to our early forefathers who, like us, had the freedom to worship their God.

—Don W. Massey

The Right Reverend Robert Poland Atkinson (left) and author Don W. Massey (right).

TABLE OF CONTENTS

PREFACE

A CORRECT HISTORY OF VIRGINIA WOULD BE THE history of North America itself," wrote Edmund Burke, "a portion of the globe, which, enjoying the invaluable privilege of self government, promises to eclipse the glory of Rome and Athens. In this part of the American Continent, the first permanent establishment was formed by the English, and it is here we must look for those ancient documents and materials, whose discovery will throw light on the history of the other States."

Virginia has a number of firsts among the colonial churches in America. Bruton Parish Church in Williamsburg was built in 1711 and is the oldest Anglican church in continuous use. The brick tower at Jamestown, built in 1639, is what remains of the church of the first parish established in the English colonies. Hebron Church in Madison County is the oldest German Lutheran congregation in the South; the building was erected in 1740. And finally, St. Luke's Church in Isle of Wight County, built in 1632, is the oldest Protestant church building in North America. It is also the only gothic colonial building in the United States, the oldest building in the English colonies of America, the oldest Anglican church in America, and the oldest building in Virginia.

Virginia was the name given by Sir Walter Raleigh to the whole country, when from London he was trying—albeit unsuccessfully—to found a colony on the Atlantic coast of North America. Raleigh named this region Virginia in honor of Elizabeth I, "The Virgin Queen." The area known as Virginia was located between the present Wilmington, North Carolina, and Charlottesville, Virginia.

The Church of England took root in America with the founding of the first permanent colony in Virginia. It was in 1606 that King James I gave charters to two companies to plant colonies in the New World. Unlike the colonies of other countries before and since, the immigrants to Virginia would enjoy all the liberties and privileges of Englishmen in the homeland. Part of this heritage, of course, was the Established Church. On 20 December 1606, three ships bearing about one hundred passengers sailed from the Thames. Since they voyaged by way of the Canary Islands and the West Indies, it was not until 6 May 1607 that the storm-worn vessels reached the Chesapeake Bay. A week later, the weary colonists disembarked on the north bank of the river, which they named the James. Some thirty miles or so from the mouth of the river, they began to build their first settlement, James Fort or Jamestown. Six weeks after the landing at Jamestown, on Sunday, 21 June 1607, the first celebration of the Holy Communion was held. It was the third Sunday after the Trinity. The next day the ships were returning to England.

The Holy Communion was celebrated by Chaplain (Rev.) Robert Hunt, whom fellow-colonist Capt. John Smith called, "an honest religious and courageous divine." The reading was from 1 Peter: 5-7: "Yea, all of you be subject one to another and be clothed with humility: for God resisteth the proud and giveth grace to the humble. Humble yourselves therefore under the mighty hand of God, that he may exalt you in due time: casting all your care upon him; for he careth for you."

John Smith said of the setting,

We did hang an awning which is an old sail, to three or four trees, til we cut planks, our pulpit a bar of wood nailed to two neighboring trees. This was our church till we built a homely thing like a barn, set upon cratchets covered with rafts, sedge and earth. Yet we had daily Common Prayer morning and evening, every Sunday two sermons, and every three months the Holy Communion.

Five years later, Virginia had a population of more than 1,200 scattered in nineteen settlements. The Assembly passed new laws concerning church affairs. Once again, uniformity was decreed and provisions made for building churches.

In June 1624, King James procured the annulment of the charter of the Virginia Company and, until the Revolution of 1776, Virginia was a royal province governed by officials appointed by the king. Therefore, the plantation period came to an end after King James took full control of the colony. The rule of the church in Virginia then passed from the Puritan party to the Conservative Church party, and thereafter the doctrine, discipline, and loyalty to the king were made to conform to the orthodoxy of the Mother Church. Puritans continued to live in Virginia in harmony until the rebellion in England, which brought to power Oliver Cromwell and the Puritans. Virginia remained loyal to both and governed herself independently during the period of the Commonwealth.

In Nansemond County, Virginia, the Puritans were concentrated, the most prominent member being Richard Bennett (see the chapter on Glebe Church, also known as the Bennett's Creek Church). From 1624 to 1634, the population of Virginia increased to five thousand. Except for a five-year interval during the Protectorate, Virginia was governed for thirty years by Sir William Berkley, who in 1641 had instruction to see that the Church was firmly maintained and no innovations permitted. Soon after his arrival, the House of Burgesses passed an act organizing the Church with vestries, similar to the parishes in England. During the years of the Commonwealth and Protectorate, the church could not give any aid to Virginia and the religious life in the colony suffered and deteriorated.

In 1660, during the Restoration, there were a dozen ministers left to administer the needs of some fifty parishes. Governor Berkeley, after being returned to power, took steps to correct the situation. He reported to the government in England in 1671, when Virginia had a population of thirty-eight thousand whites and two thousand Negro slaves, "that there are forty-eight parishes, and the ministers well paid. The clergy by my consent would be better if they would pray oftener and preach less."

Government of the Church of England in Virginia and all the American colonies differed in a fundamental respect from that of the Church in England. Anglican churches in America came under the jurisdiction of the bishop of London. No American bishop was consecrated before the Revolution and no bishop was sent from England to the colonies. This meant that priests could not be ordained in America, but had to be sent to England for ordination, nor could English priests be sent to the colonies as missionaries. William Loud, who served as the bishop of London and later as archbishop of Canterbury, was largely to blame for making no provision for American bishops. No Anglican bishop came to America before the Revolution, therefore no priests could be ordained, new members could not be confirmed, and churches could not be consecrated. Samuel Seabury was consecrated as the first American bishop in 1784, after the Revolution.

There were many other Protestants in Virginia during the colonial period. There were the Puritans, Baptists, and Friends in Nansemond County. Governor Spotswood brought in German Lutherans to work his iron industry and they built the Hebron Church in Madison County. From Pennsylvania, Friends settled in the northwest part of Virginia. They soon erected Hopewell Friends Meeting House and Goose Creek Meeting House. Presbyterians from Pennsylvania settled in the Shenandoah Valley and built Augusta Stone Church. In the Blue Ridge Mountains, at Hamburg, there is the Mill Creek Church, or Mauck Meeting House, built by the Mennonites. Nonconformists made rapid headway in the eighteenth century. Baptists and Scotch-Irish Presbyterians so increased in population that, with Quakers and others, the dissenters in 1776 outnumbered the members of the Established Church. In Virginia, the dissenting churches demanded the property of the Anglican churches and the movement was successful. In 1802, the Virginia legislature passed an act ordering the glebe lands to be sold for the benefit of the poor and for educational institutions. The Glebe Church of Nansemond County got its name as a result of that act. During these difficult years, a number of colonial Anglican churches and chapels were used by other denominations.

The Church in colonial Virginia was, from the beginning, the Church of the people rather than the Church of the clergy. The churches were built by the people and the demand for clergy was always greater than the supply. The spirit of independence exhibited in the Virginia Assembly was the spirit of the people and found expression in the vestry meetings, as well as in the halls of legislature. The people of Virginia identified themselves with the government. The church, in its parish organization, reflected the life and social standards of the Virginians. The very church building itself—with the best pews reserved for the magistrates and their families and with the private galleries erected at their own cost by the rich men of the parish—gave an added emphasis to the aristocratic nature of state and church.

History presents no more striking example of this than the churches of colonial Virginia. The people not only maintained the Church as established, but extended it to meet the needs of the growing population. They demanded that their clergy be models for people to follow and look up to. They expelled them when they fell short of their ideals. The people held loyalty to God and considered it necessary for good citizenship.

On 20 June 1907, while reading an essay at the Virginia Theological Seminary in Alexandria in celebration of the tricentennial of the Jamestown settlement, Rev. Edward L. Goodwin said, our theme is, "The fall and rising again of the church in Virginia." The story would cover, for its complete telling, about a century of her life, or say, from 1740 to 1840. At the beginning of this period, we see the church sitting as a queen upon her throne, supported and protected by her lord, the state, apparently the most stable institution among this new people. In the midst we see her dethroned, distrusted, and disqualified, vainly striving to save, from the wreck of her fortunes, some remnants of her former possessions if not of her power. At its end she appears revived, chastened, and purified, guided with humility and grave as one who serves and entered upon the holy work, in the doing of which she has outlived all calumny and been honored of God and men.

Virginia was the first colony, and quite a few of her churches still stand. Most have been restored and have active congregations. Because of its colonial association with the Church of England, the population of the Protestant Episcopal Church in America is still centered in the area of the British colonies.

THE LANDING OF THE PILGRIM FATHERS

The breaking waves dashed high
  On a stern and rock-bound coast,
And the woods against a stormy sky
  Their giant branches tossed;
And the heavy night hung dark
  The hills and waters o'er,
When a band of exiles moored their bark
  On the wild New England shore.
Not as the conqueror comes,
  They, the true-hearted, came;
Not with the roll of the stirring drums,
  And the trumpet that sings of fame:
Not as the flying come,
  In silence and in fear;
They shook the depths of the desert gloom
  With their hymns of lofty cheer.
Amidst the storm they sang,
  And the stars heard, and the sea;
And the sounding aisles of the dim woods rang
  To the anthem of the free.
The ocean eagle soared
  From his nest by the white wave's foam,
And the rocking pines of the forest roared,—
  This was their welcome home.
There were men with hoary hair
  Amidst that pilgrim-band:
Why had they come to wither there,
  Away from their childhood's land?
There was woman's fearless eye,

Lit by her deep love's truth;
There was manhood's brow serenely high,
  And the fiery heart of youth.
What sought they thus afar?
  Bright jewels of the mine?
The wealth of seas, the spoils of war?—
  They sought a faith's pure shrine!
Ay, call it holy ground,
  The soil where first they trod;
They have left unstained what there they found,—
  Freedom to worship God.

—*Felicia B. Hemans*

I AM THE CHURCH!

I AM THE CHURCH!

The great Creator drew the plans for me within His heart of love;

The Great Architect gave His dearest Possession that I might be erected;

My one and only Foundation is His Son—whose body was nailed to a tree;

My Chief Corner Stone—the Stone which the builders rejected;

My walls—placed without hammer's sound—are built by the martyrs of the centuries;

My steeple points ever toward the Great Architect—Builder throughout eternity;

From my belfry rings out the call for worship to countless multitudes of all ages;

My door swings open to all of every race and every age—bidding them welcome;

In my sanctuary there is—

Peace for tired minds,

Rest for weary bodies,

Compassion for suffering humanity,

Forgiveness for repentant sinners,

Communion for saints,

CHRIST for all who seek Him!

I AM THE CHURCH!

All the *love* of God, the great Architect,

All the *sacrifice* of Christ, the Great Builder,

All the *dreams* of dauntless prophets,

All the *faith* of hopeful pioneers,

All the *hope* of countless millions,

All the *joy* of conquering Christians are enclosed within my walls!

I AM THE CHURCH!

Without me, civilization must crumble!

With me is eternity!

—*Beulah Hughes*

ST. LUKE'S CHURCH
THE OLD BRICK CHURCH
ISLE OF WIGHT COUNTY

Erected: 1632

Denomination: Anglican

Location: 2 miles south of Smithfield on Route 10

Open Tuesday—Saturday, 9:30 A.M. to 4:00 P.M. (last tour at 3:30 P.M.);
closed during January.

St. Luke's Church in 1900. It is the oldest building of English construction in America.

S T. LUKE'S CHURCH, AFFECTIONATELY KNOWN AS "OLD Brick," is the nation's only original Gothic church and the oldest existing church of English foundation in America. Its founding date has been the subject of considerable research, but cannot be verified with absolute certainty. Anecdotally, however, it has been stated many times that Nathaniel Young, the son of Francis Young, a clerk of the county, frequently looked at the parish's first vestry book (before it became illegible and crumbled into dust) and read that the construction of St. Luke's began in 1632. Also, during a late nineteenth-century renovation, a brick was discovered engraved with the date 1632, offering further evidence to support the claim.

St. Luke's is situated in Isle of Wight County, which was formed in 1634, as one of the original eight shires, or counties, of the Virginia Colony. According to a 1634 census, the county had a population of 522 when it was established. While originally named Warrosquyoake County, after a local Indian tribe, its name was changed to Isle of Wight in 1637.

The brick church was originally in the Lower Parish (later called Newport Parish) of Isle of Wight County. This parish extended at that time from Lawne's Creek to Chuckatuck Creek.*

Because they were expensive to build, brick churches were very rare in colonial times and therefore easily identifiable. When the brick church was built in Jamestown in 1639, for example, it was called simply "The Brick Church in Jamestown." Likewise, the church at Isle of Wight County was also called "The Brick Church," and then later "The Old Brick Church." It finally received its formal designation as St. Luke's in 1828, when a young deacon named William G. H. Jones used that name in a report to the Episcopal Convention.

It has been said that it took more than twenty-five years to complete the building of St. Luke's, with its many Gothic details, including buttresses, stepped gables, brick-traceried windows, and medieval timber-trussed roof structure.

Some of the ministers from the Church of England and the Protestant Episcopal Church who served Isle of Wight County are as follows:

Reverend Falkner	1642
Rev. Robert Dienster	1651-56
Rev. William Hudsdan	1680
Rev. Andrew Monroe	1700-19
Rev. Alexander Forbes	1710-24
Rev. Thomas Baily	1720-24

Rev. John Reid	1724
Rev. John Barlow	1726-27
Rev. John Gammill	1729-43
Rev. John Reid	1746-57
Rev. John Millner	1766-70
Rev. Henry John Burgess	1773-76
Rev. William Hubardto	1802
Rev. William G. H. Jones	1826-32
Reverend Hedges	1831-33
(under whom Christ Church, Smithfield, was built)	
Rev. Thomas Smith	1834-41
Rev. John Downing	1847
Rev. John C. McCabe	1847-51
Rev. P. G. Robert	1858-62
Rev. E. T. Perkins	1862 and 1865
Rev. F. A. Meade	1873 and 1878-83
Rev. David Barr	1884-89
Rev. F. G. Scott	1892-1900
Rev. R. S. Carter	1901-08.

During the Revolutionary War, the church was threatened when Lt. Col. Banastre Tarleton's British troops camped all around it while making raids against nearby James River plantations. Confederate troops also camped at Old Brick during the Civil War.

The Old Brick Church was used as a summer chapel after a new church, known as Christ Church, was built in nearby Smithfield in 1735. Between 1785 and 1825, during the period of Disestablishment, services were held only occasionally at Old Brick.

In June 1887, a hurricane caused the roof and part of the east gable to fall. St. Luke's seemed destined for ruin, but the Reverend David Barr raised enough funds to repair it. Emmet W. Maynard supervised the removal of the debris. While engaged in this project, Maynard found the brick dated 1632. Once he learned the significance of his find, he made a careful search for other suggestive bricks. He found part of a brick inside the church with a figure 1 on it, and on the outside of the church, he found another piece with a figure 2 on it. On putting these two pieces together they fit perfectly, but the intervening 6 and 3 were gone, broken out by the force of the fall of the roof and the east wall. The whole brick with the figure 1632 on it, however, is now firmly embedded in the woodwork of the church's chancel.

Historical features at The Old Brick Church are its rood screen (carved grillwork of metal, stone, or wood, separating the chancel from the nave), the first to be restored to an ancient church in this country; the famed communion table

Above: Today, the Old Brick Church serves as a Confederate memorial.

Right: St. Luke's Church was restored and rededicated in 1894.

Far right: St. Luke's is also known as The Old Brick Church. While removing debris after a hurricane in 1887, a brick carved with the date 1632 was found.

and chairs, among the rarest such works by mid-seventeenth-century American craftsmen; its seventeenth-century American silver baptismal, which was hewn from a great log and then carefully shaped; the memorial windows and altar; a rare church organ of English origin (circa 1665) signed by its maker; and two 1629 books containing both the Bible and the Book of Common Prayer.

In 1953, the foundations, walls, and roof were in danger of giving way. Under the leadership of Henry Mason Day, a descendant of one of the earliest settlers of the region, and with funds collected from concerned citizens from all over the nation, restoration was made to the church between 1953 and 1959.

In 1966, St. Luke's was added to the National Register of Historic Places and declared a national shrine.

Soon after Pres. Dwight D. Eisenhower visited The Old Brick Church, he wrote the following:

This monument to the founders of our country is in truth a national shrine. Visitors there, inescapably, will be reminded of the deep religious convictions of the first settlers, their faith in God and their faith in themselves as children of God. St. Luke's, more than a time-hallowed relic of the past, will be an enduring witness to the spirit that animated them.

* The plantation parish of Warrosquyoake is first recorded in 1629. In 1643, the parish was subdivided into Upper (later Warrosquyoake) and Lower (later Newport) Parishes. In 1734, the lower sections of these two parishes were formed into Newport Parish and the upper sections into Nottoway Parish (which became coterminous with Southampton County fifteen years later). It is assumed that the parish, as was the city of Newport News, was named for Capt. Christopher Newport, commander of the Jamestown expedition of 1607 and commander of the *Susan Constant*.

JAMESTOWN CHURCH
JAMESTOWN ISLAND

Erected: 1639 (ruined brick tower remains)

Denomination: Anglican

Location: Jamestown Island, south of Williamsburg

Religious Services: Third Sunday after Trinity, 7:30 A.M. at the Robert Hunt Shrine

Open daily, 9:00 A.M. to 5:00 P.M.

The Old Church Tower at Jamestown and the restored church, erected as a memorial by the National Society of Colonial Dames of America.

THE ESTABLISHED ENGLISH CHURCH IN THE COLONY of Virginia originated within the present limits of James City County through the founding of its first church at Jamestown in 1607.

The prior year, in December 1606, three ships—the *Susan Constant*, the *Godspeed*, and the *Discovery*—left England with more than one hundred colonists bound for Virginia. Their numbers included the Reverend Robert Hunt, who would be appointed as the first minister of James City. Edward Wingfield, the first president of the new colony, gives the following account of Mr. Hunt's appointment:

> For my first worke, which was to make right choice of a spiritual pastor, I appeal to my Lord of Canterbury, his grace, who gave me very gracious audience in my request. And the world knoweth whom I took with me, truely a man, in my opinion, not any waie to be touched with the rebellious humour of a papist spirit, nor blemished with the least suspicion of a factious schismatic.

During the transatlantic crossing, which took eighteen weeks, Mr. Hunt was weak and sick, and many of the colonists did not expect he would recover from his illness. But the clergyman persevered, and a month after landing at Jamestown, Mr. Hunt celebrated the colony's first Holy Communion on 21 June 1607—the third Sunday after Trinity. His congregation numbered 105 people.

James S. M. Anderson, author of three most laborious and interesting volumes on colonial churches, says that a circumstance "is mentioned in President Wingfield's manuscript, which shows, in a very remarkable manner, the careful and solemn reverence manifested by the colonists for the due celebration of Christ's holy ordinance in their said extremity." He says that when "the common store of oil, sack, vinegar, and aqua-vitae, were all spent, saving two gallons of each, the sack was reserved for the communion table."

Capt. John Smith provides further evidence of the colonists' religious reverence in a pamphlet he published years later, in 1631, titled, "Advertisements for the unexperienced planters of New England, or elsewhere, &c." To the Reverend Anderson's labours we are indebted for the revival of this pamphlet.

> Now, because I have spoken so much for the body, give me leave to say somewhat of the soul; and the rather, because I have been demanded by so many, how we began to preach the Gospel in Virginia, and by what authority, what churches we had, our order of service, and maintenance for our ministers; therefore I think it not amiss to satisfie their demands, it being the mother of all our Plantations, entreating pride to spare laughter, to understand her simple beginnings and proceedings. When I went first to Virginia, I well remember, we did hang an awning (which is an old sail) to three or four trees, to shadow us from the sun; our walls were rails of wood, our seats unhewed trees, till we cut planks, our pulpit a bar of wood nailed to two neighbouring trees; in foul weather we shifted into an old rotten tent, for we had few better, and this came by way of adventure for new. This was our church, till we built a homely thing like a barn, set upon crotchetts, covered with rafts, sedge, and earth, so was also the walls. The best of our houses were of the like curiosity, but the most part far much worse workmanship, that could neither well defend wind nor rain, yet we had daily Common Prayer morning and evening, every Sunday two sermons, and every three months the holy communion, till our minister [Mr. Hunt] died. But [after that, we maintained] our prayers daily with an homily on Sundays, [and] we continued two or three years after, till more preachers came, and surely God did most mercifully hear us, till the continual inundations of mistaking directions, factions, and numbers of unprovided libertines near consumed us all, as the Israelites in the wilderness.

James City County was named for King James I, who was reigning at the time Jamestown was settled. Within its bounds were located Virginia's first church, first parish, and first attempts by settlers to establish a governmental body for the colony, and from it spread the first settlements along the James River.

In 1618, the Virginia Company of London, which had sponsored the expedition to the New World, ordered the establishment of four separate and distinct settlements under its complete control. To them, in all later records, was given the name of the "Four Ancient Boroughs," or sometimes the "Four Ancient Corporations." The four were, in order of establishment, James City, Kecoughtan (which, in 1620, changed its name to Elizabeth City), the city of Henrico, and Charles City.

The earliest established bounds of the Jamestown settlement, as proclaimed by Gov. Samuel Argall on 28 March

1619, and issued on 7 April 1619, included, in addition to the island itself, the adjacent mainland on both sides of the James River. Although mentioned as "James Towne" in chronicles and state correspondence as early as 1611, the settlement was officially named "James City," from which the county's name was later derived.

James City County was reduced in area by the establishment of Surry County in 1652. It was again reduced in 1720, when its territory west of the Chickahominy River was annexed to Charles City County—making the river the

Top left: The tower ruin as viewed from the eastern parapet of a Confederate fort of 1861.

Bottom left: The ruined tower attracts much historical interest today.

Above: Another view of the tower taken in 1898.

This photograph is from 1940, after the church was rebuilt and the original foundations protected.

dividing line between the two counties. In 1870, James City County took in the entire city of Williamsburg to simplify court jurisdiction.

The first church structure at Jamestown was built in 1608. The colonists used a "crotch" system of construction, in which both the roof and the walls were supported by pairs of crotches, or forked posts. This church did not last long. During John Smith's absence on an exploration of the Chesapeake Bay region, it was accidentally burned down. When Smith returned, a second church was erected with the help of Capt. Christopher Newport's mariners. They had delayed their return to England for the purpose of rendering aid in constructing this second church. These two churches are the only ones that Capt. John Smith ever attended in Virginia, for he departed for England in October 1609 and never returned.

Sometime around Christmas 1608 or January 1609, Jamestown's second church witnessed the first marriage in Virginia. John Layton, a laborer, married Anne Burras, the maidservant of Mrs. Forest, wife of Thomas Forest, gentleman, who was among the earliest settlers who came to Virginia in 1607 and 1608. The frail second church was still standing when Sir Thomas Gates reached Jamestown on 20 May 1610, after shipwreck on the Bermudas, and found that only sixty out of more than four hundred colonists had survived the disastrous "starving time" of the preceding winter.

The third Jamestown church of 1610 is historically memorable as the scene of the marriage of Pocahontas to John Rolfe in 1614. They were probably married by the Reverend Richard Buck, who had traveled to Virginia with Sir Thomas Gates, who served as governor. Buck presided over the church at Jamestown for at least eleven years.

It is probable that Pocahontas was baptized by the Reverend Whitaker at the settlement of Henrico, headed by Sir Thomas Dale, where she moved in 1613 and met her future husband. At the Henrico settlement, Pocahontas was educated in the Christian faith.

The frame church of 1617 was the fourth church built at Jamestown. During that same year, Capt. Samuel Argall arrived in Jamestown and began a term as deputy governor of Virginia. The fourth church seems to have been repaired in 1624, but after more than twenty years of service, the church at James City was succeeded by the fifth Jamestown church, a brick structure built during Gov. John Harvey's second administration, about 1639. This brick church was burned in 1676 by Nathaniel Bacon, when he set fire to Jamestown as a military measure in his campaign against Gov. William Berkeley. Bacon died of malaria that same year. The church was restored in 1680. Following the transfer of the colonial government to Williamsburg in 1699, the building served as a county parish church until 1758, when it closed.

Except for the existing tower, the church had fallen into complete ruin by the end of the eighteenth century. It is evident that the tower, whatever its age, once had a wooden spire above it, for Bishop William Meade records, "the testimony of an elderly gentleman who assured me that he was present when the wooden part of the tower was burned by accident." This account is supported by the modern discov-

Above: The churchyard at Jamestown. This sycamore tree grew between the tombs of Commissary James Blair and his wife and shattered the stones.

Left: An illustration that depicts the first religious service in the New World, under ship sails, conducted by Rev. Robert Hunt in 1607.

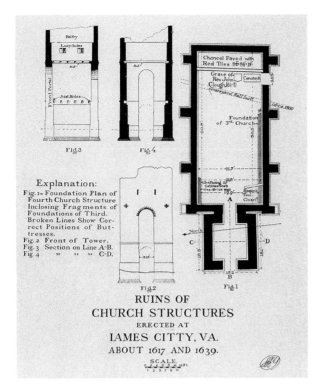

Explanation:
Fig.1= Foundation Plan of
Fourth Church Structure
Inclosing Fragments of
Foundations of Third.
Broken Lines Show Cor-
rect Positions of But-
tresses.
Fig.2 Front of Tower.
Fig.3 Section on Line A-B.
Fig.4 " " " C-D.

RUINS OF
CHURCH STRUCTURES
ERECTED AT
IAMES CITTY, VA.
ABOUT 1617 AND 1639.
SCALE

"RUINS OF CHURCH STRUCTURES ERECTED AT IAMES CITTY, VA. ABOUT 1617 AND 1639." By Samuel H. Yonge, 1907.

ery of charred timber ends in the joist holes of the tower, conclusively proving that the latter had been burned since the church was replaced in service in 1680. The foundation and the surviving portions of the tower have been saved by the efforts of the Association for the Preservation of Virginia Antiquities and the National Park Service.

Twenty-three acres of land, including the historic church tower and graveyard, were given in 1893 by Mr. and Mrs. Edward E. Barney, then owners of the island, to the Association for the Preservation of Virginia Antiquities, in whose care the reservation has since remained. The existing memorial church, designed as a restoration of the original building, was presented to the association by the National Society of Colonial Dames in 1907, upon the 300th anniversary of the founding of Jamestown. The new structure appears to rest upon the brick church's foundation, but is actually carried by a system of steel beams and concrete piers, so as not to place extra weight on the ancient brickwork, weakened by extended contact with the damp ground.

The chief service at the Robert Hunt Shrine is held on the third Sunday after Trinity in commemoration of the first recorded Holy Communion at Jamestown by the Reverend Robert Hunt in 1607.

In 1957, Virginia celebrated the 350th anniversary of the founding of Jamestown. At this celebration, the Reverend Dr. George MacLaren Brydon, the distinguished historiographer of the Diocese of Virginia, gave the address at the hymn festival. His elegant remarks speak to the Christian significance of Jamestown.

This bronze memorial, for Rev. Robert Hunt, chaplain of the first colonists, commemorates the first communion.

The statue of John Smith and the Jamestown church tower in the background.

The First Day of Jamestown: Ascensiontide

May 13, 1607—the day upon which the Settlers landed at Jamestown as their permanent settlement—was, in Anglican worship, Rogation Wednesday; and the next day (Thursday the 14th) was the Feast of the Ascension of Our Lord and Savior Jesus Christ.

As Robert Hunt, priest and prophet of God, read Morning Prayer on that Day of Taking Possession, he read that most significant Psalm LXVIII, which is appointed in the Psalter to be read on the morning of the 13th day of the month. He read these words of verse 18:

Thou art gone up on high, thou hast led captivity captive, and received gifts for men: yea, even for thine enemies, that the Lord God might dwell among them.

On that day of the first "setting of the watch," he prayed for the first time on Virginian soil the petition of the Founders' own prayer: "And seeing, Lord, the highest end of our plantation here is to set up the standard and display the banner of Jesus Christ, even here where Satan's throne is, Lord, let our labour be blessed in labouring for the conversions of the heathen."

So the Day of Occupation passed through the sunset to "the evening and the morning" of the Day that is the agelong affirmation of the Christian Faith, the Day on which man's salvation from sin has been won, and the Day that Christ in His glorious Ascension received the gifts of salvation for all mankind.

It is a momentous fact that this first religious observance of Christian settlers in a new land was the great shout of Faith in God as the Father of all mankind, and in Jesus Christ as the Saviour of all.

MERCHANTS HOPE CHURCH
MARTIN'S BRANDON PARISH
PRINCE GEORGE COUNTY

Erected: 1657

Denomination: Anglican

Location: Prince George County on Route 641, 1/2 mile west of that road's intersection with Route 10

Religious Services: Sundays, 10:00 A.M.

Merchants Hope Church gets its name from a ship that sailed between England and Virginia called Ye Merchants Hope. *Here is the church photographed in 1900.*

ERCHANTS HOPE CHURCH IS THE SECOND oldest colonial church standing in America today. The brick building is sixty feet long and thirty feet wide. The walls are twenty-two inches thick, and the rafters are of such unusual size that their weight proved a menace to the church's sturdy walls, which were braced by iron rods at one time to prevent threatened damage. The traditional date of the building's erection, 1657, is cut into one of the beams of the roof trusses. The aisles, passing from both doors and meeting at the chancel, are six feet wide and paved with the original flagstones. They are eighteen inches square and probably imported as others of that period are known to have been. Most of the wooden beams and trusses of the roof are original. The old square pews remained in use until after the Civil War when, in 1870, they were replaced with modern pews as the church was restored for worship services.

The churchyard contains no cemetery, and it is doubtful if one ever existed. At the time Merchants Hope Church was built, plantations were large and the distances between them were great. Therefore, the custom of interment in private burying grounds prevailed.

Merchants Hope Church is located in Martin's Brandon Parish. According to the Parish Lines of the Diocese of Southern Virginia, you find the following information regarding Martin's Brandon Parish. In 1616, Capt. John Martin was granted a large tract of land on the south side of the James River, which soon became one of the strong settlements. The plantation took its name from the grant, and it seems to have had the status of a group plantation parish from its first settlement. Captain Martin was one of the resourceful and aggressive leaders of the colony. Unfortunately, his grant was the subject of much controversy because the charter of that plantation made Martin virtually independent of the government at Jamestown. The result was that the representatives from Martin's Brandon Plantation, or borough, were not allowed to serve in the first General Assembly, which met at Jamestown, 30 July 1619. There is no recorded evidence of Captain Martin's death, but it is generally agreed that he died at Brandon in 1632, the last survivor of the 1607 expedition. The plantation originally granted to Captain Martin in 1618 was re-patented after his death by Symon Sturges, John Sadler, Richard Quiney, and their associates. A two hundred acre tract of this holding was subsequently given as a glebe to the parish of Martin's Brandon. The establishment of Martin's Brandon as a separate parish is fixed by an order of the Charles City County Court dated 4 June 1655.

By an act of the General Assembly, passed 25 August 1702, the county of Charles City was divided into two separate counties: one that retained the name of Charles City County and another to be called Prince George County, after Prince George of Denmark, the husband of Queen Anne who was then on the British throne. Thereafter, Martin's Brandon Parish was located in the new Prince George County.

The first church of Martin's Brandon Parish is believed to have been a wooden structure that stood in a field called the Church Pastures, at a spot a hundred yards southeast of the road leading into Brandon Plantation and less than a quarter mile southwest of a small branch of Upper Chippokes Creek.

The third church of Martin's Brandon Parish, and last of colonial design, was built around 1723 in the present village of Burrowsville, on the site now occupied by the Burrowsville Public School. It was here that Col. William Byrd is believed to have met his men on his way to run the dividing line between Virginia and North Carolina in 1728. The building, of frame construction, was abandoned for many years after the Revolution and disappeared after 1856, when construction of the existing Martin's Brandon Episcopal Church—a new brick structure with stucco finish—was completed. Brandon Episcopal Church stands today with an active Episcopal congregation in Prince George County at Burrowsville, Virginia. It is not a colonial church building, however. Merchants Hope Church still stands in the pine woods, on the north side of the old River Road, ten miles east of Hopewell, Virginia. For many years it stood dormant and inactive, but today, it conducts regular Sunday services.

In 1658, John Westrope bequeathed to the church of Martin's Brandon Parish his Bible, a folio edition of 1639; a book of Bishop Andrews's sermons; and a "Communion Cup." All of these items are still in the possession of Merchants Hope Church in the present Brandon Parish.

Merchants Hope Church takes its name from an old plantation that once stood on the property where the church was built. A bark, or small sailing vessel, called *Ye Merchants Hope* was sailing between England and Virginia in 1634 and 1635. Its captain and master was William Barker, who acquired land in Virginia in order to transport colonists to Virginia.

In 1635, Captain Barker and two London grocers mentioned earlier in relation to the re-patent of Captain Martin's property—John Sadler, who was the brother-in-law of John Harvard (founder of Harvard College), and Richard

Above, top: Merchants Hope Church is the second oldest colonial church standing in America today.

Above: Merchants Hope Church as photographed in 1930, before its restoration in 1958.

Queyning, whose brother was married to William Shakespeare's daughter, Judith—received a grant of 1,250 acres in the county of Charles City. The land was called Merchants Hope.

In his book *Colonial Churches of Tidewater Virginia,* George Carrington Mason writes that the antiquity of Merchants Hope Church has been questioned by some who consider its design too modern for the period in which it was supposed to have been built.

Bishop William Meade writes that there is neither an old vestry book nor a register of the parish, nor even a report to the bishop of London in 1724 from which to gather any materials for a notice of it in early times.

The following clergy served Martin's Brandon Parish and Merchants Hope Church from 1619 to 1787:

Rev. Robert Paulett	1619
Rev. Richard Jones	1650-55
Rev. Paul Williams	1680
Rev. James Worden	1714
Rev. Peter Fontaine	1716-20
Rev. Alexander Finney	1724-70
Rev. William Coutts	1775-76
Rev. Benjamin Blagrove	1785-87

In 1957, to celebrate the 300th anniversary of the building, an organization was chartered by the state to insure its preservation called the Merchants Hope Church Foundation. The church was restored thoroughly in 1958.

WARE CHURCH
GLOUCESTER COUNTY

Erected: circa 1690

Denomination: Anglican

Location: South side of Routes 3 and 14, 1 1/2 miles east of the
Gloucester Courthouse

Religious Services: Sundays, Holy Eucharist at 8:30 A.M.; Worship Service
at 10:30 A.M.
Wednesdays, Holy Eucharist at 10:00 A.M.

Open Monday—Friday, 9:00 A.M. to 1:00 P.M.

Ware Church in 1930. It is the only surviving rectangular colonial church that retains its three orignial entrances.

G LOUCESTER COUNTY LIES ON THE NORTH SIDE OF the York River and extends to the Chesapeake Bay. The county was formed from York County around 1651. The four parishes in Gloucester—Ware, Petsworth, Kingston, and Abingdon—were formed sometime during the period between 1655 and 1656. Of the four, Ware and Abingdon still contain colonial churches.

Ware Parish covered the southeastern section of York County to Mobjack Bay on the east, with Petsworth and Abingdon Parishes lying to the south. The early records of Ware Parish are lost. Tradition states that an earlier church had once stood in the parish, located approximately one and a half miles from the present church. The site of the earlier church is known as the "church field." In 1680, a petition was made before the Colonial Court and Council for permission to build a second church in Ware Parish. The first Ware Church was built on the opposite side of the river, near the road leading into Ware Neck, probably standing by 1660.

Although the actual date of construction of this second church is not known, the present building is the result. In 1907, the Reverend William Byrd Lee, then serving as rector, wrote an article about Ware Church in *Colonial Churches of Virginia* and thought that it must have been built in 1690, but because of its architecture, some historians have placed its date between 1710 and 1715.

The present church is constructed of brick with glazed heads. It measures eighty feet by forty feet, with walls three feet thick. The church is surrounded by a brick wall that confines a cemetery of more than half an acre of land. It is shaded by a beautiful grove of trees.

Ware Church is outstanding in several respects. It had the largest piece of land, it was the most costly of its time to build, and three of its doorways (north, south, and west) are the finest of their type. A very distinctive feature of Ware Church is the fact that it is the only surviving rectangular colonial church that retains its original three entrances. The church is lighted by twelve large windows. Of these, two double windows are located in the chancel, and each complement an above arc. The interior arrangement has been altered to one central aisle. Originally, there were two aisles covered with flagstones situated between the pews at the sides and those in the center, and a cross aisle before the chancel connecting the north and south doors. A high pulpit stood near the door.

During the Revolutionary War, American soldiers set up camp at the church. After the Disestablishment, Ware Parish became inactive, and the building was abandoned.

During 1827, the church was repaired. It was during this time that the Methodists used the building for worship. In 1854, the church was again renovated. It received a new roof. The floor of the chancel was extended over the tombs in the east end of the church. The flagstone aisles were removed and laid with boards to the level of the pew floor, and two modern blocks of pews were installed. The space under the gallery was partitioned off from the church and made into a vestibule. The old high pulpit was removed from its position near the south door and replaced by a modern pulpit that was situated within the chancel.

It is interesting to note that in 1838, the Reverend Charles Mann was authorized to place chimneys in Ware Church. They did not give satisfactory results, so they were removed, and stovepipes again projected through the walls.

During the Civil War, Federal troops camped in the yard at Ware church.

Ware Parish owns two silver chalices and two silver patens of the colonial period. Bishop Meade mentions that Augustine Warner, great-grandfather of George Washington, gave the Petsworth Parish Church one silver flagon, two silver bowls, and two silver plates. When the Petsworth Parish and Popular Spring Church became defunct—perhaps only a few years after the close of the vestry record in 1793, during the general decline of religion in Virginia and the downfall of the established church—tradition states that Ware Church received parts of their services.

Few counties in Virginia record such a large number of extended rectorships than Gloucester County, which enjoyed the service of the Reverend James Clack (forty-five years), the Reverend John Gwynn (sixteen years), the Reverend Guy Smith (eighteen years), the Reverend Emmanuel Jones (thirty-nine years), the Reverend Thomas Hughes (twenty-five years), the Reverend James M. Fontaine (thirty-one years), the Reverend Guy Smith (twenty-five years), the Reverend Emmanuel Jones Sr. (fifty-nine years), and the Reverend Charles Mann (more than forty years).

During the hard and trying years 1864 and 1865, when Federal soldiers had stripped Gloucester County of the provisions it needed to feed its citizens, a young Confederate soldier brought to Mr. Mann, during the dead of winter, a liberal quantity of flour for those times and several pieces of pork. The young soldier was the son of one of Mr. Mann's parishioners. When the aged priest was shown the provision, he said, "I did not think God would have sent you. I trusted Him and I knew I should be taken care of, though we were almost out of food." Mr. Mann's favorite hymn was reported to be "Lord, Forever at My Side."

The present Ware Church was the most expensive church building of its time.

Inside Ware Church, on the east wall to the left of the chancel, a tablet is inscribed:

> *Erected*
> *By a Loving Congregation*
> *to the memory of a*
> *faithful friend and pastor*
> *Rev. Charles Mann*
> *More than 40 years rector*
> *of this Parish*
> *Died Jan. 15, 1878*
> *in the 87th year of his age*
> *and the 60th year of his*
> *Ministry.*
>
> *The memory of the just*
> *is blessed.*

The Reverend William Byrd Lee, who served as rector of Ware Church from 1881 to the early 1900s, made an interesting observation on the spiritual condition of the members of the church during the colonial period as the result of reading private letters, extracts of wills, references in sermons and wills, and epitaphs on tombstones. He states that there were many exalted Christians who loved God and his church and tried to live godly lives. They endeavored to instill spiritual teachings and principles in the hearts of their children.

Though Ware Church and the other colonial churches were physically weak after the Revolution, it would appear that God watched over them, raising them up and sending them forward on a great commission to aid in the evangelization of mankind. Ware Church has truly fulfilled this commission; today, it is an active Episcopal congregation of nearly four hundred parishioners.

GRACE CHURCH
YORK–HAMPTON PARISH
YORKTOWN

Erected: 1697

Denomination: Anglican

Location: Church Street in historic Yorktown

Religious Services: Sundays, Holy Eucharist at 7:50 A.M. (Rite I) and 9:05
A.M. (Rite II)
First, third, and fifth Sundays, Holy Eucharist at 11:15 A.M. (Rite I)
Second and fourth Sundays, Morning Prayer at 11:15 A.M. (Rite I)
Wednesdays, Holy Eucharist at 10:00 A.M.

Open daily, 9:00 A.M. to 5:00 P.M., except during services

Grace Church in 1930. During the Revolution, Lord Cornwallis used the church as a powder magazine. It was burned in 1814 and not rebuilt until 1848.

ONE OF VIRGINIA'S EARLIEST SETTLEMENTS, YORK Plantation was patented by Gov. Sir John Harvey in 1631. It was located just west of Wormeley's Creek, on the south side of the Charles River, and included 750 acres of land, now known as Temple Farm.

In 1634, York Plantation became a part of Charles River County, one of the eight original shires, or counties, formed in Virginia. The county was named in honor of King Charles I.*

York Parish appears to have been established by York Plantation, rather than by legislative enactment. Records disclose that York Parish had an inducted minister in 1638.

The first church of York Parish was built on a plot of land that became known as "Church Field." Evidence that the church was built around 1642 is found in a deed for the two hundred acres of church land, dated 16 January 1642, given by John Chew to Robert Kinsey and Henry Lowry.

This first church was replaced by a new building around 1667. In that year, a General Court entry states that the contractor for the church of York Parish had been authorized to go on and build it. This second York Church was constructed of brick. The existence of a tombstone dated 1655, located within the ruined walls of the second church, suggests that both churches occupied the same site. The tombstone is the second-oldest legible tombstone in Virginia and marks the grave of Maj. William Gooch, a justice of York County and a member of the House of Burgesses. The inscription on the stone reads:

Major William Gooch of this parish
Dyed Octob: 29, 1655

> With in this tomb there doth interred lie
> No shape, but substance, true nobility:
> It self, though young, in years but twenty-nine;
> Yet graced with vertues morall and divine;
> The church from him did good participate
> In counsell rare fit to adorn a State.

In 1691, land from the original settlement at York was laid out to create Yorktown. The exact date of the construction of the third York Parish Church, later known as Grace Church, is not recorded, but it is generally accepted as 1697. In an entry in the county order book, dated 26 October 1696, the following pledge is made by Gov. Francis Nicholson: "I promise to give five pounds sterl'g towards building the Cott. house at Yorke town, and twenty pounds

sterling if within two years they build a brick church at the same towne."

This pledge was witnessed by the rector of York Parish, at that time the Reverend Stephen Fouace, who began officiating in 1688. The church, however, was not built of brick, but of marl, a soft stone taken from the river bluff and used in the manufacture of cement. It measured 55 1/2 feet by 28 1/2 feet, with walls approximately twenty-seven inches thick. Originally, the church was built in the form of a T, situated east and west, but is now a quadrangle with square-headed windows and doors, surmounted by a belfry in which is a bell.

In 1706, the two small and poor parishes of York and Hampton (formerly Chiskiach) united to form the parish of York-Hampton. At that time, Grace Church acquired the Hampton Parish's communion service. In continuous use at Grace Church ever since, the service consists of a chalice and flagon of antique hammered silver, made in London in 1649. Both pieces are inscribed, "Hampton parish in York County." The latter is probably the earliest English silver flagon in America. It has a flat top instead of the domed top of later periods.

In 1712, York-Hampton Parish grew again with the acquisition of Martin's Hundred Parish, one of the earliest parishes in either James City or York County.

Grace Church lost its windows and pews when it became a powder magazine for Lord Cornwallis during the Revolutionary War. It was burned in 1814, along with much of Yorktown, during a fire that spread from the waterfront to the top of the town bluff. Until the church was rebuilt and restored to service in 1848, religious services were held at the courthouse.

In his report to the Diocesan Convention of 1849, Bishop William Meade stated that during the fall of 1848, he consecrated the new church at York. Since the parish church was never called Grace Church in colonial records, it seems probable that the name was first applied to it during Bishop Meade's consecration.

During the Civil War, a signal tower was erected for Federal forces on the church's roof, and the building was severely damaged through use as a hospital. The bell, inscribed "Yorktown 1725," was also broken at this time, just as it had been once before during the War of 1812. It is uncertain whether the bell fell and broke in the 1814 fire or during the War Between the States, but all are agreed that the fragments were carried off during that war, in all probability by Union soldiers. The pieces were found in Philadelphia in 1882 and identified by the inscription. The bell

Grace Church today operates a labyrinth, a replica of European designs, that is intended for spiritual contemplation.

was then recast and restored to service at Yorktown in 1889.

One of the most prominent families of York Parish was the Nelson family. Three members of that family—a father, a son, and a grandson—lie buried in the churchyard. They are Thomas Nelson (1677-1745), William Nelson (1711-72), and Gen. Thomas Nelson Jr. (1738-89), one of the signers of the Declaration of Independence.

The first rector of the York and Hampton Parishes was the Reverend Anthony Panton, who served in 1639 and 1640. Bishop Meade also reports that an old tombstone in York County reads, "Rev. Thomas Hampton, Rector of Yorke in 1647." Other clergymen who served the parish included the Reverend William White in 1658; the Reverend James Folliott in 1680; and as mentioned earlier, the Reverend Stephen Fouace, whose service began in 1688.

Today, Grace Church has an active Episcopal congregation within the Diocese of Southern Virginia.

* In 1643, by an act of the General Assembly, Charles River County's name was changed to York County, in honor of James, duke of York, the son of King Charles I.

ST. PETER'S PARISH CHURCH
NEW KENT COUNTY

Erected: 1701

Denomination: Anglican

Location: From Route 33 (between West Point and Richmond), 1 mile north of Talleysville on Route 609 and approximately 1/2 mile on Route 642

Religious Services: Sundays, 9:00 A.M. and 11:00 A.M.

Union troops at St. Peter's Church. From an original photograph by Matthew Brady in 1862.

This peaceful church is completely surrounded by woods. One of the oldest churches in Virginia, it has the distinction of being the "First Church of the First First-Lady."

Martha Dandridge, St. Peter's most famous parishioner, was born at Chestnut Grove on 2 June 1731. She married Col. Daniel Parke Custis, a member of the vestry and a former churchwarden, in June 1749. Her father, Maj. John Dandridge, had also served as a churchwarden and vestryman, and her great-grandfather had been the first rector of nearby Bruton Parish in Williamsburg.

After eight years of marriage, Mrs. Custis was widowed with two surviving children. On 6 January 1759, she remarried to Col. George Washington. The ceremony was officiated by the Reverend David Mossom (1690-1767), who served as parish rector for four decades (and whom some say may be buried beneath the chancel of the church). Due to the cold weather that day, the couple was not married at St. Peter's Church, as many people believe, but at "White House," the Widow Custis's home, located several miles from the church on the Pamunkey River.

New Kent County was carved away from the upper part of York County by the General Assembly on 20 November 1654. It commenced on Scimon's Creek, on the north side of the York River, some distance above Williamsburg, and extended to the heads of the Pamunkey and Mattaponi Rivers, then north of the Mattaponi to the Prepotanke Creek, north of the York River, including what are now the counties of King William, King and Queen, and Hanover to the west. St. John's Parish was located on the north side of the York and Pamunkey Rivers, and St. Peter's Parish was located on the south side.

St. Peter's Parish was created out of Blisland Parish by a general court held at James City on 29 April 1679. (It is generally accepted that Blisland Parish was created in 1653, although there is no evidence to support this contention.) At the present time, St. Peter's Parish includes all of New Kent County except the easternmost part, which is still officially listed by the Diocese of Virginia as a dormant parish, although the only church in modern Blisland Parish stands in James City County and the Diocese of Southern Virginia.

St. Peter's Parish was originally divided into an Upper and a Lower Parish. In 1704, Upper Parish was laid off to form St. John's Parish. What remained of St. Peter's Parish had two churches, one of which was an old frame building, "Commonly known as the Broken-Back'd" church because of its structural weakness, which was, perhaps, erected as early as 1685.

According to the first entry in the vestry book, dated 13 August 1700, the vestry instructed Gideon Macon and Thomas Smith to purchase one acre of land from Thomas Jackson on which to erect a church, designed by Will Hughes. The "Brick Church," as it was originally described, was built in 1703, at a cost of 146,000 weight of tobacco. In 1722, a belfry was built at the west end of the church to house a bell given to the parish. The tower, with its three large semi-circular openings, is one of the most remarkable features of the church.

In vestry minutes, dated 20 November 1752, The Brick Church was referred to as "St. Peter's Church" for the first time, although during the years 1684 and 1698, one of the churches in St. Peter's Parish was frequently referred to as "St. Peter's Church" by the clerk of the vestry.

After the Revolutionary War, the congregation of St. Peter's was scattered, and the church was inactive until 1820, when it was repaired and used exclusively by Presbyterians until 1843. At that time, Episcopal services were revived, and the two denominations alternated weekly services until the Presbyterians erected a church of their own in 1856.

Just before the Civil War, St. Peter's had a large and prosperous congregation, but during the war, the church was defaced by Federal soldiers, who stripped it of its furnishings and stabled their horses inside the building. A company of soldiers from Hartford, Connecticut, wrote their names on the inner walls and left many other marks of their occupancy. After the war, the Reverend Henry S. Kepler was very instrumental in bringing the people together to renew and repair the church.

In 1922, a group of people from many denominations took steps to save the historic building by forming the St. Peter's Church Restoration Association.

Above: St. Peter's today is the "First Church of the First First-Lady."

Opposite: St. Peter's Church in 1930. The St. Peter's Church Restoration Association is responsible for saving this historic building.

The churchyard at St. Peter's is very beautiful, with many varieties of trees, including large oaks, cedars, dogwoods, and walnuts. There are also a number of colonial graves, located near the east and south walls of the church.

St. Peter's vestry book (1684-1758) and register (1685-1786) have been published twice, most recently in 1937. They reveal the names of some of St. Peter's early ministers:

Rev. Richard Squire	1703-07
Rev. Daniel Taylor	1707-08
Rev. Daniel Gray	1708-09
Rev. Benjamin Goodin	1709-10
Rev. William Brodie	1710-20
Rev. Henry Colings	1722-25
Rev. David Mossom	1727-67

They also include the names of vestry members, such as George Jones, William Bassett, Cornelius Dabney, Gideon Macon, Thomas Butts, John Park, Nicholas Merriwether, Richard Littlepage, Samuel Gray, David Patterson, Michael Sherman, George Webb, Jesse Scott, William Vaughan, William Clayton, John Roper, Thomas Massie, Matthew Page, John Lydall, Charles Massie, William Waddell, Henry Childs, and William Chamberlayne.

Today, after more than 290 years of authenticated history, St. Peter's Church remains, to all intent and purposes, a monument to all of those who built it and worshipped God in it.

YEOCOMICO CHURCH
WESTMORELAND COUNTY

Erected: 1706

Denomination: Protestant Episcopal

Location: 4 miles west of Tucker Hill Post Office. North of Warsaw on Route 203

Religious Services: First, third, and fifth Sundays, 11:15 A.M.

Yeocomico Church is the oldest colonial church built in a T form. This photograph is from 1930.

ACCORDING TO BISHOP WILLIAM MEADE IN HIS book *Old Churches, Ministers, and Families of Virginia,* Westmoreland County had two parishes: Washington Parish in the upper section and Cople Parish in the lower. The latter parish, established in 1664, contained two colonial-era churches: Yeocomico Church and Nominy Church, both of which took their Indian names from local waterways. (Nominy Church, in Mount Holly, was destroyed by fire in 1814; its two remaining walls were incorporated into the present structure when the church was rebuilt around 1848.)

The first vestry of Cople Parish was chosen in 1655. According to the Reverend G. W. Beale of Hague, Virginia, the earliest vestrymen of the parish were Nicholas Turner, John Powell, and Richard Holder.

Also in 1655, the first Yeocomico Church, a frame structure, was built on land two miles from the Yeocomico River. It was replaced in 1706 by the existing brick church. The Reverend Samuel Gray was rector at the time this second church was built.

Yeocomico is the oldest colonial church built in a T-form. Its swag roof recalls that of Merchants Hope Church, built in 1754 in Prince George County. The lower half of the front wall of Yeocomico Church is laid in Flemish bond, and the upper half, as well as the east-end wall, is laid in English bond. At the top of the front wall, under the dentilated cornice, is a molded brick tile bearing the construction date of 1706.

The interior of the church has an unconventional arrangement, whereby the congregation has to pass by the lectern and pulpit on the way to the central aisle. The chancel is located in the east gable, surmounted by a Georgian window. At the south end of the church stands a large door—an original from the 1655 frame church—that features a battened wicket door for use in cold weather. At the north end of the church is a gallery, said to be the seating place of the early slaves and carriage drivers. Yeocomico is the only surviving colonial church in Westmoreland County.

One historic figure associated with Yeocomico Church is Mary Ball, who attended the church from 1721 to 1730 while under the tutelage of her guardian, Col. George Eskridge of Sandy Point. (Her father, Col. William Ball, had been a parishioner of St. Mary's White Chapel.) In 1730, Mary became the second wife of widower Augustine Washington. They had six children. The first was born in Westmoreland County on 22 February 1732 and named George, after Mary's guardian. This son would not only

usher in the fourth generation of the Washington family in Virginia, but he would later help usher in a new nation and serve as the country's first president.

According to Bishop Meade, the Reverend Charles Rose served as rector from 1754 to 1758. Colonial clergy that served Cople Parish include Rev. William Scrimgour, 1680 (et ante) to 1693; Rev. Samuel Gray, 1698; Rev. James Breechin, 1702, and again, 1714 (circa); Rev. Walter Jones, 1724-1727; Rev. Charles Rose, 1754-1758; and Rev. Thomas Smith, 1773-1789.

In an election held in 1755, the following vestrymen were chosen: John Bushrod, Daniel Tebbs, Richard Lee, Benedict Middleton, Willowby Newton, Robert Middleton, George Lee, John Newton, Samuel Oldham, Robert Carter, Fleet Cox, and James Steptoe.

At an election held immediately after the Revolutionary War, a new vestry was chosen. Its members included Vincent Marmaduke, Jeremiah G. Bailey, John A. Washington, Samuel Rust, John Crabb, Richard Lee, George Garver, George Tuberville, Patrick Sanford, John Rochester, and Samuel Templeman.

When Reverend Smith left the church's service, his replacement was unpopular. People drifted away from the church, leaving it unused by the Episcopal Church for many years. Instead, in the years after the Revolution, Yeocomico Church served as a courthouse, a school, and a Methodist chapel.

Yeocomico Church suffered along with many other churches during the stormy times of the nation's history. During the War of 1812, for example, it was shamefully abused by the soldiers who were quartered in it. The communion table was removed into the yard, where it served as a butcher's block, and was entirely defaced. It was restored to its former place in 1820 and is now used for the holy purposes for which it was originally designed. Bishop Meade also mentions the fact that the canvas on which the Ten Commandments, the Lord's Prayer, and the Apostles' Creed were impressed, was so torn by the soldiers that it was necessary to remove it, and repairs were made by a gentleman from New York.

During the Civil War, the old church again was used as a barracks by the home guard.

In 1906, on the 200th anniversary of the building of the brick church, the Association for the Preservation of Yeocomico Church was formed in order to maintain this historic house of worship. An extensive restoration of the church's foundations and walls occurred during this time; both of these projects were initiated by the Archdeacon of

Yeocomico Church is known today for its colonial architecture and historic communicant families.

Virginia John Poyntz Tyler, a native of Cople Parish, and later, from 1914 to 1931, the bishop of North Dakota.

Yeocomico Church, which is noted both for its architecture as well as for its historic communicant families—the Lees, Carters, Turbervilles, Corbins, and Eskridges—was included on the National Register of Historic Places in 1966 and has received, along with Stratford in Westmoreland County, the highest monument status, which means the highest historical significance, of a National Historic Landmark.

In 1976, the church's carriage yard, one of the last surviving examples in the United States, disappeared when a landscaped circular drive flanked by Georgian brick portals was installed in its place. An old sundial, which bears on its face the name of Philip Smith and the date 1717, has been removed from the post before the church and is now kept in the rectory. The old pews have been replaced with modern ones, and the original pulpit and sounding board also have been replaced. The present pews probably derive from 1873. The pulpit and sounding board derive from 1928. The wooden floors were replaced in 1928 and refinished in 1959. Repairs and renovations have been made to Yeocomico Church in 1773, circa 1820, 1906, 1928, and 1958 to 1959.

CHRIST CHURCH
MIDDLESEX COUNTY

Erected: 1712

Denomination: Anglican

Location: 2 1/2 miles east of Saluda on Route 33. Christ Church and Christchurch School are connected.

Christ Church in 1900 after rennovation. Bishop William Meade once referred to the church's decaying condition, as it was quite neglected from 1813 to 1840.

THE COUNTY OF MIDDLESEX IS LOCATED ON A narrow peninsula lying between the Rappahannock and Piankatank Rivers. Middlesex was originally part of Lancaster County, which once embraced the territory on both sides of the Rappahannock for a considerable distance. From this, Middlesex was formed on the southern shore. Records in Richmond show that this division occurred as early as 1669.

In 1657, Lancaster was divided into two parishes separated by the river, and the parish on the south side was subdivided into an upper parish named Lancaster and a lower parish named Peanckatanck (for the river on the southern boundary). In 1666, Lancaster and Peanckatanck Parishes were united to form Christ Church Parish.

Unlike those of many colonial parishes, the records of Christ Church Parish are intact, and a vestry book, which has been published, runs from 1663 to 1767. It is the only vestry book in Virginia antedating Bacon's Rebellion of 1676. According to these records, the Reverend Samuel Cole was the minister of both the Lancaster and Peanckatanck Parishes in 1657. The first entry states the appointment of Henry Corbin, according to a late Act of Assembly, to keep the register of the parish.

The vestry of Lancaster Parish agreed to build a church after the model of the Williamsburg Church, either on the north or the south side of Sunderland Creek. By a lot drawing, it fell on the north side but was never built. In 1666, some dissension as to the bounds of the two parishes and other matters led to a reunion, at which the vestry agreed to build a mother church by the name of Christ Church, also after the model of the Williamsburg Church.

The church was built midway between Brandon and Rosegill in the parish and was used until 1712, when a new church was built in the same place. The date of the existing church's erection is 1714. This date can be seen on three bricks now located over the doorway of the church. On one of these bricks are the letters J. H., which probably stand for John Hipkins, who performed most of the carpentry, plumbing, and glazing. No personal markings or inscriptions are found from the other contractor, Alexander Graves. The brick of the rectangular building was laid in Flemish bond with glazed headers, but many of the original features no longer exist in the present remodeled building.

The church measures thirty-three feet by sixty feet on the outside. The original specifications called for dimensions of sixty feet by thirty feet, with walls fourteen feet high that were increased later by five courses of brick and a half-hipped or clipped gable roof, as seen in the Lower Chapel. They also called for a large arched window in the chancel end, ten feet wide and six feet high, but the large window has been reduced considerably in size, very similarly to the one in St. Peter's Church in New Kent County.

Rood screens were specified in 1710 for all three churches, but not one has survived in a colonial church in Virginia. These carved grillworks of wood, metal, or stone separate the chancel from the nave and are surmounted by a crucifix. The use of a rood screen seems to have been inherited by the 1666 to 1667 churches of Christ Church Parish from the 1660 church at Middle Plantation (later Williamsburg) that served as their model.

In 1719, a cupola, or small dome, was built on the west end to house a bell that had been presented the year before by the bishop of London, but it was gone by the year 1843. The interior of this church had practically vanished when the church was reconstructed in that year.

From 1813 to 1840 there is little record of active church participation, except that James Chewning was a lay delegate at the Diocesan Council meeting in 1821. In 1840, Bishop William Meade referred to the sad conditions of Christ Church: "And what has become of the mother church, the great church as she is styled in her journal, standing in view of the wide Rappahannock, midway between Rosegill and Brandon?" The church building stood abandoned for half a century. Its roof decayed and fell in. A sycamore tree sprung up within its walls and two feet of loam covered the flagstones of the aisles.

Christ Church was remodeled in 1900 and again in 1930. The sacristy was added on the northeast side in 1931. The flagstones down the central aisle were purchased from the former Upper Church at Church View in 1931 for the sum of $265. The brick walls around the churchyard were erected by the Garden Club of Virginia in 1942.

In the old churchyard rest the remains of many of the people who figured prominently in the affairs of church and state, including John Grymes; the Honorable Ralph Wormley; Lucy Berkeley, who died in 1716; the Reverend John Shephard; and the Honorable Lady Madame Catherine Wormley (wife of Ralph Wormley), who died in 1685. One of the most recent additions to the cemetery at Christ Church was Gen. Lewis B. "Chesty" Puller, who died in 1971. He and Mrs. Puller were married at Christ Church and attended Sunday church services there after their retirement.

There are five persons buried in the chancel and two others in the aisle. The Reverend John Shepherd is buried at the head of the aisle. One of the graves under the chancel holds

Above: This photograph of Christ Church was taken in 1930, after its second remodeling.

Above top: Christ Church now shares its name with a neighboring preparatory school operated by the Diocese of Virginia.

the remains of Sir Henry Chicheley, who was governor from 1678 to 1680, died in 1682, and was buried here in the first building of the Parish Church.

In 1665, the vestrymen in this parish were Henry Corbin, Richard Perrott, Abraham Weeks, John Hastewood, Richard Cock, and Robert Chewning. In 1692, the Reverend Matthew Lidford was appointed minister of the parish for one year. In 1699, the Reverend Robert Yates was named minister and continued until 1704 when he returned to England. His son, the Reverend Bartholomew Yates, succeeded him and served faithfully for eighteen years. The Reverend John King served the parish from 1767 to 1795. (The parish register of 1653 to 1812, with some more recent additions, can be seen at the Virginia State Library in Richmond.)

On the land adjoining the churchyard is Christchurch School, a preparatory school for boys and girls operated by the Diocese of Virginia.

Christ Church today has an active Episcopal congregation.

BRUTON PARISH CHURCH

WILLIAMSBURG

Erected: 1715

Denomination: Protestant Anglican

Location: Colonial Williamsburg, Duke of Gloucester Street

Religious Services: Sundays, Holy Eucharist at 7:30 A.M. and 5:30 P.M.
Second, fourth, and fifth Sundays, Holy Eucharist at 9:00 A.M.
First and third Sundays, Morning Prayer and Sermon at 9:00 A.M.
First, third, and fifth Sundays, Holy Eucharist at 11:15 A.M.
Second and fourth Sundays, Morning Prayer and Sermon at 9:00 A.M.
Tuesdays, Holy Eucharist at 7:00 A.M. in St. Mary's Chapel
Wednesdays, Holy Eucharist and Healing at 11:00 A.M.
Monday—Saturday, Noonday Prayers at 12:00 .P.M.

Bruton Parish Church completely restored on Duke of Gloucester Street in Colonial Williamsburg.

BRUTON PARISH WAS LAID OUT FROM THE COUNTIES of James City and Charles River. The latter county was, in 1642, changed into York County. The parish of Bruton, in the year 1723, was reported to the bishop of London as ten miles square. The vestry book of Bruton Parish commenced in 1674 and continued until 1769, a few years before the Revolution.

The first rector of Bruton Parish (1674-88), Rowland Jones, was a great-grandfather of Martha Washington. He was initially buried at the second church building. His grave was moved to the present church on the north side of the chancel near the baptismal font.

In 1674, the parish of Marston, established in York County in 1654, and Middleton Parish were united under the name Bruton Parish. The source from which the name was derived is suggested by the inscription on the tomb of Sir Thomas Ludwell that lies at the entrance of the north transept door and states that he was born "at Bruton, in the county of Summerset, in the Kingdom of England and departed this life in the year 1678."

There was a church building in Williamsburg in 1665 that, in 1674, had come to be known as the "old church." The Old Brick Church of 1674 soon became inadequate due to membership growth and, in 1710, under the leadership of the Reverend James Blair, it was determined that a new church be built. Plans were furnished by Gov. Alexander Spotswood. The new church, called Bruton, was completed in 1715 and has remained continuously in use, withstanding the injure of war and the devastating touch of time. Most of the early ministers at Bruton Church were men of superior culture, having received masters of arts from the universities of Oxford and Cambridge, and some being full graduates of the College of William and Mary.

With the approach of the American Revolution, the services in Old Bruton assumed a tone of tenderness and thrilling interest, unique in character and fervent power. The congregation, as they listened, saw clearer the vision of liberty. George Washington makes mention in his diary of attending services at Bruton Church. This noble band of patriot legislators also had ties with Bruton Church: Nelson, Wythe, Harrison, Cabell, Bland, the Lees, George Mason, Peyton Randolph, Edmund Pendleton, and Patrick Henry.

Bruton Church is the inheritor and custodian of several sacred memorials of the past. The original pulpit Bible is preserved together with the old parish registry, noting George Washington's name eleven times and recording the baptism of 1,122 Negro servants within a twenty-five year period. The old prayer book, which bears the inscription "Bruton Parish," is also preserved. The old Jamestown baptismal font and communion silver are still in use at Bruton Parish Church, together with a set of communion silver made in 1686, given by Lady Gooch to the College of William and Mary, and a set bearing the royal arms of King George III.

In 1752, the chancel was enlarged by twenty-five feet to accommodate an organ and, in 1754, the wall was built around the churchyard. In 1769, the church was completed as it now stands, with the addition of the tower. In its wooden belfry hangs the "Liberty Bell of Virginia," donated in 1761 and rung for the Declaration of Independence, the surrender of Cornwallis, and the signing of the peace treaty in 1783.

The gallery in the west end, which dates from 1715, was assigned to students of the College of William and Mary during the colonial period; the railing bears initials carved over two hundred years ago. It was reached by a covered outside stairway that has since been removed.

In 1840, the congregation, yielding to the spirit of innovation, allowed the interior form and appearance of the church to be changed, and at that time a partition wall was built across the church. The high corner pulpit, the colonial pews, flagstone chancel, and aisles were removed.

The church was partially restored from 1905 to 1907 under the leadership of the rector, Dr. W. A. R. Goodwin. The restoration was inaugurated on 15 May 1905 with a sermon preached by Rev. Beverly D. Tucker, D.D. The plan was to restore Bruton Parish Church with absolute fidelity to colonial type and historic verity, reproducing the form and feeling of the past. The tower woodwork, together with the clock that was originally in the House of Burgesses, was reconstructed and the bell engraved, "the gift of James Tarphey to Bruton Parish, 1761." The high pulpit is a memorial to the Reverend James Blair, D.D. and the other clergy of the colonial period. Of the twenty-eight graves found in the aisles, nine could be identified from writing, which was done by driving brass tacks into the coffins. Among the graves were Governors Francis Fauquier and Edmund Jennings, as well as Dr. William Cocke, secretary of state for Virginia.

The pulpit Bible, given by King Edward VII, and the lectern, presented by Pres. Theodore Roosevelt, are dedicated in memory of the 300th anniversary of the establishment of the British Church and English civilization in America. Preserved and restored, the old church is typical

Bruton Parish Church in 1930. The wooden belfry houses the "Liberty Bell of Virginia," which was rung for the presentation of the Declaration of Independence and the surrender of Cornwallis.

of strong and simple architectural designs of the colonial period. Old Bruton Parish Church stands, as a former bishop said, "the noblest monument of religion in America."

LOWER CHAPEL
MIDDLESEX COUNTY

Erected: 1717

Denomination: Methodist

Location: Just east of the Hartfield Post Office on Route 33

Religious Services: Sundays, Early Worship at 8:30 A.M.; Worship Service at 11:00 A.M.

Open Mondays, Wednesdays, and Fridays, 9:00 A.M. to 1:00 P.M., or by appointment

Lower Chapel as photographed in 1995. It is one of three colonial churches to possess brickwork laid in English bond.

IN *VIRGINIA COUNTIES*, BY MORGAN POITIAUX ROBINSON, the date of the formation of Middlesex County is said to be 1673. Since the publication of that most interesting work in 1916, additional information has been brought to light. In an article by Floyd W. Sydnor, titled "Middlesex County, Virginia: The Date of Its Origin," the creation of Middlesex County is dated 1669.

Other than the court records referred to in Mr. Sydnor's article, there is no known record of the formation of Middlesex County by the General Assembly. It was taken from Lancaster County, being the portion that lies between the south side of the Rappahannock River and Dragon Swamp, the northern boundary of Gloucester County. As will hereafter be shown, it was the southern part of Christ Church Parish in Lancaster County and retained the same parish name. Christ Church is the only parish coterminous with Middlesex County. In 1675, the General Assembly called on Middlesex County to furnish twenty-five men for military purposes.

In tracing the history of the colonial churches of Christ Church Parish in Middlesex County, Virginia, it is necessary to start with the formation of Lancaster County, out of Northumberland and York Counties, in 1651. The original Lancaster County covered both sides of the Rappahannock River. On 7 August 1654, Lancaster County was divided by a county court order into an upper and lower parish, each including territory on both sides of the Rappahannock River. On 1 April 1657, Lancaster County was again divided by court order into two parishes separated by the river; on 27 May 1657, the south-side parish was subdivided into two additional parishes, the upper named Lancaster and the lower recorded later as Peanckatanck. In 1666, Lancaster and Peanckatanck were reunited to form Christ Church Parish, and when Middlesex County was cut off from Lancaster County in 1669, the new county and parish became coterminous, remaining so to this day.

On 29 January 1666, the vestry book records the creation of Christ Church Parish, by action of a general vestry for the south side of Lancaster County, as follows:

> We doe accord and Agree that the two prishes Formerly called Lancaster and Peanckatanck from henceforth be united as one and called Christ Church prish...it is agreed That Major Genrll Robert Smith and Henry Corbin Esqr be requested to move to the Assembly for Continueing the Union of the Two late Parishes of Pyancktanke and Lancaster.

The Act of Assembly confirming this order was not passed until 26 October 1666, nine months later, but the vestry did not wait for its ratification before ordering the construction of a parish church, as the wording of the original order reveals:

> That a Mother Church be built in the small Indian Field next the head of Capt. Brocas his ground. It being Adjudged to us to be about the Middle of the parish...That the Mother Church be forthwith built by the Undertakers [contractors] Capt. Cuthbert Potter and John Appleton...in every Respect to be done and finished according to the Middle Plantacon Church, to be finished in six months, Glass and iron work convenient time to be given for its transportation out of England.

The first vestry meeting at the new Christ Church was held on 31 December 1666, but the church building was at that point incomplete, since Mr. Cuthbert Potter was ordered to "Finish the Mother Church."

The first church mentioned was the existing parish church, or Chapel of Peanckatanck. The Peanckatanck Parish Church appears to have been the earliest church building in the combined parish of Christ Church, Middlesex. The Methodist church has adopted the name of Piankatank Parish for their circle of churches served by the minister of the present Lower Church. (Varied spellings of this Indian name occur in the colonial vestry book: it is spelled thirteen different ways in twenty-nine entries.) The old Peanckatanck Chapel stood at the head of Scroggin's Creek, which flows into the Piankatank River, at the site where Lower Chapel now stands, about six miles below Christ Church.

On 4 January 1710, the vestry ordered three churches to be built in the parish. In 1714, it ordered "That a new church be built as soon as convenienty may be in the Lower Precincts on the north side of the old church...that the above church be fifty feet long in the cleare and five and twenty wide in the cleare," and "that the Roofe of the sd. church be hipped above the wind beams." The vestry's decision to build so small a church must have met with some opposition, for, at a meeting on 11 November 1714, they agreed that the dimensions chosen were too short by ten feet and ordered the chapel to be built sixty feet long but of the same width. Later, on 6 December 1714, the size of the chapel was changed by the vestry to be fifty-two feet long by thirty feet wide. The outside dimensions on the present building are fifty-six feet by thirty-four feet. The brick work is laid in English bond above and below the water table. The only other colonial churches in Virginia to possess English bond brick work are

Today, Lower Chapel is used by a Methodist congregation.

Yeocomico Church in Westmoreland County, St. Peter's Church in New Kent County, and the Jamestown Tower. This chapel was the smallest and the least expensive to build of the three churches.

The new Lower Chapel was ordered to be built by Capt. Henry Armistead and Maj. Edmond Berkeley and was to be completed by 3 January 1717. The first service in the new church was held on 25 October 1717, and it was conducted by the Reverend Bartholomew Yates, the rector of the parish. A brick to the left of the west doorway is marked "17A15," the "A" probably being the initial of Armistead and the date midway in the course of construction. Another brick, on the opposite side of the doorway, is marked I. W., probably for James Waller, an overseer for the vestry. The quaint Dutch roof of the Lower Chapel is similar to that of the Old Stone Church near Fort Defiance, Virginia. The vestry record shows that for each of the three churches ordered in 1710, a price was set in sweet-scented tobacco, the amount being 126,000 pounds for the Mother Church, 110,000 pounds for the Upper Chapel, and 90,000 pounds for the Lower Chapel.

Sometime after the Revolution, the Lower Chapel was abandoned. It has been said that the Baptists and Methodists utilized the building, and it was also used for a school during the early 1800s. One informant to Bishop William Meade, the Reverend Carraway, mentioned that the old Lower Chapel had been taken over by the Methodists, but still retained some appearance of antiquity, in spite of having been remodeled so as to destroy "all evidence of Episcopal taste and usage." The one remaining original remnant of the colonial period still in the possession of the Lower Chapel is a carved oak chest that dates back to 1677. It formerly held linens and plates as well as other articles for the Holy Communion. It is apparently the chest mentioned in a vestry levy of 20 November 1677, and if so, it is now over 325 years old. The vestry book states that another chest was purchased for the Upper Church in the same year and one for the Mother Church in 1706; both have since disappeared.

The communion vessels of the Lower Chapel were purchased in 1846 by the vestry of St. Paul's Church in Richmond. The inscription on one indicates it was given to the Lower Chapel in 1722. The interior of the church still remains quite attractive. The Lower Chapel, sometimes referred to as the "Old Church," is still active today and is called the Methodist Lower Chapel.

VAUTER'S CHURCH

ST. ANNE'S PARISH CHURCH

ESSEX COUNTY

Erected: 1719

Denomination: Anglican

Location: North side of Route 17, 1/2 mile from Loretto and 12 1/2 miles southeast of the junction of Routes 17 and 301 near Port Royal

Religious Services: Sundays, 9:00 A.M.

Vauter's Church in 1900. It escaped physical damage during the Revolution, the War of 1812, and the Civil War.

Vauter's Church is the second Upper Church of St. Anne's Parish, which was created out of Sittingbourne Parish.

In 1656, Rappahannock County was formed from Lancaster County. At that time it contained Littlebourne Parish, which lay on both sides of the Rappahannock River.

In 1692, Rappahannock County was divided into two new counties: Richmond and Essex. Then Littlebourne Parish divided three ways into North Farnham Parish in Richmond County, South Farnham Parish in lower Essex County, and St. Anne's Parish in upper Essex County.

The first Upper Church of St. Anne's Parish was built sometime around 1710. During colonial times, the parish also consecutively maintained two lower churches. The first was a frame church that stood on Occupacia Creek, probably built around 1665. The second was Sale's Church, which replaced the first Lower Church in 1735; it was named after Cornelius Sale, who donated the land.

Vauter's Church was erected on a branch of Blackburn's Creek, formerly Lucas' Creek. The church is a fine example of T-form colonial brick church architecture. The original portion of the church was built around 1719, and the south wing was added in 1731. The wing is also thirty feet by two inches wide and projects sixteen feet. The outside dimensions of the original rectangle are fifty-six feet six inches by thirty feet two inches.

Bishop William Meade's book *Old Churches, Ministers, and Families of Virginia* contains a communication concerning Old Vauter's Church from Mr. Richard Baylor of Essex:

Upon a branch of Blackburn's Creek, called Church Swamp, stands Vauter's Church, built, as indicated by a date inscribed upon its walls, in 1731. This church, as you know, is in a good state of preservation. The walls over the doors and windows have cracked somewhat but with proper attention old Vauter's will yet serve many generations. The first thing that I recollect, as connected with the old sanctuary, is that my father used to keep the old English Bible at Marl Bank, and when the casual services of a passing Episcopal Minister were to be held there, a servant took the old Bible on his head, and accompanied the family, a near walking-way, across this same Blackburn's Creek, and after service brought it back. I still have this old Bible at Kinlock [the name of Baylor's residence], valued for its antiquity, and on its blank leaves are numerous references in my father's handwriting.

I was told by the late Robert B. Starke of Norfolk that many years ago he attended, as surgeon, one of a party who fought a duel in Vauter's Church yard, before the door facing Loretto, Virginia. The parties were the late General Bankhead and a Mr. Buckner, who, after an exchange of one or two shots without physical effect, retired satisfied. According to Mr. P. S. Hunter of Loretto, in an article written in 1907 about Vauter's Church, he mentions a legend that existed over a long period of time concerning a communion service that was given to Vauter's Church by Queen Anne of England; the old cup of the church service was lost. It was reported later that someone in New Jersey was shown a communion cup in the collection of a friend and marked "St. Anne's Parish, Essex County, Virginia." No doubt, this was the missing cup presented to St. Anne's parish by the Queen, and as she died in 1714, the presentation must have been prior to 1731, when the church was supposed to have been built.

Vauter's Church is oriented with the main entrance in the west end. The chancel is at the east end; while now furnished in modern style, the original high pulpit and reading desk still stand at the church's north end. Much of the interior of the church is of colonial origin, but some of it dates to 1827. The flagstones of the nave are original. It is said that remnants of a brick floor lie under the present wooden floors of the pews. The original box pews survive, although their high sides have been cut down. The doorway in the south wing is of classic pedimented design with Tuscan influence, a style that was fashionable among the colonial churches in the first half of the eighteenth century, and of which Ware Church in Gloucester County affords the earliest example.

The rector of St. Anne's Parish in 1724 was the Reverend John Bagge, who died soon after assuming the rectorship. He was succeeded by the Reverend Robert Rose (1705-51) who served the parish for twenty-one years. In 1746, Mr. Rose became rector of another St. Anne's Parish in Albemarle County, near Scottsville, Virginia. When the city of Richmond was about to be laid out, he was invited by the officials to be their counsel. During this time he became ill, and on 30 June 1751, he died at age forty-seven. He rests in the graveyard of the old church on Richmond Hill, with the inscription, "Here lyeth the body of Robert Rose, Rector of Albemarle parish. His extraordinary genius and capacity in all the polite and useful acts of life, though equalled by few, were yet exceeded by the great goodness of his heart."

Bishop William Meade records that a brother, Charles

Rose, was rector of Yeocomico Church, Westmoreland County, from 1754 to 1758. The Reverend Smelt succeeded Robert Rose in Essex County in 1749 and was there until 1758. Afterward, there is no record of clergymen in Essex until 1774 and 1776, when two Virginia almanacs of that period list the Reverend John Matthews as the minister of St. Anne's Parish. Bishop Meade, in speaking of the earliest church conventions after the Revolution, says:

> In 1814 Thomas Matthews and the Hon. James Hunter were delegates from St. Anne's Parish. Then after a long interval, Rev. John Reynolds was minister in 1822, succeeded in 1825 by Rev. John P. McGuire, 1852-1867; Dr. Charles Goodrich, in 1869; Rev. Alexander Overby, 1873-1880; Rev. W. S. Campbell, 1881-1884; Rev. J. C. Koon, 1885-1888; Rev. D. T. C. Davis, 1890-1899; Rev. E. W. Cowling, 1900-1902; and Rev. J. F. Burks, 1902.

Vauter's Church apparently escaped physical damage during the Revolution, the War of 1812, and the War Between the States—which many of Virginia's colonial churches did not. The glebe house of St. Anne's Parish still stands about six miles from the church on Occupacia Creek. There are two colonial-period gravestones in the yard at Vauter's, one dated 1761 and the other dated 1764.

Vauter's Church owns a silver communion service made in 1724 and 1725 by William Pearson of London, England. All of the silver except one chalice was stolen during the War Between the States. Two pieces, a paten and another chalice, were returned to the parish in 1909. Each of the pieces is

inscribed "St. Ann's Parish Essex County."

In 1969, an extensive restoration of the church took place, this time under the guidance of Mr. Milton Grigg of Charlottesville, Virginia. The building is now as close as possible to the original.

Today, Vauter's Church has an active Episcopal congregation and conducts services every Sunday morning. The rector serves both Vauter's and St. Peter's Church in Port Royal.

Above: Vauter's Church as photographed in 1930, before its restoration in 1969.

Above top: Vauter's Church today with its historic marker, which makes note of the church's communion set that was given by Queen Anne.

ST. JOHN'S CHURCH
ELIZABETH CITY PARISH
HAMPTON

Erected: 1727

Denomination: Anglican

Location: Corner of West Queen and Court Streets in Olde Hampton, downtown

Religious Services: Sundays, 8:00 A.M. and 10:00 A.M.

Open Monday—Friday, 9:00 A.M. to 3:30 P.M., and Saturday, 9:00 A.M. to 12:00 P.M.

The remains of St. John's Church at the close of the Civil War, 1865.

UNDER THE CHARTER OF 1609, THE VIRGINIA Company of London was given authority to establish communities in addition to Jamestown, and the settlers looked forward to the granting of land to private owner-ship, but it was not until 1618 that the first grants of land were made to individuals. By order of the company in 1618, four separate and distinct settlements were established—the only four established directly by the Virginia Company and under its control. To them was given, in later years, the name of "the Four Ancient Boroughs," and they were sometimes referred to as "the four ancient incor-porations." These four were, in order of establishment, James City, Kecoughtan (later Elizabeth City), the city of Henrico, and Charles City.

In 1618, for administrative purposes, the Virginia Company ordered the organization of the four ancient bor-oughs into four corporations. This order was carried out in 1619 by Sir George Yeardley, the British colonial governor of Virginia. The formation of the corporations of James City, Elizabeth City, Henrico, and Charles City carried with it, in each case, the creation of a parish coterminous with the cor-poration.

The pioneer settlement of 1610 at Kecoughtan constitut-ed a typical parish, which formed the nucleus of the later parish of Elizabeth City. William Mease is recorded as the parish priest there from 1610 to 1620.

Elizabeth City County/Parish was named for His Majesty King James I's "most virtuous and renowned Daughter," Princess Elizabeth. A large county, it extended south from the York River, across the Peninsula, and across the James River to include the former Nansemond County and the cities of Chesapeake and Virginia Beach. It also covered the area previously known as the corporation of Elizabeth City. In 1629, the upper and lower parts of the county were rep-resented in the General Assembly for that year.

In 1636, when New Norfolk County was formed, the parish was divided. Elizabeth River Parish encompassed that portion of the parish located on the south side of the James River. Elizabeth City Parish included everything on the north side of the river.

The site of the first Elizabeth City Church, known as Kecoughtan Church, was possibly built as early as 1613. Its remains were discovered on the old glebe in 1910 through the use of a sounding rod, under the direction of Jacob Heffelfinger. The foundation proved to be of cobblestone with a few bricks and is clearly that of a wooden building, probably of framed timber, like the contemporary Argall

Church at Jamestown. The outside dimensions of the foun-dation, as given by Heffelfinger, are fifty-three feet six inches long by twenty-three feet wide, and inside it were found fragments of the church floor, made of brick tiles. A granite cross, erected by the local chapter of the Daughters of the American Revolution, commemorates the existence of this historic pioneer church.

Definite proof that an Elizabeth City Parish church was in service just prior to the incorporation of the city of Hampton is found in the journal of the Reverend George Keith, believed to be the grandson of the minister of the same name, who had officiated at Elizabeth City prior to 1624. In this journal, Mr. Keith, who had been a Quaker but was then a minister of the Established Church, records that on Sunday, 2 May 1703, he preached at "Kecoughtan Church [on] the James River." The church thus mentioned was evi-dently the second Elizabeth City Parish Church, which may be assumed to have been built not long before 1667, in response to an Act of Assembly passed in March 1661, requiring that there be a church decently built in each parish of this county.

The same diary suggests the existence of a chapel-of-ease in Elizabeth City Parish: "May 9, Sunday [1703], I preached at a chapel in Elizabeth [City] County." This entry probably refers to the Charles Parish Church, which stood just over the county line in York County.

The brick foundation of the second church of Elizabeth City Parish has also been excavated. It appears to have been a frame building measuring about fifty feet by twenty-seven feet outside—only slightly larger than its predecessor.

In his book Old Churches, Ministers, and Families in Virginia, Bishop William Meade states that the only surviving vestry book of Elizabeth City Parish opens in the year 1751. Until this time (and on one list after this date) the parish was called Hampton Parish, but from the beginning of this par-ticular vestry book, it was changed to Elizabeth City Parish. The list mentioned by Bishop Meade is apparently one of the two lists of Virginia rectors (ministers), published in 1754 and 1755, respectively, both of which gave the parish's name as Hampton for those years.

The list of rectors who served during the years 1610 to 1727 is as follows:

Rev. William Mease	1610-20
Rev. George Keith	1617-25
Rev. Frances Bolton	1621-23
Rev. Mr. Fenton	1624
Rev. Jonas Stockton	1627

A photograph of St. John's Church in 1910, taken from Queen Street. The colonial communion from 1619 set is still in the church's possession.

Rev. William Wilkensen	1644
Rev. Philip Mallory	1661
Rev. Jusinian Aylmer	1665-67
Rev. Jeremiah Taylor	1667
Rev. William Harris	1675
Rev. John Page	1677-87
Rev. Cope D'Oyle	1687
Rev. James Wallace	1691-1712
Rev. James Falconer	1720-24
Rev. Thomas Peader	1727

The third Elizabeth City Parish Church, built in 1728, is the building now known as St. John's Church, which stands in the northwest corner of Queen and Court Streets in Hampton. The brick structure forms the shape of a Latin cross, with chancel and transept wings of exactly the same length and the nave nearly twice as long. The outside dimensions of the cross are seventy-five feet two inches (east to west) by sixty feet eight inches (north to south). The body of the church and the transept are both of the same width, thirty feet four inches (outside), and the three wings of the cross

each project fifteen feet two inches, while the nave measures twenty-nine feet eight inches in length. The walls are two feet thick.

As in most cruciform colonial churches, there is a main entrance at the west end of the nave and a secondary entrance at each end of the transept. A gallery was built in the north transept wing, some time before 1763 by Alexander McKenzie.

Only slight damage was incurred by St. John's Church during the bombardment of Hampton by the British in 1775, but the building was desecrated by British troops through use as a barracks in the War of 1812. After the War of 1812, the church and yard went to ruin. Nothing was left of the church except the walls and a "leaking roof." When Hampton was sacked and plundered in 1812 by the British under Rear Adm. Sir George Cockburn, great indignity was inflicted on the people by the troops. The Reverend John C. McCabe says that "the Church of God was not spared during the saturnalia of lust and violence. His temple was profaned and desecrated. The church in which our fathers worshiped stabled the horse and stalled the ox."

Bishop Meade also mentions the British ruthlessness in volume one of his *Old Churches*. In 1824, the bishop inspired the parishioners with his presence, holding a service in the ruins of the church. The restoration process began soon thereafter. Work was completed in 1827, at which time, by the action of the vestry, the church was named St. John's. Bishop Moore consecrated the building on 6 March 1830.

After three decades of active use, the old parish church of Elizabeth City was once again reduced to ruins when it was burned, along with the town of Hampton, on the night of 7 August 1861, by Confederate forces under the command of Brig. Gen. John Magruder. Following the close of the Civil War, services were held occasionally at the Odd Fellows' Hall on Court Street until St. John's Church was restored to use on 13 April 1870.

The old church shares with the city of Hampton the glory of three historic priorities: first, the town is the oldest continuous settlement of English origin in America; second, the parish is the oldest Protestant parish in continuous existence in America; and third, it possesses a set of communion silver that has been in use longer than any English communion service in the United States.

This ancient communion set consists of a silver-gilt cup inscribed, "The Communion Cupp for Snt Mary's Church in Smith's Hundred in Virginia," and two silver patens, one of which is inscribed, "If any man eate of this Bread he shall

Above: St. John's Church in 1925. This building survived the bombardment of Hampton by the British in 1775.

Above top: This early photo of St. John's Church shows the surrounding churchyard, which includes beautiful old magnolias and cypresses.

St. John's Church and its cemetary has lasted three wars.

live for ever John VIth." All three pieces bear the London date letter for 1618/19. This old silver was given in 1619 by an unknown person to the church at Smith's Hundred, an early settlement founded by the bequest of two hundred pounds in the will of Mrs. Mary Robinson of London, at her death in 1618. The church stood at Smith's Hundred on Dancing Point, between the Chickahominy and James Rivers, in what is now Charles City County. The settlement was so badly damaged by the Indian massacre of 1622 that it was abandoned, and the surviving colonists transferred to a new site, while the silver was given to Sir George Yeardley, commander of the hundred and, later, governor of the colony, for safekeeping.

After Yeardley's death in 1726, his widow delivered the vessels to the general court at Jamestown, and since Smith's Hundred had been renamed Southampton Hundred in 1620,

in honor of the earl of Southampton, it is supposed that the court thought it fitting to give the silver to the new church of Elizabeth City on Hampton Creek, then called Southampton River, after the same nobleman.

The only English church silver in the United States that is older than these St. John's Church vessels are a chalice and paten made in London in 1611 and owned by St. Peter's Church at Perth Amboy, New Jersey. This church was not founded until 1698 and 1699, and its communion silver was imported at that time, eighty years after the Hampton plate came to America.

Elizabeth City Parish has prospered and grown under the blessing of God and the devoted Christian people who have served it. The church has passed through and survived three wars. It remains today a strong and developing force for God and righteousness.

SLASH CHURCH

UPPER CHURCH OF ST. PAUL'S PARISH
HANOVER COUNTY

Erected: 1729

Denomination: Disciples of Christ; before the Revolution, it was known as the Upper Church of St. Paul's (Episcopal) Parish

Location: Located on Route 656 between Peaks and Ashland in Hanover County. From Ashland, take Route 54 across I-95 bridges, and turn right onto Route 656

Religious Services: Sundays, Worship Service at 10:45 A.M.
Second and fourth Wednesdays, Disciple Night (contemporary worship) at 6:00 P.M.

Slash Church gets its name from the slashes, or ravines, that form in the sandy clay soil on which it was built.

Hanover County was named for George I of England, who also was the duke of Hanover in Germany. It was formed from New Kent County in 1721.

The first minister of St. Paul's Parish, whose boundaries are contiguous with Hanover County, was the Reverend Zachariah Brookes, who was still vicar of Hawkston and Newton in England, leaving a curate there. In 1724, he informed the bishop of London that his Virginia parish was sixty miles in length and twelve in width (before Louisa County was cut off) and that its two churches and two chapels served 1,200 families. He also reported that there were one hundred communicants at each of the churches.

The existing Slash Church, constructed in 1729, was the second Upper Church of St. Paul's Parish. The first Upper Church stood about one and a half miles north of the current church and had been constructed in 1702. This first church was known at that time as the "Mechumps Creek" chapel.

Its replacement, Slash Church, takes its name from the slashes, or ravines, that form in the poorly draining sandy clay soil on which it was constructed.

Slash Church was constructed by Edward Chambers and Thomas Pinchbeck using frame construction. Its outside walls measure approximately sixty feet by twenty-six feet.

According to James Scott Rawlings, the following are possibly original colonial features of Slash Church: some of the clapboards on the east, south, and west walls; the modillon (form-of-bracket) cornice; the double doors and door trim on the west; the sills of the lower two windows in the east; the wooden sills of the foundations (which have now been raised and set on brick foundations); the horizontal board wainscotting; and the hand rail (though not the balusters)

and flooring of the west gallery.

The Reverend Patrick Henry, uncle of the famous orator, served as minister of St. Paul's Parish from 1737 until his death in 1777. It is believed that both Mr. Henry's well-spoken nephew and Dolley Madison attended religious services at Slash Church.

In 1789, the Reverend Talley became minister of St. Paul's Parish. Later, Mr. Talley became a Universalist.

Unfortunately for the Episcopal Church, the congregation at St. Paul's declined during the difficult times after the Revolution and the Disestablishment. The church was abandoned and stood idle for a period of time. After the Episcopalians abandoned the building, they began attending St. Paul's Church at Hanover Courthouse, and Slash Church began to be used by other denominations, including Methodists and the Disciples of Christ. The latter congregation is predominantly American communion, non-creedal, but Biblical in doctrine. Historically, the Disciples of Christ have been committed to the dual goals of Christian unity and the restoration of the simple Christianity of the New Testament. In 1842, the Disciples of Christ purchased the Slash Church and property.

In May 1862, Slash Church became the headquarters for Confederate Brig. Gen. Lawrence O'Brian Branch. On 27 May, two battles fought in the vicinity of the church (later called the Battle of Slash Church in the South) resulted in a victory for the Union. After the engagement, local homes and Slash Church were used as hospitals for more than three hundred wounded soldiers. In the 1950s, old trees cut down on north side of Slash Church were found to contain bullets from these battles.

Today, the Disciples of Christ continue to use Slash Christian Church, as it is now called, for their services.

UPPER CHURCH
STRATTON MAJOR PARISH
KING AND QUEEN COUNTY

Erected: 1724-1729

Denomination: Methodist

Location: On Route 14, about 5 miles northwest of Centerville and 8.6 miles south of King and Queen Courthouse

Religious Services: Sundays, 11:00 A.M.

Upper Church was used for only nine years before it was abandoned. In 1825, it was pulled down and its bricks used for other purposes. Here is a photograph of Upper Church in 1910.

THE DEVELOPMENT OF THE ENGLISH SETTLEMENT UP the York River was marked by the formation of King and Queen County, which was named for the joint sovereigns of England: King William III, Prince of Orange, and Queen Mary.

Knowledge of the early churches in this region is somewhat limited, since the archives of both King and Queen County and King William County (which was split off from King and Queen in 1701) were destroyed by fire, and almost all their parish records have been lost, with the principal exception of one eighteenth-century vestry book for a parish in King and Queen.

The present King and Queen County once formed part of Charles River County, one of the eight original shires into which the Virginia Colony was divided in 1634. The original county's name was changed to York in 1643. The area north of the York and Mattaponi Rivers became Gloucester County in 1651. The northwest extension of York and Gloucester Counties was cut off above Scimino and Poropotank Creeks in 1654 to form New Kent County. Stratton Major Parish, established in 1655 as New Kent's first parish, may have been named for Stratton in Cornwall, England, but the origins of the name have not been clearly established.

By an act of the General Assembly in 1691, New Kent County was divided, and King and Queen County was created; thereafter, Stratton Major Parish fell within the bounds of King and Queen County.

Churchill Gibson Chamberlayne, in the introduction to his vestry book of Stratton Major Parish, discusses the probable boundary lines and sums up his conclusions as follows:

Following the history notes just given, a word or two on the geography of Stratton Major Parish will not be out of place here. Stratton Major Parish, which from the year of its establishment until 1691 was in New Kent County and after that date in King and Queen County, of which it forms the southeastern third, is bounded on the southeast by Poropotank Creek [which separates King and Queen from Gloucester], on the southwest by the York River [which separates King and Queen from New Kent] and the Mattapony [which separates King and Queen from King William], on the northeast by the Dragon Run [which separates King and Queen from Middlesex], and on the northwest by the southeast line of St. Stephen's Parish. The territory embraced within the limits of Stratton Major Parish is strictly rural in char-

acter, there being no towns at all and few villages of any considerable size. There are many water courses, of which the majority empty into either the Mattapony or the York.

Of the nine colonial churches built in the area of the original King and Queen County, five are still standing: two in the present King and Queen County and three in King William. The two in King and Queen comprise the third Upper Church of Stratton Major Parish and the second Mattaponi Church, respectively.

The third Upper Church of Stratton Major Parish was built between 1724 and 1729. It apparently occupies the exact site of an earlier chapel, probably a wooden structure, that was built sometime around 1675. It is said that footings of this earlier church were uncovered by a bulldozer some years ago.

The colonial brick of the third Upper Church is laid in Flemish bond with dark glazed headers. The upper walls are two feet thick, and the church measures sixty-four feet by thirty-four feet on the outside. The building was oriented with the chancel at the east end. There are two windows in each side of the nave, one in each side of the chancel, and two in the east end. Few details of the old church's original interior arrangement are given in the vestry book, but it was apparently of conventional design, having the pulpit on the north side, directly opposite the south doorway, and a central aisle leading from the chancel to the main entrance in the west end.

It is recorded that a gallery was built in the church in 1739, probably at the west end of the nave. A marble font was given to the Upper Church in 1730 by Col. Cavin Corbin, and a sundial was installed in the churchyard sixteen years later.

The original 1729 to 1783 vestry book of Stratton Major Parish is on deposit at the Virginia State Library in Richmond. It lists the following vestrymen, commencing in 1739, who were the leaders in all the civil and ecclesiastical matters in Stratton Major Parish and King and Queen County: Richard Roy, Richard Johnson, Henry Hickman, Edward Ware, Thomas Dudley, John Collier, Roger Gregory, Philip Roots, Francis Gaines, John Whiting, Thomas Reid Roots, Richard Corbin, Richard Bray, and John Kidd.

The first record of the vestry's intention to replace both of the existing churches in Stratton Major Parish is found in a vestry order of 30 November 1759. The land for the new church, to be situated midway between the two older structures, was given by Richard Corbin, a member of the Church

Upper Church as it appears today. It was completely rebuilt in 1850 and used by Baptists and Methodists.

Council and the receiver-general of Virginia.

When the church was completed in 1768, it was not only the costliest but also the largest colonial church of which there is any record in the state. It was specified to be eighty feet by fifty feet, with side walls twenty-seven feet high and three feet thick, resting on a foundation with footings five brick lengths wide.

Like Ware Church at Gloucester, this new church had four rows of high box pews in the body of the church. Since the men did the seating, they put the women on the south side, and typical colonial seating arrangements of this character are recorded in the vestry books for Bruton Parish Church in Williamsburg and Donation Church in Virginia Beach.

The new church was accepted by the vestry on 4 March 1768, and the two older church buildings were retired from service. On 3 October 1768, the vestry ordered that the Upper Church be boarded up and closed.

The new church was used for only nine years. In 1777, in the face of opposition from both the Crown and the Church of England, services ceased. The beautiful church building was sold, and in 1825, it was pulled down and its bricks were used for other purposes.

The third Upper Church (built circa 1724-29), although closed, seems to have been used for worship by Baptists and other groups until about 1842. It was used as a school, taught by Robert Stubbs, until its roof and interior woodwork were destroyed by fire.

In 1850, the Upper Church was completely rebuilt and then used for services by both the Baptists and Methodists for a number of years. The Methodists finally bought out other interests in the building, including the claims of the owner of the surrounding land, and have occupied the church ever since. The minutes of the Gloucester Circuit of Methodist Churches shows that the church was considered a member of the circuit from 1818 to 1826.

The vestry book (1729-83) of Stratton Major Parish has been published and is available at most libraries.

WREN CHAPEL
WILLIAMSBURG

Erected: 1729

Denomination: Nondenominational

Location: The campus of the College of William and Mary

Religious Services: Wednesdays, Eucharist at 6:00 P.M. (while college is in session)

Wren Chapel of the College of William and Mary in the early 1900s. It is the oldest academic building in the nation. (The statue is of Norborne Berkeley, Baron de Botetourt, an early Virginia governor and benefactor of the college.)

THE WREN BUILDING IS THE OLDEST ACADEMIC building in use in America; the cornerstone was laid in 1695. It was named for Sir Christopher Wren, one of the most famous English architects. It is uncertain but possible that Sir Christopher Wren supplied the design for the first form of the building. The Reverend Hugh Jones, the first professor of mathematics at the college, wrote in his "Present State of Virginia," in 1722, "The building is beautiful and commodious, being first modelled by Sir Christopher Wren, adapted to the nature of the country by the gentlemen there; and since it burned down, it has been rebuilt and nicely contrived, altered and adorned by the ingenious direction of Governor Spotswood and is not altogether unlike Chelsa Hospital."

The college building was planned by Sir Christopher Wren, and it was designed, says Beverly, "to be an entire square when completed." The first commencement exercises were held in 1700, "at which there was a great concourse of people."

The General Assembly of Virginia was held at his Majesty's Royal College of William and Mary, from 1700 until 1705, when, with the library and philosophical apparatus, it was destroyed by fire. The second building was commenced during the service of Governor Spotswood, but due to the lack of materials and workmen, it was not completed until 1723. The following is an extract from *Beverley's History of Virginia, 1722*: "The College was burned in the first year of Governor Mott's time [the cause was not known]. It was not rebuilt till Governor Spotswood's time, when it was raised to the same bigness as before." In 1719, the building was occupied by the Convention of the Colonial Clergy.

The founder and first president of the college was James Blair (1656-1743). He was a native of Scotland and an Episcopal clergyman. He was appointed to the office by the Charter. At the request of the bishop of London, he came as a missionary to Virginia in 1685. He died in 1743, after having filled the office of president of the college for half a century. It is interesting to note that eight presidents of the College of William and Mary have been rectors of Bruton Parish Church, and two presidents have been bishops of the Episcopal Church.

On the night of 8 February 1859, at a time when the alumni of the college were on the eve of celebrating the 166th anniversary of its foundation, the Wren building, with most of its interesting antiquities, was destroyed by accidental fire. It was believed that the fire started in the cellar, below the laboratory. A man was cutting wood in the cellar, by the light of a candle, and it was his carelessness that caused the fire.

Early in May 1861, the college suspended its exercises and closed its doors. The building was seized by the military and used as a barracks and, later, as a hospital, until the evacuation of Williamsburg in May 1862. A conflict occurred on 9 September 1862 between a detachment of Confederate cavalry and a Federal garrison, then consisting of the Fifth Regiment Pennsylvania Cavalry, which received the worst of the battle. The Confederates took control of the town early in the day, but withdrew in a few hours. Drunken Federal soldiers, provoked by their defeat, set fire to the Wren building, and the entire structure and all furniture were destroyed. The grounds and buildings not destroyed were held by the United States Army, from May 1862 to September 1865, for depots and other purposes. In July 1869, the Wren building was substantially restored; the faculty was reorganized, with a sufficient corps of academic professors; the course of studies were revised and modified; and the college was opened for the first time since 1861.

The walls of the chapel remained intact after each of the fires of 1705, 1859, and 1862. They were reused in each new form, including the restoration of the second form that was accomplished by Colonial Williamsburg in the years 1928 to 1931. The seventeenth-century plans called for a quadrangle enclosing a courtyard, but the first and second forms were built only in the shape of an L. The main range is 138 feet by forty-six feet on the outside, running north to south, and the north hall is sixty-four feet by thirty-two feet, running east to west. The interior of the chapel features high paneling on the walls in the late Jacobean style.

A number of influential people lie buried in vaults beneath the chapel. Among them are Gov. Lord Botetourt, Sir John Randolph, Peyton Randolph, and the Right Reverend James Madison, the first bishop of Virginia.

Among the prominent men in Virginia, many were alumni of the college. These include James Monroe, John Marshall, Thomas Jefferson, Henry Lee, John Tyler, and William Wirt. George Washington was chancellor for eleven years. Four of the first ten presidents of the United States were associated with the College of William and Mary.

The Wren building at the College of William and Mary includes English-bond brickwork; the only other surviving colonial churches in Virginia with this feature were all built within two decades after 1699, the date recorded for the construction of the Jamestown tower. These churches are St. Peter's (1703) in New Kent County, Yeocomico (1706) in Westmoreland County, and the Lower Methodist Chapel

The chapel was named for Sir Christopher Wren, the famous English architect. Photograph by F. S. Lincoln.

(1717) in Middlesex County.

The College of William and Mary is located in one of America's oldest and most historical cities. It would be more accurate to say that one of America's oldest and most historic cities has grown up around the College of William and Mary. The college was established before the town. It is certain that there never would have been any restoration of Williamsburg had not been for the College of William and Mary. The idea of restoring Williamsburg came about in 1924 when Mr. John D. Rockefeller Jr. was persuaded to undertake the project. The first building restored was the Wren building. This was no easy task, as fires and centuries had considerably changed the building. During the research process, however, a plate was found at the Bodelian Library at Oxford. On this plate an eighteenth-century artist had engraved actual drawings of the principal buildings that the college was attempting to restore.

Not far from the historic Wren building is the lovely Bruton Parish Church, restored to authenticity. We have in Williamsburg one of the most significant landmarks in America's history preserved for future generations of Americans. In one book about Colonial Williamsburg, there is a verse that ends,

For if the things you see give you no gain
The lives of many men were lived in vain.

MANGOHICK CHURCH

CHAPEL OF ST. MARGARET'S PARISH

UPPER CHURCH OF ST. DAVID'S PARISH

KING WILLIAM COUNTY

Erected: 1706

Denomination: Protestant Episcopal

Location: 4 miles west of Tucker Hill Post Office. North of Warsaw on Route 203

Religious Services: First, third, and fifth Sundays, 11:15 A.M.

Mangohick Church as photographed in 1910.

KING WILLIAM COUNTY WAS NAMED AFTER WILLIAM of Orange, king of England, who reigned with Queen Mary, from 1688 to 1694, and alone, from 1695 to 1702. The county was laid off from King and Queen County in 1702. St. John's Parish was originally formed in 1680 in New Kent County, but came into King William the year the county was created.

In 1720, the upper section of St. John's Parish, which was coextensive with King William County, was laid off, by Act of Assembly, to create St. Margaret's Parish. The same act provided that both churches in the county would fall into the Lower Parish (St. John's). This circumstance made it necessary to build a new church in the new St. Margaret's Parish. The vestry of St. John's Parish was ordered to donate twenty-five thousand pounds of tobacco toward the construction of the new church. The result was the present Mangohick Church, which was finished around 1730 as a chapel of ease. It seems likely that several years elapsed before the new parish was financially able to undertake the construction—despite donations from the old parish—since the church was still new when Colonel Byrd visited it in 1732.

Mangohick seems to have been mentioned in petition of 1738 to the colonial Council by Benjamin Walker, Gentleman. In this petition, the inhabitants of St. Margaret's Parish complain that John Brunskill, clerk of the parish, had "neglected to perform divine service at a Chapel of Ease built several years ago for the convenience of a great number of families living remote from the church of the said parish and refusing to preach or read prayers there as by he is obliged." The date and wording of this petition are consistent with a date of erection, prior to 1732, for Mangohick Church.

When St. David's Parish was formed in 1744, Mangohick Church became the Upper Church of St. David's. It was abandoned by the parish, however, soon after the Revolutionary War.

The name "Mangohick" is Indian, and it is also applied to a nearby creek. The church measures approximately sixty-two feet by twenty-eight feet on the outside. The brick is laid in Flemish bond with glazed headers. The church has the conventional west and south doors, and there is the usual gallery in the west end of the nave, lighted by a pair of small, rectangular windows above the main entrance. Another small window in the north side indicates that there were once a great number of pews between the pulpit and the chancel, in addition to the two on either side of the communion table. The floor of this church has been raised, and the present interior bears no resemblance of a colonial—or Anglican—church.

After many years as a "free church," available to any denomination for services, the property was deeded to an African-American congregation. In 1825, Union Baptist Church, a congregation made up of blacks and whites, was organized at Mangohick Church. In 1854, the white members moved to a new church building. Since that time, the church has been called Mangohick Baptist Church.

Unfortunately, Mangohick Church no longer resembles a colonial church.

WESTOVER CHURCH

CHARLES CITY COUNTY

Erected: 1731

Denomination: Anglican

Location: 6401 John Tyler Memorial Highway (Route 5)

Religious Services: Sundays, Communion at 8:30 A.M., and Worship at 11:00 A.M.

Westover Church as it appeared in the early 1900s. During its early years, it served as the county seat and courthouse.

WESTOVER CHURCH IS SITUATED IN ONE of the oldest and most interesting counties in Virginia. Charles City, which lies on the James River, was one of the eight original shires, or counties, into which the Virginia Colony was partitioned in 1634. Yet, while it held so central a position among the first counties, little of the civil or ecclesiastical history stemming from its first century of existence is known. One exception is the great Indian massacre of 1622, which either destroyed or greatly damaged Westover Hundred, Weyanoke Hundred, and Charles City Hundred—the earliest settlements in Charles City County.

Originally, Charles City County contained two parishes—Westover (or the Upper) Parish and Weyanoke (or the Lower) Parish. Each of these was divided by the James River into two parts, northern and southern.

In 1720, the northern parts of Westover and Weyanoke Parishes, together with a part of another parish called Wallingford (which extended to the Chickahominy River), were all united into one parish, which retained the name of Westover. Likewise, the southern parts of the original Westover and Weyanoke Parishes were united into one parish called Martin's Brandon, located in Prince George County.

The Reverend Peter Fontaine officiated in Wallingford, Weyanoke, Martin's Brandon, and Jamestown before the new arrangement.

In 1724, the Wilmington Parish was dissolved, and its section south of the Chickahominy was added to Westover Parish. From that time to the present, Westover Parish has been coextensive with Charles City County.

The first church of Westover Parish stood a few hundred yards up the James River from the Westover plantation house, nearly two miles from the site of the present church. There, the old churchyard contains tombstones that date from 1637—the year that Capt. Thomas Pawlett patented two thousand acres that became known as Westover. He was influential in the decision to locate the church on this part of his land, which he subsequently left to the church in his will. The churchyard also contains the tombs of Benjamin Harrison of Berkeley and his wife, Elizabeth Burwell, who were the parents of Benjamin Harrison, speaker of the House of Burgesses; the grandparents of Benjamin Harrison, one of the signers of the Declaration of Independence; the great-grandparents of William Harrison, who died in 1841 while serving as president of the United States; and great-great-great-grandparents of Benjamin Harrison, twenty-third president of the United States.

For many years, Westover served as the seat of Charles City County and the courthouse, as well as the church, which stood near the plantation house. In 1731, that first church was replaced by the present building, located about a mile and a half from the house on the north side of Herring Creek. The rectangular building, of brick laid in Flemish bond, was designed in the conventional Georgian style.

In his book on early Virginia churches, Bishop William Meade wrote of the present building:

> The old Westover church still stands, a relic and monument of ancient times. It is built of the glazed-end bricks, generally used in Colonial structures. It has been subject to terrible mutilation, having been used in the days of general depression in the Episcopal Church in the beginning of the 19th century as a barn. Repaired then by the families of Berkeley and Shirley, and again repaired just prior to the [Civil] War, it was used by the Federal troops as a stable. In 1867 the

"A relic and monument of modern times," Westover Church as it appeared in 1930.

The present Westover Church was rennovated with funds raised by the Ladies Aid Society in 1907.

Westover Church was opened and used again for the first time since the close of the War. Not a door, window, or floor was left, but by the blessing of good God and kind friends, we have repaired it.

In 1907, the Ladies Aid Society raised a considerable sum toward the restoration and beautification of the church. In the course of repairs, the colonial design was modified. The door on the south side was replaced by an additional arched window; in the east end, a window was replaced by a door; and the high-backed box pews were replaced by modern pews.

The parish's early vestrymen included Lightfoots, Minges, Byrds, Carters, Harrisons, Tylers, Christians, Seldons, Nelsons, Lewises, Douthats, and Willcoxes.

Of the ministers of this parish, Bishop Meade reports that the earliest on record was the Reverend Charles Anderson, who died in 1718, after having been the minister of the parish for twenty-six years. He was followed by the Reverend Peter Fontaine, who died in 1755, and then Rev. William Davis, who served from 1758 to 1773; the Reverend James Ogilbie began service circa 1776; and the Reverend John Dunbar started in 1786.

The Reverend Sewell Chapin, last occupant of the glebe, or parsonage, came to the church in 1793. He baptized John Tyler, tenth president of the United States, who was born at Greenway, Charles City County, in 1790. Mr. Chapin died at "Weyanoke," the residence of Mr. F. Lewis, and was buried in the aisle and under the present chancel of Westover Church.

The parish owns a pater and chalice made in London in 1694 and 1695. On the cover of the chalice is inscribed the name of the donor, Sarah Braine. Today, Westover continues as an active Episcopal parish church of the Diocese of Virginia.

CHRIST CHURCH
LANCASTER COUNTY

Erected: 1732

Denomination: Anglican

Location: 3 miles north of Irvington, Virginia, off Route 3

Religious services: Used by Grace Episcopal Church, Kilmarnock, from Memorial to Labor Day (Sundays, 8:00 A.M.)

Open daily

Christ Church, as photographed in 1900, is one of the most perfect examples of colonial architecture.

THE MOST PERFECT EXAMPLE OF COLONIAL CHURCH architecture now remaining in Virginia is Christ Church, Lancaster County. The first mention of Lancaster County is made in "Henning's Statutes at Large," as early as 1652, when it is represented in the House of Burgesses by Capt. Henry Fleet and Mr. William Underwood. At that time, and for four years afterward, it included the area that currently comprises Lancaster, Middlesex, Essex, and Richmond Counties. In 1656, Rappahannock County was cut off from Lancaster and divided into the counties of Richmond and Essex in 1692. (Rappahannock County is no more.) In the county of Lancaster, when including Middlesex, there were four parishes—two on each side of the Rappahannock River. Those on the south side of the river were called the Lancaster Parish and the Piankatank Parish, until at an early period they were merged and jointly called Christ Church. Those on the north side were St. Mary's and Christ Church until, at a much later period, they were united into what is now known as Christ Church.

According to Bishop William Meade in the second volume of *Old Churches, Minisers, and Families* (1857), the vestry book of Christ Church commenced in 1654. He first saw the book in 1852 and once again three years later. He took extracts from it, some of which were published. Soon after, the vestry book disappeared and was not located. Fortunately, the county records are intact from 1652 and can supply more information as regards to church history. Bishop Meade also describes the construction of the earlier church and the Carter family's influence in the erection of the new building.

In 1654, the name of John Carter, the patriarch of that family, appears at the head of the vestry lists. The same can be said of the eldest son, John, and the youngest son, Robert, alias "King" Carter. Their names always preceded the minister's and were written in large, bold hand. Robert "King" Carter was quite wealthy and acquired numerous servants and tenants. Tradition has it that the congregation did not enter the church on Sundays until the Carters' coach had arrived and he and his family were inside.

The present church was built on the site of an older one, which was completed in 1670, under the direction of John Carter, the first of that name and the great ancestor of the Carters of Virginia. By the side of the chancel is a large marble slab, on which are the names of John Carter and his three wives and several children, who all died before him and were buried in that spot.

When the church became too small for the increasing population, Robert "King" Carter offered to build a new one at his own expense. The offer was cheerfully accepted, and

the present church was completed in 1732, about the time of Mr. Carter's death. The most perfect example of colonial church architecture now remaining in Virginia is Christ Church, Lancaster County. It is now, with the exception of some minor details, almost as it came from the hands of the builders in 1732.

Bishop Meade commented,

> ...in such a house surrounded by many memorials, it was delightful to read the word of God and the prayers of the church from the old desk, to pronounce the commandments from the altar near which the two tablets of the law, the Creed, and the Lord's Prayer, are still to be seen in large and legible characters; and then to preach the words of eternal life from the high and lofty pulpit, which seemed, as it were, to be hung in the air. Peculiarly delightful it was to raise the voice in such utterances in a church whose sacred form and beautiful arches seemed to give force and music to the feeblest tongue beyond any other building in which I ever performed or heard the hallowed services of the sanctuary.

Many years ago, Mr. R. S. Mitchell of Irvington, who was a vestryman of the parish for numerable years, furnished measurements of the building. It is in the form of a Greek cross, the main body of the church and the transepts measuring externally sixty-eight feet. As the walls are three feet thick, the interior dimensions are sixty-two feet. The ceiling, which forms a groined arch (the sharp-curved edge formed at the junction of two intersecting vaults) over the intersection of the aisles, is thirty-three feet from the floor, and the top of the roof is ten feet higher. The flooring of the aisles, slabs of freestone, is still solid and smooth, while the raised plank flooring of the pews is, in most instances, in fair condition. There are three round windows in the gables and twelve others, which are six by fourteen feet. The high pews of solid black walnut, with seats running around them, are still solid and strong. There are twenty-five pews, twenty-two with a seating capacity of twelve each, and three that will contain twenty persons each. These latter were for the Carter family and attendants, and for the magistrates.

Bishop Meade records that the old box pews now stand without the brass rods and damask curtains that formerly divided them. The mortar and white plaster were clinched behind the thick laths and the original walls have stood solid and intact.

Robert "King" Carter died on 4 August 1732, in his sixty-ninth year, and was buried in a large sarcophagus (limestone coffin) outside the east end of the church. Next to his final resting place is the sarcophagus of Betty Carter, his second wife, who died in 1710, and beyond it is that of Judith Carter, his first wife, who died in 1699. A long inscription in Latin, accompanied by the family coat-of-arms, relates that Robert had served as rector of the College of William and Mary, speaker of the House of Burgesses for six years, governor of the colony for more than a year, and treasurer in the reigns of William, Anne, George I, and George II.

Tradition says that Christ Church is built of bricks brought over from England. Robert Carter had so many vessels from England assigned to him, he may, at little cost, have had English bricks put in as ballast and then conveyed in flatboats up the creek within a short distance of the church.

Christ Church is the only colonial church in Virginia erected by one man, and it is the only one of that period that has come down to us unaltered. It is a monument to the generosity as well as the great estate of Robert Carter and the intimate generational ties with the Carter family

Above: Christ Church in 1930. King Carter may have had its bricks shipped from England.

Below: Christ Church's building remains as it did at its creation in 1732.

Opposite: Robert "King" Carter, who is responsible for the construction of Christ Church, built Carter's Grove on the James River about 1730.

MATTAPONI CHURCH
LOWER CHURCH OF ST. STEPHEN'S PARISH
KING AND QUEEN COUNTY

Erected: 1730-1734

Denomination: Baptist

Location: On the west side of Route 14, 5.7 miles north of King and Queen Courthouse and 1/2 mile south of Cummon Post Office

Religious Services: Sundays, 11:00 A.M.

Mattaponi Church in desperate need of repair in 1910.

THE FIRST LOWER ST. STEPHEN'S CHURCH WAS succeeded by the existing second church of that name—a magnificent cruciform structure of colonial brick walls laid in Flemish bond with glazed headers and doorways with classical pediments. Long known as the Mattaponi Church, it is located in King and Queen County, which was named for joint sovereigns of England: King William III, Prince of Orange, and Queen Mary.

King and Queen County was formed from New Kent County by an act of the General Assembly in 1691. Stratton Major Parish, previously a part of New Kent County, fell within the boundaries of the new King and Queen County. Sometime between 1660 and 1674, Stratton Major Parish was divided to create St. Stephen's Parish. (Patent records show that St. Stephen's Parish was in existence by 1674; on 18 February of that year, William Herndon was granted land in St. Stephen's Parish in New Kent County.)

St. Stephen's Parish lay on both sides of the Mattiponi River, beginning at Heartsease Creek, but the exact bounds of it are not known. In 1723, the parish was divided, creating the Drysdale Parish. St. Stephen's Parish was represented in the first convention of the church held in 1785.

The first church of St. Stephen's Parish is believed to have served originally as the Upper Church of Stratton Major, before being cut off with the new parish as its first Lower Church. It was built sometime around 1664.

The present Mattaponi Church was built on the site of the first Lower Church. This beautiful structure measures approximately eighty-five feet (east and west) by sixty-four feet (north and south), with a nave measuring forty-three feet four inches long and 32 1/2 feet wide. The walls are three brick lengths thick. There are two windows in each side of the nave and in the east end of the chancel, and one window in each side of the other three arms of the cross. The main entrance stands at the west end, and a secondary entrance can be found at each end of the transept. Originally, the church had a three-decker pulpit, with a sounding board in the north angle of the cross, but this pulpit disappeared after a subsequent modernization took place.

The date of erection of Mattaponi Church has not been definitively established. One possible clue may be taken from what appears to be the builder's name, David Minetree, deeply cut into a brick above the west doorway of the church. Minetree is believed to have been the English builder/architect imported by Carter Burwell in 1751 to construct his mansion at Carter's Grove Plantation. But since there were other builders possessing this name during the colonial period, it is possible that some other Minetree, working at a different time, constructed the church.

Most likely, it was erected between 1720 and 1760. The date 1733 appears on the cover of a Bible of "the Lower Church of St. Stephen's Parish," but George C. Mason, in his *Colonial Churches of Tidewater, Virginia,* suggests that the Bible might have belonged to an earlier church. He is led to believe that this church was built sometime around 1755, because it has a great deal of similarity to Abingdon Church, which was built in 1754 near White Marsh in Gloucester County. Both of these colonial churches were built in the form of a Latin cross.

Mattaponi Church is the only surviving colonial church at St. Stephen's Parish. Its preservation is due to the fact that, having been abandoned by its minister and people a few years after the Disestablishment of the Church of England, the deserted building was taken over by a group of Baptists around 1803. This group repaired the church thoroughly in 1817. Remaining a branch of Lower King and Queen Baptist Church under the ministry of the Reverend William Todd until 1828, the congregation was then formed as the Mattaponi Baptist Church.

The colonial interior was modernized in 1834, and a deed to the church (and to the 2 1/4-acre churchyard) was issued in 1841. The original colonial font (the bowl that holds the water used in baptismal services) was later given to The Fork Church near Doswell in Hanover County.

During the winter of 1922 and 1923, Mattaponi Baptist Church was completely gutted by fire, although the walls were left undamaged. Soon afterwards, the church was rebuilt and is still being used by a Baptist congregation.

During the winter of 1922 and 1923, Mattaponi Church was damaged in a fire. The building was rebuilt, however, and is being used today by a Baptist congregation.

ST. JOHN'S CHURCH
KING WILLIAM COUNTY

Erected: 1734

Denomination: Protestant Episcopal

Location: From West Point take Route 30 North

Religious Services: Sundays, Holy Eucharist at 8:00 A.M. (without music)
First and third Sundays, Holy Eucharist at 10:30 A.M.
Second and fourth Sundays, Morning Prayer at 10:30 A.M.
Fifth Sundays, alternate Morning Prayer and Holy Eucharist at 10:30 A.M.
Homecoming Service, fourth Sunday in September at 11:00 A.M.

St. John's Church, photographed in 1930, would have become a ruin had it not been for the St. John's Church Restoration Association.

ST. JOHN'S PARISH CAME INTO BEING IN 1680 WITH THE division of Stratton Major Parish (which covered the equivalent of several modern counties) into smaller, more compact areas.

There were two churches in the parish at an early date. John Fontaine, who accompanied the governor, records in his journal that Gov. Alexander Spotswood and his party stopped for Sunday services at the upper church during the "Knights of the Golden Horseshoe" expedition that explored the Blue Ridge in 1716.

The lower part of the parish was served by Pamunkey Neck Chapel, constructed between 1650 and 1680 within the boundaries of what later became the town of West Point. The only physical evidence left of the chapel is what was apparently the graveyard, located near the side entrance of West Point's First Baptist Church.

One of the headstones, legible until some years ago, marked the last resting place of a seafaring man:

Though Boreas' blasts and Neptune's waves
  Have tossed me to and fro,
In spite of all, by God's decree
  We anchor here below.
Now here do we at anchor lie
  With many of our fleet,
Yet once again we must set sail
  Our Savior Christ to meet.

In 1729, the vestry of St. John's Parish expressed concern about the decay of the two churches and agreed to set about replacing them. The church to serve the lower part of the parish was to be built first, and both churches were to be of "equal dimensions and goodness."

To finance the two churches, the vestry levied a tax of 19,050 pounds of tobacco on the parishioners. The proceeds from the sale of this commodity, however, were insufficient to construct both churches. So in 1731, a decision was made to build only one church on a site to be selected by agreement among the vestrymen.

The site chosen for St. John's Church was a piece of land on the colonial road between King William Courthouse and Pamunkey Neck, where the town of West Point grew up in the mid-nineteenth century. It is approximately ten miles from West Point and 150 yards west of Virginia State Route 33.

Though it has been conjectured that the church was built in 1732, it seems more likely that it was completed in 1734. As it happens, someone had carved the latter date in the

brick of the door facing the highway, on a wing or transept that was added on the north side some time after the date of the original construction. Except for this addition and the raising of the floor of the nave approximately twelve inches, St. John's in its structural aspects remains the same today as it was in 1734.

The brick is laid in English bond below the water table, but in Flemish bond with all glazed headers above the water table. The west and north doorways are gauged brick. The west doorway has a segmental head, and the north one has a triangular pediment, of which the field is gauged. The west doorway is flanked by pilasters, one of which went to pieces and has recently been restored. In its construction the church offers a fine example of the colonial brick mason's art.

The first rector of St. John's on record was the Reverend John Monro Jr., a Scot who came to the parish in 1693. Monro's tenure fell during a period of stormy relations between church and state in Virginia. He was a brother-in-law of the Reverend James Blair, commissary of the church, who strongly opposed the administration of Gov. Francis Nicholson.

Politically powerful vestrymen like Thomas Claiborne, Henry Fox, and John West supported Nicholson, and Monro took the part of Blair. Monro was accused of slandering the royal governor. The minister, in reply, denounced the vestry for failing to make provision for his living and for having "nay'd and lock'd" the chapel door to keep him from preaching. The vestry denied this, and also denied any prejudice against Mr. Monro because of his Scottish birth, but did admit they believed an Englishman "would be more acceptable" in the pulpit. The quarrel was eventually patched up, and Mr. Monro remained rector until his death about 1723. His widow died in 1725 and was buried beneath Bruton Parish Church in Williamsburg.

The next rector of St. John's Parish was the Reverend William Nelson, who remained only briefly, until about 1724. The first rector to minister to the newly built St. John's Church was the Reverend Daniel Taylor Jr., son of the Reverend Daniel Taylor of Blisland Parish, New Kent County. Young Mr. Taylor studied in the grammar school of the College of William and Mary. In 1723, when he was about nineteen years of age, he entered Cambridge University, studying at St. John's College and Trinity College.

After receiving his bachelor of arts degree, he took holy orders, and on his return to Virginia in 1727, he was chosen rector by the vestry of St. John's Parish. Mr. Taylor remained rector until his death on 9 September 1742.

Apparently, Mr. Taylor was an exemplary minister, and the building of the new church during his rectorate is a testimonial to the unity of the parish under his charge. His wife was Alice Littlepage, daughter of Richard Littlepage of a well-known Virginia family.

For nearly ten years after Mr. Taylor's death, St. John's was without a regular clergyman, though the Reverend James Maury (one of several Anglican clergymen in Virginia who filed suit in the renowned "Parson's Cause" court case of 1763) seems to have served a year or more in the parish. This long deprivation ended with the coming of the Reverend John Robertson as minister in 1752. We know little about Mr. Robertson and his ministry. Apparently he served until around 1756, though there is no record of his being at St. John's after 1756.

During the years 1760 to 1764, St. John's was served by the Reverend Robert Reade, of whose ministry also little is known. Then the church acquired one of the truly gifted clergymen of colonial Virginia: the Reverend Henry Skyren.

Mr. Skyren was born in the port of Whitehaven on England's east coast in 1729. In 1763, he emigrated to the colonies and preached alternately in King and Queen and King William Counties before being elected rector of St.

John's. He married Lucy Moore, daughter of Col. Bernard Moore and Anne Catherine Spotswood, daughter of the royal governor. Colonel Moore was master of the great plantation "Chelsea" in lower King William County.

The vestry of St. John's was impressed with Mr. Skyren's abilities. In 1771, they sought legislation in the House of Burgesses to increase the glebe (the land that yields revenue to a parish church) in order to keep him as rector. He remained at St. John's until he was in his sixties, an advanced age for the day, and he brought to the church its golden years as a house of worship.

Mr. Skyren was blessed with remarkable eloquence. H. I. Lewis, in a series of articles on King William County, wrote of him: "Crowds attended services held in this church to listen to the eloquent sermons from the above celebrated divine, Parson Skyren. Many families brought with them to the church chairs that they might be seated in the aisles, so great were the crowds attending the same."

During Mr. Skyren's early years at St. John's, the vestry was the cockpit of a sharp rivalry between two members, Carter Braxton and Thomas Claiborne, who were bitter political opponents in King William County. They vied for power in the church as well as in politics. Their disagreement was

St. John's Church is structurally the same today as it was in 1734. Phase I of its restoration, which calls for basic preservation, is almost complete. The next phase will see the church ready for use.

carried to the House of Burgesses, which ordered the vestry to be dissolved and new members to be chosen.

Despite the disunity, which ended in the supremacy of the Braxton faction, Mr. Skyren was able to pack his church with supporters of both sides. Again in 1775, the people of the church raised the glebe in order to provide him with a more adequate living.

The Claiborne-Braxton disputes seemed to foreshadow the deep divergence that developed in the parish during the struggle with Great Britain. Claiborne became an outspoken Tory, while Braxton took the part of the colonies as a signer of the Declaration of Independence. Tory raiders burned Braxton's home in 1780, while he was attending a session of the Continental Congress.

St. John's suffered more than many other Anglican churches from the effects of the Revolution. Many of its members either went away to war and never returned or, like Col. John West, owner of the West Point tract and a descendant of the third Lord Delaware, they fled the New World.

Unlike many Anglican clergymen, Mr. Skyren remained with his church to lead it through this difficult period and to assist in its rebirth without its historic ties to the royal government. In 1785 and 1786, we find Mr. Skyren and Carter Braxton listed as delegates from St. John's Parish to the first two Episcopal Conventions. In 1787, Mr. Skyren and William Claiborne served as delegates.

Also in 1787, Mr. Skyren ended his long ministry at St. John's, probably because of advancing age. In 1790, he moved to Hampton and five years later, he died there. St. John's was never to be the same without him.

With the end of Mr. Skyren's ministry, the church could find no clergyman able to measure up to him as a spiritual leader. In 1792, the Reverend James Price became rector, but he left in 1796, apparently having accomplished little. (Reverend Price appears to have been the son of the Reverend Thomas Price of Gloucester County.)

The Reverend John Dunn succeeded Price around 1797. It is not known how long he served, although it is clear that he had left St. John's by 1799, when he shows up as rector of Manchester Parish in Chesterfield County. Mr. Dunn appears to have been St. John's last full-time rector. However, Bishop William Meade states in his book *Old Churches, Ministers, and Families in Virginia* that a Rev. John McGuire often served St. John's while he was a pastor in Essex County.

In a legal sense, St. John's seems to have become state property after the Revolution along with other Crown properties, but as long as it was being used by an Episcopal congregation, there was no question of the state asserting any legal title.

There is no record of St. John's last years as an active Episcopal church or of when it closed its doors as such. The fact is, however, that the Episcopalians ceased to worship there, leaving the way open for other denominations to occupy it in subsequent years.

Capt. J. Churchill Cooke wrote in 1930 that St. John's appeared to be a free church and that "any and all of the various denominations had the right to worship there." He stated that the Baptists and Methodists held regular services in the church after the War Between the States and that they

probably did so before the war, as well.

A Methodist congregation attempted to take over the church, and probably would have obtained legal title to the property had it not been for the efforts of Capt. Robert E. Lee Jr. of "Romancoke" and Dr. Buchan Richards of "Tuckoman."

In 1876, Captain Lee and Dr. Richards ran a survey of the property and began proceedings through the State Land Office to claim the building and its site. By treasury warrant No. 30284, dated 14 April 1877, they purchased the two-acre lot for the current land-grant price of one dollar per acre, and the site, with the church, became their personal property.

Meanwhile, an Episcopal congregation was growing up in the town of West Point, which had been incorporated in 1870 and was developing as a railway port terminal. By 1882, the members had built their own church, also called St. John's. Since the old St. John's was no longer used by any denomination, it was rapidly becoming a ruin.

Dr. Richards died, leaving Captain Lee and his wife, Juliet Carter Lee, the sole possessors of the church and its site. By deed of 12 December 1913, the Lees gave old St. John's to the vestry of the new church. At that same time, the St. John's Church Restoration Association was formed. Since then, this interdenominational association has worked to preserve and restore old St. John's.

Among those who have given their time and money to this effort, none is more deserving of mention than the late Dr. G. MacLaren Brydon, a former rector and later historiographer of the Diocese of Virginia, one of the founders and organizers of the Restoration Association.

Two other leaders in the restoration movement are Capt. J. Churchill Cooke and Rev. Arthur P. Gray Jr. for many years rectorship at St. John's in West Point. In 1931, we find Mr. Gray moving that the association and the parish encourage the people of the country to use the church for religious services and to "consider old St. John's as a shrine belonging to this country." Mr. Gray worked tirelessly during his lifetime to encourage national recognition of the historic site.

At present the association is engaged in a well-organized and realistic program of preservation looking toward ultimate restoration of this lovely colonial church. Phase I of the plan calls for basic preservation and is now virtually completed. Phase II consists of structural replacement and is being carried out as funds become available. Phase II envisions preparation of the church for services or for similar use as a shrine.

To raise money, donations from individuals and organizations are solicited and collected. The restoration movement is not a church or sectarian movement, but is interdenominational in every sense.

When completed, the restoration should bring about a new period in the history of the ancient church. Situated as it is on George Washington's Burgess Route to Williamsburg —a road that was used by Washington and so many other famous Americans—the old church has probably looked upon as many great men from our country's past as any other in the nation. It seems fitting that it should be preserved and one day restored to its former glory.

BLANDFORD CHURCH
PETERSBURG

Erected: 1735

Denomination: Anglican

Location: On the east side of Crater Road in Blandford Cemetery in Petersburg (Routes 301 and 460)

Religious Services: Annual Memorial Service, 9 June

Open daily, 10:00 A.M. to 5:00 P.M.

Old Blandford Church as photographed in 1900, shortly after its first rennovation.

LANDFORD CHURCH OF BRISTOL PARISH IS NAMED for the colonial town of Blandford, which long ago became a part of the city of Petersburg. It has also been known as the Brick Church on Wells's Hill and, for a time, St. Paul's Church. Bristol Parish, which was established on both sides of the Appomattox River by Act of Assembly in 1643, was laid off from Martin's Brandon Parish. It extended from the mouth of the Appomattox at the James River up to Peter's Point and the falls, where Petersburg is now located.

George and Eleazar Robertson, Robert Ferguson, Thomas Wilkerson, William Harrison, John Cameron, and Andrew Syme were the names of the ministers who once preached the Word of God at Blandford Church.

In 1720, according to the vestry book and register of Bristol Parish, there were 848 parishioners in the parish and two places of worship: a church and a chapel. During the fourteen years between 1720 and 1734, the number of parishioners in Bristol Parish more than doubled to 2,084, and the places of worship had increased from two to five. Besides the mother church and the Ferry Chapel, there were now chapels on Namozine, Sapponey, and Flat Creeks, all south of the Appomattox.

By separate Acts of Assembly in 1734, all of Bristol Parish north of the Appomattox was laid off to form two new parishes in Chesterfield County: the parish of Raleigh and the parish of Dale. The former act went into effect on 25 March 1735, the latter, on 31 May of the same year. The creation of these new parishes very much reduced the area of Bristol Parish, as well as the number of parishioners, which shrank to 1,349. Of the five places of worship formerly in the parish, only two remained: the Ferry Chapel and the chapel on Sapponey Creek. Both of these featured frame construction, and one was in a state of deterioration.

The passage of the acts in regard to Raleigh and Dale Parishes placed the vestry of Bristol in an embarrassing situation. Before that time, at a vestry meeting held on 7 March 1733, it was "ordered that a new church be built of brick on Wells's Hill for the convenience of this parish sixty foot long and twenty-five foot wide in the clear eighteen foot pitch with compass sealing and compass windows the isle eight foot wide laid with Portland stone or Bristol marble...etc."

It was also ordered that Col. Robert Bolling, Capt. William Stark, and Maj. William Poythres negotiate with the workmen for building a new church according to the 1733 vestry order. At the laying of levies for that year, twenty-five thousand pounds of tobacco were laid toward building the church. There was a delay in starting the construction as

parishioners over the river, who were to be cut off from the parish in 1735, objected to paying the tax for a church that would not be theirs. The issue was decided by the governor at Williamsburg, and work on the present church began in 1735. When it was completed in 1737, the Ferry Chapel was abandoned. There were now two churches in the newly defined Bristol Parish: the new Brick Church (Blandford) and the Sapponey Chapel, later to be called a church.

The addition of the long transept on the north side of Blandford Church, which gave the building its T-shape, was ordered in 1752 and completed in 1764. In 1757, the brick wall was built around the churchyard. The basic design of the building remains unchanged since then.

After the Revolutionary War, the town of Blandford, which lies between Wells's Hill and the river, rapidly declined in importance as a tobacco port, while the new town of Petersburg to the west grew steadily. Between the years 1802 and 1808, the new St. Paul's Church in Petersburg was built, thus sealing the fated decline of the Blandford Church on Wells's Hill. Services at the old Brick Church were eventually discontinued, and the church was left alone in its glory. Abandoned, it gradually fell into ruins. The Reverend Andrew Syme, who served the Bristol Parish faithfully for forty-five years was the last rector to conduct services at the Blandford Church on a regular basis.

Writing in 1879, a short while before the Brick Church underwent its first "restoration," Dr. Philip Slaughter said, quoting in part Charles Campbell:

"Blandford is chiefly remarkable for the melancholy charm of a moss-velveted and ivy-embroidered, ante-Revolutionary church (whose yard is the Petersburg cemetery), at present in the most picturesque place of dilapidation." And we add that it is the pride of Petersburg, and the most attractive of all her historical surroundings. The pilgrim and the stranger who tarry but a night is sure to wend his way and pay his homage at this shrine. Time, too, in its revolvings, "brings in other revenges." The children, and the children's children, of the scattered worshippers who were baptized at this font or knelt at this shrine, when they have finished their course on earth, are borne back in solemn procession and laid in the bosom of old Mother Church, which invests her with a charm, in the eyes and hearts of the whole community.

Necessary repairs for the preservation of Blandford Church were made by the city of Petersburg in 1882. In

Above: The church is located near the battlefield of the Crater in Petersburg.

Above top: The basic design of Blandford Church remains unchanged since 1757.

1901, the city delegated to the Ladies Memorial Association of Petersburg the privilege of developing the church into a memorial chapel and a Confederate shrine in memory of the thirty thousand soldiers who were buried in the cemetery where this old Brick Church stands.

The Confederates honored their soldiers by placing memorial windows in the church. These windows were designed and executed by Louis Comfort Tiffany, who became known for the development of Tiffany Favrile Glass during the years 1875 to 1930.

A visit to Blandford Church recalls many memories of the historic past. Wandering outside the church through the cemetery, one sees old tombstones with half-obliterated inscriptions, calling to mind the full ancient glory of Blandford Church, which possesses a character of its own.

The following poem, found on the wall in the church, was written about 1841 by an unknown author:

Thou art crumbling to the dust, old pile,
Thou art hastening to thy fall,
And 'round thee in thy loneliness
Clings the ivy to thy wall.
The worshippers are scattered now
Who knelt before thy shrine,
And silence reigns where anthems rose,
In days of "Auld Lang Syne."

And sadly sighs the wandering wind

Where oft in years gone by,
Prayers rose from many hearts to Him,
The Highest of the High:
The tramp of many a busy foot
That sought thy aisles is o'er,
And many a weary heart around
Is still forever more.

How doth ambition's hope take wing,
How droops the spirit now;
We hear the distant city's din,
The dead are mute below.
The sun that shone upon their paths
Now gilds their lonely graves;

The zephyrs which once fanned their brows
The grass above them waves.

Oh! Could we call the many back
Who've gathered here in vain—
Who've careless roved where we do now,
Who'll never meet again;
How would our weary souls be stirred
To meet the earnest gaze
Of the lovely and the beautiful
The lights of other days.

Blandford Church in 1930. Its memorial windows were designed by Louis Comfort Tiffany of Tiffany Favrile Glass (1875-1930).

THE FORK CHURCH
HANOVER COUNTY

Erected: 1735

Denomination: Anglican

Location: On Route 738, approximately 4 1/2 miles west of Gum Tree (Route 1), 3 miles south of Doswell, and 4 1/2 miles north of Ashland

Religious Services: Sundays, Morning Prayer at 11:00 A.M.

Above: Fork Church in 1930. Patrick Henry attended services here as a child.

Opposite: Fork Church in the present. Actress Katherine Hepburn's grandfather, Parson S. S. Hepburn, was rector of the parish at the turn of the century.

HANOVER COUNTY WAS ESTABLISHED IN 1720. It contained St. Paul's Parish. In his 1884 account of the recovery of "the Rectory Book" of St. Paul's Parish (published in *Southern Churchman*), the Reverend Dr. Philip Slaughter mentions that members of the following families served on the early vestries of St. Paul's Parish: Pollard, Cross, Darracott, Chapman, Pierce, Macon, Abbott, Pendleton, Meredith, Bickerton, Winston, Henry, Crawford, Merewether, and Gryms.

Six years later, in 1726, St. Paul's Parish was divided, resulting in the creation of St. Martin's Parish, named after St. Martin-in-the-Fields, London.

A church was built for the parish in 1735. It was called St. Martin's but soon became more commonly known as The Fork Church—a reference to its location at the fork of the Pamunkey River (formed from the joining of the North Anna and South Anna Rivers).

Two other churches once stood in the western part of St. Martin's Parish—Allen's Creek and Hollowing Creek—but no trace of either exists. In the place of these churches, two others have been erected, but the old Fork Church survives as a noble monument to colonial parishioners. The Slash Church of St. Paul's Parish still stands.

The brick for The Fork Church, which measures more than seventy-five feet in length, was laid in Flemish bond with glazed headers. Tradition states that many colonial churches were built of brick from England, but this contention has been disputed.

There is a door located at Fork Church's southern end and another on the side, near the northeastern corner. Over each door is a portico on brick columns, which is admired by many lovers of architecture.

In the early 1800s, the high-backed pews were replaced, and the pulpit was moved from the side to the end.

The Fork Church is rich in historic associations. As a child, patriot Patrick Henry would come here for services from "Scotch Town," the Henry family plantation five miles away. His father, John Henry, was a vestryman, and his uncle, for whom he was named, was a rector in the parish for forty years.

Patrick Henry's cousin, Dorothea Payne, also traveled to The Fork Church from Scotch Town. Better known as Dolley, this woman would one day become the wife of James Madison, the fourth president of the United States. When Dolley Payne first met James Madison in Philadelphia, she was a Quaker.

St. Martin's Parish still owns a beautiful communion serv-

ice. The paten and chalice are inscribed with the following: "For the St. Martin's parish in Hanover and Louisa Counties, 1759." It is believed that they were brought from England that year by Thomas Nelson Jr., one of the signers of the Declaration of Independence, who had gone to England to receive a private education. The service was presented to the church by his father, William Nelson, a merchant descended from an English family.

Thomas Nelson Jr. also served as a general in the Revolutionary War and later as governor of Virginia. His son, Francis Nelson, represented the St. Martin's Parish in church councils for many years. By the beginning of the present century, the Nelson family had produced at least twenty-four clergymen.

Among the ministers furnished by this parish, Bishop William Meade mentions in *Old Churches, Ministers, and Families of Virginia* the Reverend W. N. Pendleton, Washington Nelson, Robert Nelson, and Farley Berkeley. It was to this parish, and to the home of Dr. Carter Berkeley, that Bishop Meade came to choose his second wife, Thomasia Nelson, stepdaughter of Dr. Berkeley. She, too, is buried at The Old Fork Church.

The marble baptismal font at The Fork Church came from another one of Virginia's colonial churches, Mattaponi Church in King and Queen County. The Baptists had taken over Mattaponi Church and had no use for the vessel.

Parson S. S. Hepburn, grandfather of the actress Katherine Hepburn, was the rector of St. Martin's Parish from 1893 to 1903.

Bishop Meade mentions many devoted friends of the parish; they are the Fontaines, Nelsons, Morrises, Wickhams, Taylors, Winstons, Pollards, Robinsons, Pages, Prices, and Shepherds, as well as the Berkeley family already mentioned.

The only monument inside the church is a beautiful tablet to three of its faithful sons, the Reverend Robert Nelson, missionary to China; William Nelson, late colonel of the C.S.A. (Confederate States of America); and John Page, late major of the C.S.A.

OLD DONATION CHURCH

LYNNHAVEN PARISH

VIRGINIA BEACH

Erected: 1736

Denomination: Anglican

Location: 4449 Witch Duck Road, off Route 58 (between Norfolk and Virginia Beach)

Religious Services: Sundays, Holy Eucharist at 7:45 A.M. (Rite I), 9:00 A.M. (family oriented), and 11:00 A.M. (Rite II).
Tuesdays and Wednesdays, Morning Prayer at 10:00 A.M. and Evening Prayer at 5:30 P.M.
Thursdays, Holy Eucharist and Healing at 10:00 A.M. and Evening Prayer at 5:30 P.M.

Open for private prayers, Monday—Thursday, 7:30 A.M. to 5:30 P.M., and Friday, 7:30 A.M. to 3:30 P.M.

Above: Old Donation Church today is in an area known as Witch Duck, named for when Grace Sherwood survived her "ducking," or dunking, in the water after being tried as a witch in 1705.

Opposite: Old Donation Church was destroyed by fire in 1882 and reconstructed in 1916. Courtesy of Old Donation Episcopal Church.

CAPE HENRY, SITUATED AT THE ENTRANCE TO THE Chesapeake Bay and the James River, was probably the first point that Virginia colonists touched upon reaching America in April 1607. Soon after, a fort was established there, followed by other settlements along the three sides of the coast and bay.

Lynnhaven Parish, with Cape Henry at its northeast corner, was one of the three parishes created out of Lower Norfolk County and Parish after the county was formed in 1637. It takes its name from the Lynnhaven River, which in turn was named by colonist Adam Thoroughgood in honor of King's Lynn, his early home in Norfolk, England. (Thoroughgood came to the Virginia Colony as an indentured servant in 1621 and later became a prominent member of society, among other things serving as a member of the Virginia House of Burgesses.)

The first church of Lynnhaven Parish was built in 1639 on Thoroughgood's land at what has ever since been known as Church Point, located on the west side of the western branch of the Lynnhaven River. At his death in 1640, Thoroughgood left one thousand pounds of tobacco to Lynnhaven Parish Church "for the purchase of some necessary and decent ornament." The remains of this church were still visible in 1850.

Repeated references to this first Lynnhaven Parish Church in court orders and wills of Lower Norfolk County, from 1637 to 1687, evince its continued use for at least half a century. The old church's increasing age, however, made frequent repairs necessary. Consequently, on 28 March 1691, the vestry ordered that the first church be replaced by a new building. (Also that year, Princess Anne County was created, and its boundaries coincided with the boundaries of Lynnhaven Parish. The county was named for Princess—later Queen—Anne of England.)

There are no seventeenth-century vestry records available for Lynnhaven Parish (although the 1723-86 vestry book was published by the Virginia Historical Society in Richmond and may still be available). However, Princess Anne County's court-order book contains an agreement, dated 1 April 1691, between the vestry and Mr. Jacob Johnson, for the construction of "a good and substantial Brick Church" for the parish of Lynnhaven. According to this document, the new church was specified to be forty-five feet long, twenty-two feet wide, and thirteen feet high, with brick gable ends to the ridge of the roof. Furthermore, the agreement called for the structure to be completed by the end of June 1692, under penalty of one hundred thousand pounds

of tobacco, thus allowing only fifteen months for its construction.

In his writings, Bishop William Meade also notes that benches in the chancel, such as those specified in the court order, were provided for the use of the poor, who occupied them after the wealthier members of the congregation were seated in the pews.

This second parish church was located on the "Western shore of the Lynnhaven, upon the plantation belonging to Mr. Ebenezer Taylor, near the ferry." The ferry had been established a few years earlier, across the western branch of the Lynnhaven River, near the point known today as Witch Duck, where Grace Sherwood survived her "ducking," or dunking, in the water after being tried as a witch in 1705. Near this ferry was a fifty-acre tract, still called the Ferry Farm.

The plan to build a third Lynnhaven Parish Church was accepted by the vestry on 25 June 1736. In view of recorded facts, there seems to be no doubt that the present Old Donation Church is, in fact, this third church, but if further proof of Old Donation's identity be required, it may be found in the exact agreement between its dimensions and those specified for the third church and in the date 1736, cut in a brick to the right of the front door.

The name "Donation" doesn't appear to have been applied

Courtesy of Old Donation Episcopal Church.

to the second or third church during the colonial period. At that time, the churches were called either Lynnhaven Church or Lynnhaven Parish Church. The first published use of the name "Donation" in connection with the third church building seems to have taken place in 1822, when the vestry ordered that "the church called the Donation Church in this parish" be put in repair. According to Bishop Meade, the name "Donation" originated from the gift to the parish of adjoining lands, still known as Donation Farm, by the former rector, the Reverend Robert Dickson, at his death in 1776. The gift was to serve as an endowment for a free school.

Now known as Old Donation Church, the building was neglected after the Disestablishment and then completely restored in 1824. Sometime after 1843, however, the church was abandoned for nearly forty years. The interior was burned out by a woods fire in 1882, leaving behind a roof-

Old Donation Church in 1930, after its complete reconstruction.

less ruin in which trees would eventually grow. In 1916, the church was restored in a modern style with a low pulpit and slip pews. It became the parish church again in 1943.

Lynnhaven Parish owns colonial communion silver, including a 1711 paten, a 1712 cup, and a 1716 flagon. The paten was a gift of Maximilian Boush, a wealthy Norfolk merchant, and bears his arms. The parish also owns a red marble font and a pewter alms basin, both of which are believed to have descended from the first parish church.

The oldest stone in the Old Donation Church cemetery is dated 1768. It was moved there, along with several others from neighboring plantations, in 1930. It is the only colonial-period marker in the graveyard.

The reredos, altar, pulpit, lectern, and communion rail were given to Old Donation Church in 1916 by St. Paul's Church in Norfolk.

NORTH FARNHAM CHURCH
RICHMOND COUNTY

Erected: 1737

Denomination: Anglican

Location: The village of Farnham is 11 miles east of Warsaw. The church sits off Route 3, approximately 1/4 mile from its junction with Route 607.

Religious Services: Sundays, 9:30 A.M.
First, third, and fifth Sundays, Morning Prayer at 9:30 A.M.

North Farnham Church in 1930. This building replaced an earlier church that was erected circa 1660.

ORTH FARNHAM CHURCH WAS BUILT IN 1737. This handsome brick structure, built in the form of a Greek cross with a single tier of windows, dominates the village of Farnham, which is situated in the lower section of Richmond County. During Holy Communion services, the church uses a flagon and paten that were made in London in 1720 by Joseph Fainell.

Named in honor of the duke of Richmond, Richmond County was established in 1692, when the old Rappahannock County was divided into Richmond County, on the north side of the Rappahannock River, and Essex County, on the south side. According to court records, the county once contained three parishes—Lunenburg, St. Mary's, and North Farnham (so named to distinguish it from South Farnham Parish in Essex County).

Each of these counties had separate ministers. Of the three ministers mentioned in the records from 1693 to 1742, the account is depressing. According to Bishop William Meade, the first two, John Burnet and John Alexander, were always in court, "suing or being sued." The third minister, the Reverend Thomas Blewer, was presented by the grand jury as a common swearer.

The Reverend William Mackay served North Farnham Parish from 1754 to 1774. After his departure, the Reverend John Leland from Northumberland presided.

In 1796, the vestry obtained the services of the Reverend George Young. Reverend Young agreed to officiate at Farnham every third Sunday and at Lunenburg Parish, which adjoined Farnham, on the two Sundays in between in exchange for an annual fee of $250, plus the use of the glebe. In 1799, the Reverend John Seward agreed to a similar arrangement, receiving a payment of two hundred dollars annually along with the glebe.

The following vestrymen served Farnham from 1787 to 1802: William Peachy, William Miskell, John Fauntleroy, John Sydnor, Leroy Peachy, Griffin Fauntleroy, Thaddeus Williams, J. Hammond, Benjamin Smith, Samuel Hipkins, Epaphroditus Sydnor, Walter Tomlin, Richard Eale, Bartholomew McCarty, David Williams, Ezekiel Levy, Charles Smith, Abner Dobyns, William McCarty, William Palmer, John G. Chinn, Vincent Branham, W. T. Colston, George Miskell, Peter Temple, and J. M. Yerby.

North Farnham Church replaced an earlier church built sometime around 1660 and located several miles west of Farnham Village. It was probably deserted by 1737 when the present church was built.

After the Revolution and the Disestablishment of the Church of England in Virginia, beginning in 1784, the church was abandoned for many years. Some of the bricks were taken from the churchyard wall, and the building was used as a stable and a distillery.

During the War of 1812, North Farnham Church was struck by bullets during a skirmish between soldiers of the Virginia militia and raiders from the fleet of British Navy Rear Adm. Sir George Cockburn. The bullet holes are located on the south face of the transept.

In 1820, the neglected church stood in ruins. By the time the building was restored in 1834, only its walls were standing.

During the Civil War, North Farnham Church was once again abused, and by both the Confederate and Federal armies. The building was once again restored to use in 1873, but unfortunately, fourteen years later, in 1889, fire gutted the building.

North Farnham Church stood in that condition until it was restored a third time in 1921. In 1959, the reredos and shelves were put in, and the interior was painted. According to James Scott Rawlings, author of *Virginia's Colonial Churches,* colonial precedent has not been closely followed in either of the most recent restorations.

The Right Reverend F. D. Goodwin was elected bishop of Virginia while serving as rector of Cople, Lunenberg, and North Farnham Parishes. He was consecrated at North Farnham Church in 1930.

As with many colonial churches in Virginia, North Farnham Church has withstood the tests of time—the neglect, the wars, and the fire of 1889. Progress has not surrounded this colonial church as it has surrounded Christ-Alexandria, Pohick-Lorton, Falls Church, or Abington in Gloucester County. As a result, its churchyard, as Rawlings put it so well, still "has an air of a village green."

The present North Farnham Church and its historic marker. Bullet holes from the War of 1812 can be found in the south face of the transept.

GLEBE CHURCH
BENNETT'S CREEK CHURCH
NANSEMOND COUNTY

Erected: 1738

Denomination: Anglican

Location: Route 337, less than 1/2 mile from the village of Driver in Nansemond County

Glebe Church as photographed in 1930. Its name recalls the fact that the parish still retains its colonial glebe land.

THE INDIAN NAME NANSEMOND MEANS "FISHING point or angle" and was given by the Indians of the region to their town that was situated in the angle created by the junction of the Western Branch with the main stream of Nansemond River. Nansemond County lies on the south side of the James River west of Norfolk and extends to the North Carolina line. It was a part of the Elizabeth City Corporation, one of the four divisions of the colony in 1618 and one of the eight original shires of 1634. New Norfolk County was laid off in 1636 and was also subdivided that year into Lower and Upper Norfolk. In 1646, the name of Upper Norfolk County was changed to Naismum, which evolved several times to reach its present spelling, Nansemond.

The history of the earliest churches in the present county of Nansemond is vague as a result of the destruction of the county records by three successive fires, in the years 1734, 1779, and 1866. Vestry books for both of its eighteenth-century parishes have been preserved and furnish an authentic account of its two surviving colonial churches.

In 1642, the county was divided into three parishes known at that time as South, East, and West. Lists of Virginia parishes published in 1680 and 1714 reveal that the South Parish soon became known as the Upper Parish, the East as the Lower Parish, and the West as the Chiccocatuck or Chuckatuck Parish. Sometime around 1725, the Lower and Chuckatuck Parishes were united to form Suffolk Parish.

From the time of the early settlement, the Puritans, as well as Quakers and other dissenters, came to Nansemond County. A land grant, dated 3 June 1635, allotts 150 acres "on the Nanzamond River" to "George White, Minister of the Word of God." This service was probably held in a private home, which accounts for the fact that no church buildings are mentioned in the Act of 1643, dividing Upper Norfolk into three parishes, although disposition is made of an existing glebe and parsonage within the bounds then laid down for the East Parish.

One of the earliest settlers in Nansemond County was Richard Bennett. In 1635, George West granted to Richard Bennett two thousand acres on the Nansemond River. Bennett played a very large role in the life of the county and colony. In 1641, he sent his brother to New England to request that several Puritan ministers be sent to Virginia. These ministers gained their strongest foothold in Nansemond County, where a flourishing church numbering 118 members was soon organized and selected a Reverend

Harrison as its minister. Another body of dissenters in the county fared better than the Puritans. The Society of Friends was founded in 1648.

Sometime around 1725, Chuckatuck and Lower Parish were united to form one parish called Suffolk Parish. The name of the parish antedates the town of Suffolk by at least seventeen years and, strangely enough, Suffolk is not in Suffolk Parish, but rather in the Upper Parish of Nansemond.

In 1737, the vestry of Suffolk Parish, "upon evident proof of the ruinous condition of the church" in Lower Parish, gave order for the erection of a new brick church at a more convenient site called Jordan's Mill Hill. The members of the vestry from the Chuckatuck side of the river refused to assist in the construction, and the matter was appealed to the governor in Council, who ordered the immediate erection of the building. The order of the Council fixes the construction date of Glebe Church—or Bennett's Creek Church, as it was called in the vestry book—as 1738. (The Council also ordered that since Chuckatuck had a majority in the vestry and seemed determined to maintain it, none of the inhabitants of Chuckatuck could be elected to the vestry until it acheived an equal number of members from each side of the river.)

The building, Glebe Church, is situated on high ground at the head of the west fork of Bennett's Creek. Its present name commemorates the parish's being one of the few left in Virginia that still retains its colonial glebe lands.

The Glebe Church is small and very plain, measuring forty-eight feet six inches by twenty-five feet four inches on the outside, and is considered one of the smallest surviving colonial churches in Virginia. In 1777, a private gallery was added for use by a new vestryman.

After the Disestablishment of the Church of England, in 1785, the Glebe Church became inactive and was in ruins until 1856. The north wing was dismantled—the bricks used to complete the north wall and to erect a vesting room at the west doorway.

According to James Scott Rawlings, who is an authority on architectural designs of colonial churches, Bennett's Church bears a remarkable resemblance to St. George's (Pungoteague) Church on the Eastern Shore, for both are of the same age and display the same superb masonry. The vestry book (1743-93) of the Upper Parish, Nansemond County, has been published, and the original is on deposit at the Virginia State Library in Richmond. Bennett's Creek Church is first mentioned in the Suffolk vestry book as "the church" or the "Lower Church," while the other church in

the combined parish is always distinguished as "Chucka-tuck Church." It is apparent that the new building erected in 1737 and 1738 was regarded as the parish church. The Glebe Church has remained active in Lower Parish, served by the rector of St. Paul's Church in Suffolk.

Glebe Church, photographed with its additions, was originally called Bennett's Creek Church.

ST. GEORGE'S CHURCH
PUNGOTEAGUE CHURCH
ACCOMACK COUNTY

Erected: 1738

Denomination: Anglican

Location: Virginia Route 178, northeast of junction with Route 180 in Pungoteague.

St. George's Church, also known as Pungoteague Church, and its graveyard in 1900.

I N 1623, THE SETTLEMENT IN ACCOMACK HAD A MINISTER, Rev. Francis Bolton, and it is evident that the settlement constituted a plantation parish. Accomack County was one of the original shires created by an act of the General Assembly in 1634. By Act of Assembly, in 1663, the county's name was changed to Northhampton County. In 1663, Northhampton County was divided, but no enactment has been found to fix the exact date of the division. The lower county remained Northhampton County, and the new county resumed the name of Accomack County.

Conclusive evidence reveals that a church was established on the Eastern Shore as early as 1621. The general assumption is that it represented a plantation parish that took the name of Accomack Parish. When the division of Northhampton County occurred, that portion of Northhampton County that was included within the bounds of the new Accomack County became known as Accomack Parish. It also absorbed Occohannock Parish, which was partially within its boundaries.

Accomack Parish was first divided in 1763, by an Act of Assembly, which provided that

From and after the third day of January next, the said parish of Accomack shall be divided into two distinct parishes, by a line to begin at the mouth of Parker's creek, thence to run up the said creek to the head of Rooty Branch, and from thence by a direct line to be run to the head of the branch called Drummond's new mill branch, and thence down the said branch to the mouth of Hunting Creek; and all that part of the said parish of Accomack which lies above the said bounds, and to the northward thereof, shall be one distinct parish, and retain the name of Accomack: and that all the part thereof which lies below the said bounds shall be one other distinct parish, and shall be called and known by the name of St. George.

Accomack Parish was again divided when the Council of the Diocese of Southern Virginia, in 1896, created Trinity Parish. St. George's Church was one of eight colonial churches built in Accomack County and the only one that survives today. George C. Mason, in his *Colonial Churches of Tidewater, Virginia,* mentions two churches not previously revealed by other historians. These are Nandue Church, built in 1653, and Occahannock Church, erected in 1656, both in the southern part of the county, on the bay side. In the upper section of the county, above St. George's, there were

Assawaman and Onancock Churches, both of about 1680; Middle Creek of 1723; Lower Church of 1773; and New Church of 1767.

The Indian name for the Eastern Shore territory was "Accomack," meaning "the other side place"; this name was given to this second permanent settlement on King's Creek. Like most names of Indian origin, Accomack can be found in a variety of spellings, ranging from "Acchawmacke" in the earliest times, to "Accomako" in a parish report of 1724.

In the year 1724, there were three churches in the upper parish (Accomack), about ten miles apart from each other. The first minister of the parish was the Reverend William Black, who, in the years 1709 and 1710, wrote the bishop of London that he had taken charge of it and that the parish had been without a minister for fifteen years. Reverend Black preached at three churches and had two hundred communicants and four hundred families under his charge. In 1762, when St. George's Parish was laid off from Accomack Parish, Pungoteague Church became the parish church and was called St. George's Church.

A study of the early land grants has been made by two Eastern Shore residents, Mr. Ralph T. Whitelaw of Accomack and Ms. Anne Floyd Upshur of Nassawadox. They believe that the earliest establishment on the Eastern Shore was the old Plantation Creek, which traditionally gave this tidal waterway its historic name. It seems probable that the first church was built soon after the Reverend Francis Bolton's arrival on the Eastern Shore in 1723. Although no church appears to be listed at Accomack in the Virginia Company's census of 1624, Whitelaw and Upshur believe that the first church was the one traditionally located near Fishing Point, as described in an early chronicle. The chronicle states that the early church was built "neare the fishinge poynte" and describes it as being "of insignificant dimension." The Fishing Point is thought to have received its name as the principle scene of fishing operations by the Dale's Gift colonists. The Fishing Point Church was traditionally the first built on the Eastern Shore and has therefore been assigned a construction date as early as 1623, by previous writers.

The first St. George's Church was probably completed in 1678. A court record of 1666 and 1667 is conclusive proof that St. George's Church could not have been constructed prior to that date. The completion of the church at Pungoteague is established by a deposition of May 1678, by Robert Watson, in which he mentions "being at Pungoteag [sic] Church about Shrove Tuesday in the year 1677" (1678). The first minister of the church seems to have been Henry Parke,

Above: At one time, all that remained of St. George's Church was its roof and walls.

Opposite: The present St. George's Church is in the form of a Latin cross.

who, in a deposition made two months later, identified himself as "Henry Parke, Minister of Accomack Parish, age thirty-three years." A court record reveals that he died in or before that year.

Several significant items were found by Whitelaw and Upshur. After their intensive search of Accomack records, the researchers suggest that the existing St. George's Church at Pungoteague is the second building on this site and was not built until about 1738. "An assignment of all tobacco tc. to be levied for building of Pongoteague Church from John Snead Gent to William Andrews Gent." The whole record strongly discounts the original church's survival for two more centuries, through the most destructive sort of abuse, and accordingly strengthens the case for its having been replaced in 1738 by a new building.

In its original shape, the present building is in the form of a Latin cross. It is apparent from soundings made on the site, that the church was built fifty-four feet (north and south) by sixty-nine feet (east and west) inside, exclusive of the apse (eastern end or eastern arm of a church). The nave was about twenty-four feet six inches long, and the chancel twenty-one feet, while all four arms of the cross had an inside width of twenty-one feet six inches, the aspe being about six feet narrower. A sketch of 1819 reveals that there was a window in each side of the chancel and transept wings.

Old St. George's Church, unlike most of Virginia's colonial churches, was not abandoned following the Disestablishment of 1785, but remained in service until the War of 1812. Upon the general revival of religion on the Eastern Shore in 1819, it was repaired and restored to use as an Episcopal church, and it was again thoroughly repaired about 1858. During the Civil War, the church was inexcusably desecrated when the Federal forces used it as an army stable; one of the wings had been raided for bricks to build a cook house for the Federal troops. Afterwards, nothing remained except the roof and walls. The present church consists of only parts of the original transepts. The nave and chancel wings were in ruins, then torn down, the bricks used to close the openings left in the trasept walls. The church today stands as a plain rectangular building, retaining little of its original charm.

The ancient communion silver of old St. George's Church is still in use there today. Both chalice and paten bear the inscription, "This belongs to the Parish of Accomack," and show the London date-letter of 1734 to 1735. Another valued relic of this old building is still owned by its modern successor, Emmanuel Church, at Jenkins Bridge. This is a silver communion cup inscribed: "For the use of the Parish Church of Accomack at Assuaman." It is believed to have been purchased with money left to the parish by Col. George Douglas in 1748, and it bears the London date-letter of 1749 to 1750. The cup was discovered, long after the church had gone to ruin, in a field on Col. Thomas Croopers's farm, where it had been used as a drinking cup by farm hands.

The first rector of the restored church was the Reverend S. H. Wellman, and he was succeeded by the Reverends John Anderson, F. M. Burch, John McNabb, Henry L. Derby, Cary Gamble, John S. Meredith, W. Cosby Bell, and Benjamin Bosworth Smith, who later became the first bishop of Kentucky.

The churchyard at St. George's holds no marked grave sites from the colonial period.

ST. PAUL'S CHURCH – BOROUGH CHURCH
ELIZABETH RIVER PARISH
NORFOLK

Erected: 1739

Denomination: Anglican

Location: 201 St. Paul's Boulevard; corner of North Church Street and City Hall Avenue in downtown Norfolk

Religious Services: Sundays, 8:00 A.M. and 10:30 A.M., and Wednesdays, 12:00 M.

St. Paul's Church in 1930. The church was restored in 1892 and 1913.

THE FIRST SETTLEMENT OF THE ENGLISH AT Jamestown occurred at Sewell's Point. This was the site of one of Virginia's earliest colonial churches, the parish church of Elizabeth River Parish. The early history of what is today called St. Paul's Church is practically the history of Norfolk County, from the establishment of the Virginia Colony to the close of the Revolution.

Elizabeth City County was one of the first eight counties created in Virginia in 1634. Two years later, the House of Burgesses created New Norfolk County from a portion of Elizabeth City County. The new county was large; it included all of Elizabeth City County south of the James River and extended north to the Nansemond River and east to the Atlantic Ocean.

In 1637, only a year after its creation, New Norfolk County was divided into Upper Norfolk County and Lower Norfolk County. In 1691, Lower Norfolk County was renamed Norfolk County, and a new county, Princess Anne, was split off from it. This latter county was named for Anne, Princess of Denmark, daughter of James II, who subsequently came to the throne of England in 1702; as Queen Anne, she did a lot for Anglican churches in the American colonies.

The records of Norfolk County show that in 1637 there were two well-organized churches, one located in the lower part of the county on Lynnhaven Bay and the other at Sewell's Point. Up to that time, the settlement at Elizabeth River (the site of the present city of Norfolk) had greatly increased, and by 1638, its residents were finding it difficult to attend a parish church more than eight miles away. As seen by the following order, the inconvenience to the people would be remedied by erecting a chapel of ease at Elizabeth City:

The Church in Lower Norfolk County
The First Church from Records of Norfolk County

At a Court holden in the Lower County of New Norfolk 21 of November 1638.

Capt. Adam Thorowgood, Esq. Capt. John Sibsey, Mr. Willie Julian, Mr. Edward Windha, Mr. Francis Mason, Mr. Henry Seawell.

Whereas there hath beene an order of court granted by Governor and Counsell for the building and erecting of a Church in the Upper * * * * of the County with a reference to the Commander and Commis-

sioners of sd County for apointing of a place fitting and convenient for the situation and building thereof the sd order being in part not accomplish. But standing now in elsortoin [sic] to be voyde and the work to fall into ruine. We now the sd Commissioners taking it into consideration doe appoint Captain John Sibsey and Henry Seawell to procure workmen for the finishing of the same and what they shall agree for with the sd workmen to be levied by the appointment of us the Commissioners.

It appears from the records that Ye Chappell of Ease was completed in the fall of 1641. Documentary references to this old building suggest that it was made of brick and stood in what is now the Cove Street corner of the yard. An entry on an October 1641 court record mentions that services were regularly held at the Chappell of Ease at Elizabeth River.

When the Chappell of Ease at Sewell's Point was given up, a new building was erected at Elizabeth River, adjoining the old church, as parish church. In 1682, the town of Norfolk was founded. Four years later, Virginia Gov. Francis Howard, Baron of Effingham, gave one hundred acres of land adjoining Norfolk as a glebe (a parcel of land that yields revenue) for the Elizabeth River Parish.

In 1736, Norfolk was incorporated as a borough by royal charter, and for many years St. Paul's Church was known as the Borough Church, although this name does not seem to appear in the county records.

In 1739, the present church structure was erected. A brick in the south wall church bears the date 1739, and the initials "S. B.," most likely for Samuel Boush I, who gave the land for the church and served as a vestryman. His son, Capt. Samuel Boush, also served as a vestryman and, in 1682, gave a chalice to the church.

The only surviving colonial vestry book of Elizabeth River Parish, which opens in October 1749 and closes in April 1761, records that on 9 October 1750, it was ordered that James Pasteur have the bricks and timber from the old church to build a schoolhouse. It appears that this privilege was not exercised by Mr. Pasteur, since it was offered, exactly ten years later, to Joseph Mitchell, who was given the bricks of the old church on condition that he clear the churchyard of all rubbish. This act probably explains the final disappearance of the old Chappell's ruins.

St. Paul's Church is a brick structure built in the form of a Latin cross, with the chancel and transept wings of nearly equal length, and the nave considerably longer. From the

In 1776, a Revolutionary cannonball struck St. Paul's and made an indentation in the wall. Three-quarters of a century later, the buried cannonball was unearthed and cemented into the indentation.

outside, it measures eighty-six feet six inches (east to west) by sixty-three feet six inches (north to south). The main body of the church is thirty-three feet wide, and the transept is twenty-six feet three inches wide. The walls of the church are nearly thirty inches thick. Like most cross-shaped colonial churches, the existing St. Paul's Church has a principal entrance at the west end of the nave, and a secondary entrance at each end of the transept.

The following ministers are known to have served the church in the eighteenth century:

Rev. William Rudd	1703
Rev. James Falconer	1718
Reverend Garzia	1724

Rev. Moses Robertson	1734
Rev. Charles Smith	1749-61
Rev. Thomas David	1773-76
Rev. Walker Maury	1786-88
Rev. James Whitehead	1789-1800
Rev. William Bland	1791-1803

The church was struck by a British cannonball during the bombardment of Norfolk by Lord Dunmore's fleet in January 1776 (Dunmore was the last colonial governor of Virginia). Shortly afterward, the entire town was burned by the American forces, with or without orders from the Virginia Convention, and the old church's roof and interior woodwork were completely destroyed.

Its massive walls survived the fire, as was the case of several other colonial churches, but they stood in ruins for nine years before the church was rebuilt, with the original walls, and replaced in service about 1785.

Nearly three-quarters of a century after the bombardment, the cannonball that had struck the church was found buried in the ground beneath the indentation it had made in the brickwork. It was later cemented into the indentation, and a historical marker was placed beneath it, which reads:

Fired By
Lord Dunmore,
Jan. 1. 1776.

The cannonball is reputed to have been fired by the *Liverpool*, a British frigate.

One highly interesting relic found in the St. Paul's Parish museum is the chair in which John Hancock sat when he signed the Declaration of American Independence. A mahogany arm chair, upholstered in leather, it was bought by Col. Thomas M. Bayley of Accomack County, Virginia.

The beautiful yard that surrounds the church contains nearly two acres of trees and shrubs. The wall around the yard was constructed in 1759.

The Reverend Beverly D. Tucker served St. Paul's Church as rector from 1882 to 1906 before becoming bishop coadjutor of Southern Virginia (1906-18) and bishop of the Diocese in 1918. Several volumes of poems came from his pen, among them *My Three Lovers, Poems on St. Paul,* and *Memorial Poems.* In prose, he contributed the *Confederate Army* and *Washington as a Churchman.*

The oldest tombstone in the cemetery is located on the south side of the church and bears the following inscription: "Here lies the body of Dorothy Farrell who deceased the 18th of January 1673." There are other stones from 1691 and 1694, as well as numerous eighteenth-century graves.

During the Civil War, Norfolk was captured by Union soldiers, and military forces took possession of the church, prompting the members of St. Paul's to worship with the parishioners of nearby Christ Church. On 29 October 1863, the commanding general ordered the wardens of St. Paul's Church to provide religious services according to the liturgy of the Episcopal Church of the United States.

Special Order No. 46.
Norfolk, VA., Nov, 1, 1865
St. Paul's church, of Norfolk, Virginia, being no longer needed by the military authorities, is herby turned over to the old Presbytery and congregation.
By order of Brevet Major-Gen. A. A. Torbert.
John L. Warden, Jr., Asst. Adj.-Gen.

In November 1865, seven months after the surrender of Confederate Gen. Robert E. Lee, the church was returned to its rightful owners, and in 1892, the church was repaired to its early style. The present interior, with its high pews, was restored in 1913 following colonial precedent.

Although St. Paul's has suffered from wars, neglect, and congregational strife, it still stands in a churchyard of outstanding beauty and offers much historical interest.

HEBRON CHURCH
MADISON COUNTY

Erected: 1740

Denomination: Lutheran

Location: Route 231, from Madison to Sperryville, to Route 638, and then Route 653. Church is 3/4 mile north of the junction of Routes 638 and 653.

Religious Services: Sundays, Worship at 11:00 A.M.

Hebron Church, as photographed in 1930, is the result of the first permanent Lutheran colony of Dutch immigrants in Virginia.

THE FIRST REPRESENTATIVES OF THE LUTHERAN Church in the territory of the United States were not to be found among the Germans, but among the Dutch colonists from Holland, who settled at New Amsterdam, now New York City, near the close of the first quarter of the seventeenth century. The Swedes followed them and settled along the Delaware River and built their churches. Then came the Germans in small numbers toward the close of the seventeenth century. In the next fifty years, great numbers of Lutheran immigrants had settled in New York, Pennsylvania, Virginia, and the Carolinas.

Among the colonies that sailed for Pennsylvania, one—small in number, poor in material wealth, but rich in faith—was cast on the shores of Virginia following a disastrous voyage. This colony took root and became the first permanent Lutheran settlement in Virginia. Other colonists of the same faith followed a few years later. Together, they established Hebron Church a few miles east of the Blue Ridge, in the valley of the Robinson River and White Oak Run, which is located in Madison County. For years it was known as the "Old Dutch Church."

Hebron Church represents the oldest Lutheran congregation in the south, and its building is the oldest church erected and still used by Lutherans in all America. It is one of the four surviving wooden churches of Virginia's colonial heritage.

Hebron Church is also the only existing colonial church with a name derived from the Old Testament. Hebron (hĕ-bron) is one of the oldest cities of the world, located nineteen miles southwest of Jerusalem. It was an early camping place for Abraham.

The congregation was established prior to 1726 by Germans who had migrated from the vicinity of Germanna, on the Rapidan River, where, from 1717 until their migration, they had worked in Gov. Alexander Spotswood's vineyards and iron ore mines. The first church was built of unhewn logs in 1726 and occupied the same site as its successor.

Building a new church during the colonial era was no small undertaking. It required much labor to cut trees, hew the logs for the strong framework, saw the weatherboarding and ceiling with whipsaws, and joint the shingles. All of the nails were made by a blacksmith.

According to the date on the great girder, the church was completed in 1740. The framed structure, rectangular in form, measures fifty feet long and twenty-six feet wide. The small vestry on the north side that was part of the colonial building has been replaced several times.

The year the church was completed, the congregation addressed a letter of thanks to all their benefactors. It was dated "Orange County in America, August 19, 1740," and signed in the name of the congregation, accepting the unaltered Augsburg Confession.* George Samuel Klug, Pastor; Michael Cook; Michael Smith; Michael Holt; Michael Clore; and George Utz signed on behalf of the church congregation.

In 1748, Hebron Church consisted of about eighty families that lived within a circle of a few miles.

The pastor's salary on 25 November 1743—for Rev. George Samuel Klug—was eight hundred pounds of tobacco. One of the longest pastorates in the history of Hebron Church was that of the Reverend William Carpenter, who served for twenty-six years, from 1787 to 1813. When he was sixteen years of age, Mr. Carpenter entered the Revolutionary Army and fought under the command of the Reverend Peter Muhlenberg, who had raised and commanded the Eighth Virginia (German) Regiment and became a commissioned brigadier general of the Continental Army in 1777. Mr. Carpenter continued in military service until the surrender of Lord Cornwallis at Yorktown, which he and his father witnessed.

It was during Mr. Carpenter's ministry that the present south addition was built onto the original church structure, sometime between 1790 and 1802. The present organ, built in 1800 by David Tannenburg of Lititz, Pennsylvania, was installed during the construction of the south addition. John Yager, a member of the congregation, went to the factory to purchase it. It was then hauled on wagons by parishioners Jacob Rouse and Michael House from Lititz to Madison County. It was installed in the church in 1802 by Philip Broughman, a parishioner who was extremely knowledgeable of organs. The organ has four octaves and eight stops.

Hebron Church has fared better than most other colonial churches in Virginia. It went through several wars without sustaining any damage to its building.

Strange as it may seem today, slaves were bought by the congregation between the years 1739 and 1743 to work the church lands. The Reverend John Stoever, who served from 1733 to 1739, used them for farming and clearing the church property. He thought that by treating them well and instructing them in the word of God, they might become Christians. In later years, some of the slaves became communicants of the church.

Hebron Church had no cemetery during the colonial period. On 2 September 1899, Capt. J. C. Crigler, at a meeting of the Church Council, offered a gift of two acres of land, located on a hill east of the White Oak Run and on the road lead-

Hebron Church in the present. The name Hebron is derived from one of the oldest established cities near Jerusalem.

ing to Madison, that finally allowed the creation of a church cemetery. The first burial to take place there was that of Ruth Elizabeth, the young daughter of the Reverend and Mrs. William P. Huddle. She was buried on 2 January 1900, but a few days later, her body was moved to Rural Retreat for a permanent burial. There were only four other people buried in this cemetery.

A new cemetery nearer the church was debated, and finally a deed for an acre of ground was secured from Mr. H. B. Fray on 6 February 1904, although the first interment of Mrs. E. Belle Fray on 28 October 1903, settled the question of a new cemetery. The people could see the importance of a cemetery close by the church, where it would be better cared for and where they could easily visit when they came to worship, the resting places of those whom they have loved for so long. The ground was enclosed by a beautiful iron fence and laid off in lots. The price of the land was $153 and the cost of the fence was $470. The bodies of those buried on the hill and some from other cemeteries were moved to the new cemetery.

Hebron Church owns many communion vessels, including a tray, two patens, two flagons, and a baptismal bowl, all in pewter and all given by Thomas Giffin of London, England. The pair of flagons is stamped 1729, the rest are dated 1727. The tray is engraved with the Institution of the Lord's Supper; on the patens is Christ on the cross. All of the church's communion pieces were hidden by courageous women of the congregation when the neighborhood was ransacked by Federal soldiers during the Civil War, although a Federal soldier did manage to steal a pewter wafer box.

In 1940, the bicentennial of the church building was celebrated, and for that occasion, a historical account was published by William Harrison Lamb, the fourth generation of his family to belong to the congregation.

Sitting outside of Hebron Lutheran Church are three stile blocks waiting to help ladies onto the backs of horses that no longer come. The stiles, which look like stairways to nowhere, are strategically placed outside three doors on each side of the church, serving as a reminder of a time when attending church was the major event of the week.

This simple white church sits in the shadow of the mountains, where Pres. Herbert Hoover once went trout fishing.

Lucy Frances Coppage, a parishioner, remembers when large white buckets were placed inside the church for travel-weary congregation members to have a sip of water before the service began. Mrs. Coppage also remembers summer picnics in the shade of huge virgin oak trees outside the church. Those trees have since been destroyed by tornado-force winds that swept through the valley in 1969.

In 1990, Hebron Church celebrated its 250th anniversary with a special German communion service for descendants of the German settlers and a rededication ceremony.

* The Augsburg Confession was a statement of Lutheran beliefs presented to Emperor Charles V at the Diet of Augsburg in 1530. Philipp Melanchthon, friend of Martin Luther, wrote the confession in an attempt to reunite the Christian world and to prevent civil war in Germany. He hoped that his statement would mend the differences between Roman Catholics and Protestants in Germany.

MAUCK MEETING HOUSE
MILL CREEK CHURCH
PAGE COUNTY

Erected: 1738-1740

Denomination: Mennonite

Location: On Route 766, across from the historic Calendine in the village of Hamburg

Open by appointment

The origin of Mauck Meeting House is debated, although, it was probably built by Mennonites.

NEAR LURAY IN PAGE COUNTY STANDS THE primitive, but well-maintained building called The Mauck Meeting House (sometimes Mill Creek Church). It was built for religious purposes by the "neighbors," namely Mennonites from Switzerland and Southern Germany. Early Mennonite ministers were Jacob Strickler, Abraham Heiston, John Roads, and Michael Kauffman.

The church got its name from Daniel Mauck, who granted the 270 acres of land on which the church sits in 1730. The Mauck Meeting House is constructed of rough-hewn logs; the pine-log outside walls were covered with white weatherboards in 1851. It is approximately thirty-five feet eleven inches (east to west) by twenty-nine feet eight inches (north to south). There are two doorways set in the centers of the south and west walls. Each of the doors look quite old and might be colonial. The floor is made from pine timbers of random width, ranging from six to twelve inches. The interior window frames may possibly derive from the eighteenth century.

There seems to have been two periods of early construction for The Mauck Meeting House. The logs and beams may derive from the first period (possibly 1738-40), and the galleries and columns may come from the second period (possibly 1770).

The origin of the meeting house is a matter of some debate. Some claim that it was erected after the Revolution as a Union meeting house, of which both Mennonites and Primitive Baptists had an interest. Others believe it was constructed around 1770 by a Primitive Baptist elder named John Koontz from Pennsylvania. Still others think it to have been built around 1738 to 1740 by Mennonites, who had also come from Pennsylvania.

Inasmuch as Union churches were not common before the Disestablishment, and inasmuch as Mennonites were not like-

ly to partner with a Union body, the first claim is unlikely. However, the second and third claims may be partly true. It is most likely that the building was started by the Mennonites in 1738 to 1740. In 1770, perhaps, either Elder Koontz converted many of the Mennonites to Primitive Baptist beliefs, or the Mennonites, as pacifists, withdrew from the house during expeditions against warring Indians. Also, the Mennonites are said to have wanted a Sunday school, which the Primitive Baptists disliked. For some or all of these reasons, the Mennonites withdrew to worship at the White House Fort around 1770. This latter structure, which seemed to function as a dwelling and a fort and which still stands, was probably erected around 1760 by Martin Kauffman II. Mennonite worship didn't last there either, for Kauffman was converted to the Primitive Baptist faith, later becoming one of their ministers.

The deed that granted The Mauck Meeting House to "...Sundry persons...friends of religion & good order" was made in 1807, ordered to be certified in 1811, and recorded in 1818. It was then situated on land belonging to Joseph Mauck, son of Daniel Mauck, the settler.

After the Mennonites left the meeting house, the Primitive Baptists used it until the brick church at the top of the hill was completed around 1888 to 1890. After that time, Baptists of the New School, Methodists, and others held Sunday school and services there for over fifteen years.

The Mauck Meeting House was initially erected as a Nonconformist chapel within the Augusta Parish of the Established Church. It fell into Frederick Parish in 1753 and into Beckford Parish in 1769. It remained within the boundaries of Beckford Parish until 1872, when Luray Parish was created. It is obvious that The Mauck Meeting House has served a variety of Christian faiths. In one of his books, Vernon Davis wrote, "Not far from the eastern slope of the Massanutten Range in Page County stands a remarkable building, remarkable principally for its primitive, rugged simplicity."

ST. MARY'S WHITE CHAPEL

LANCASTER COUNTY

Erected: 1740

Denomination: Anglican

Location: Junction of Routes 354 and 201, 3 miles from Lively

Religious Services: First and third Sundays, Morning Prayer at 11:15 A.M.
Second, fourth, and fifth Sundays, Holy Eucharist at 11:15 A.M.
Third Thursdays, 10:30 A.M.
Holy Days, 12 M.

St. Mary's White Chapel, as photographed in 1930, is of cruciform construction.

L ANCASTER COUNTY PARISH DATES BACK TO 1650, when Lancaster and Middlesex were combined. A few years later, in the absence of a vestry, the court appointed the Reverend Samuel Cole the minister of the entire county. This is the same minister who appears in the vestry book of Middlesex in the year 1664. The court also appointed church wardens; they were John Taylor, William Clapham, John Merryman, Edmund Lurin, George Kibble, and William Leech. Other names also appear in the records, such as Thomas Powell, Cuthbert Powell, Edward Digges, Robert Chewning, David Fox, Henry Corbyn, and John Washington. In 1661, a general vestry was formed and Mr. John Carter, Henry Corbyn, David Fox, and William Leech were appointed to the take up subscriptions for the support of the minister.

In the upper section of the county, at the present town of Lively, the first church called St. Mary's White Chapel was erected. The early vestry book and numerous county records were destroyed during the Civil War, and the history is very fragmentary. The first church is believed to have been erected about 1669. Bishop William Meade, in his *Old Churches, Ministers, and Families of Virginia,* states that, according to the vestry book, the old building was razed and a new one built in 1740. The second building was cruciform, like its contemporary, Christ Church. In the course of repairing the building in 1830, after it had stood abandoned for many years, the building was remodeled; after the chancel and nave wings had been removed, the transept was restored, and the new rectangular church measured sixty feet by thirty feet, which is the present building. The high pulpit originally stood at the north end facing the south door of the present building. The present long aisle, running from the south door to the north end, is intersected by a wider aisle from the door on the west side, which evidently was the main aisle in the nave of the cruciform buildings.

In 1740, Maj. James Ball and Mr. Joseph Ball were allowed to build a gallery in the church for their families, provided it be completed by the time the church was completed and finished in the same style as the west gallery. Leave was also granted to two of the Balls and a Mr. Burgess to build an end-gallery on the same terms.

The high pews and the pulpit, which had its own stairway with a banister rail, existed until prior to the Civil War. In 1882, the high pulpit was removed. In that same year, the old tablets were also removed from the gallery, where they had laid in dust. They were restored at a cost of one hundred dollars.

Rev. H. L. Derby, then the rector of the parish, was extremely active in this project. Often called reredos, or partitions behind the altar, there were four in St. Mary's. Two contain the Ten Commandments and were the gift of David Fox in 1702. The remaining two were given by his son, William Fox, and contain the Apostles' Creed and the Lord's Prayer. There are no dates inscribed on these, but they were made in 1717, as shown by the will of Capt. William Fox, dated 1717, and in which he directed: "My Wife shall send for the Lord's Prayer and Creed, well drawn in gold letters, and my name under each of them, set in decent black frames, as a gift to St. Mary's White Chapel." He also left in his will, "the font that came in that year." The tablets are of solid walnut wood and the letters are hand-carved, cut in, and heavily gilded in gold gilt. They are oval at the top with the square base, in keeping with the deep-seated windows and oval ceiling. The font of unpolished marble stands on a square base, which is exceedingly heavy, and from which a round marble pedestal supports on its top a very large, round marble basin, all of which stands four feet and six inches. The chalice is a solid silver goblet inscribed, "the Gift of David Fox, 1669."

Mr. George Spencer, in his will dated 23 March 1691, gave twenty pounds of sterling for a communion plate for St. Mary's White Chapel, as well as a small silver salver, which is used with the goblet. The old Bible was given by Rawleigh Downman, of Belle Isle, in 1838. The beautiful, circular communion railing remains authentic.

In the churchyard are a number of old tombs of massive marble, bearing dates from the sixteenth and seventeenth centuries. Nearly all of the oldest stones are inscribed with the name of Ball, mainly David, seventh son of William Ball, born 1686. Some of the others are Mildred; Juduthum; Mary Ann, daughter of Rev. John Bertrand; Jesse Ball; and Mary Ball, daughter of Edwin Conway and wife of James Ball. Among the earlier ministers are Rev. Samuel Cole, died 1659; Rev. William White and Benjamin Doggett, died 1682; Rev. John Bertrand, died 1701; Rev. Andrew Jackson, died 1710; Rev. John Bell, died 1743; Rev. David Currie, died 1793; Rev. David Ball, died 1791; and Rev. Ephraim Adams, died 1838.

Unlike most colonial churches, St. Mary's did not suffer during the War Between the States (1861-65). The Federal gunboats came up the Rappahannock River near the church and shot bomb shells over and around it, but the only damage incurred was a few broken tree tops. A company of Ninth Virginia Calvary, C.S.A., were stationed at the church for a few months in 1861 and pitched tents in the church-

yard. Col. Meriwether Lewis, who was a captain at that time, was joined by Robert Tunstsall Pierce (First Lieutenant) and James K. Ball of Beaudley (Second Lieutenant). All three are buried in the churchyard at St. Mary's.

Today, St. Mary's White Chapel is well preserved. Both the interior and exterior are neat in appearance. Today it has an active Episcopal congregation in the Diocese of Virginia.

Today, St. Mary's White Chapel is well preserved, and its churchyard contains grave markers from the seventeenth century.

ST. JOHN'S CHURCH
HENRICO COUNTY
RICHMOND

Erected: 1741

Denomination: Anglican

Location: 2401 East Broad Street, Richmond

Religious Services: Sundays, Holy Eucharist at 8:30 A.M. (Rite I: sermon, no music) and 11:00 A.M. (Rite II)

Parish Office open Monday—Friday, 9:00 A.M. to 3:00 P.M.
Tour Operations open Monday—Saturday, 10:00 A.M. to 4:00 P.M., Sunday, 1:00 P.M. to 4:00 P.M.

St. John's Church as photographed in 1925. It was here that Patrick Henry delivered his famous words, "Give me liberty, or give me death!"

Reenactments of Patrick Henry's speech at the Second Virginia Convention occur at 2:00 P.M. on Sundays between Memorial Day and Labor Day and are preceded by a musical recital, which starts at 1:30 P.M.

CAPT. JOHN SMITH WAS IN A PARTY OF EXPLORERS, under Capt. Christopher Newport, which sailed up the James River in 1607 and planted a cross on an island by the site of the present day city of Richmond. Henrico Parish was formed in this region in 1611, only four years after the settlement of Jamestown.

The Reverend Alexander Whitaker, called the "Cambridge Apostle to Virginia" and perhaps best known as the minister who baptized Pocahontas, served as Henrico Parish's first rector. He was the son of Dr. William Whitaker, master of St. John's College, Cambridge.

The Reverend Thomas Bargrave became rector in 1619. It was during his administration that the parish of Henrico was chosen as the site of a great university; fifteen thousand acres of land between Henricopolis and where Richmond now stands were set apart as college land by the Virginia Company. King James, through the archbishop of Canterbury, appealed for and obtained large subscriptions in England. Mr. Bargrave donated his library.

For the next one hundred years, the annals of Henrico Parish are fragmentary, although it is known that the Reverend James Blair served as rector from 1686 to 1694. The oldest record book of the parish vestry begins on 28 October 1730. This book was found in 1867 among the old records of Henrico County and was given to the vestry.

When the book was begun, the principal church in the parish was Curle's Church, located a few miles below Richmond on the north side of the James River. Also, at that time, the Reverend James Keith was rector. He left the service of the church in 1735, at which time, the vestry arranged with the Reverend David Mossom to preach at the church every fifth Sunday in exchange for four hundred pounds of tobacco. Mr. Mosson, who served as rector of St. Peter's, New Kent County, for forty years, officiated at the marriage of George Washington and Martha Custis. He was the first Native American to be ordained a Presbyterian in the Church of England.

In 1736, the Reverend William Stith, who was educated at William and Mary and in England, became rector of the parish. During his rectorate, St. John's Church was built in 1741, and he wrote the *History of Virginia from the First Settlement to the Dissolution of the London Company* in 1747.

The original church building was sixty feet long and twenty-five feet wide, and consisted only of the present east-west transepts, with, as usual, the altar in the east, the doors in the south (near the chancel) and the west, and the pulpit probably on the north wall just west of the chancel. In 1772, a north wing with galleries was added; it was this T-shaped structure that provided the meeting place for the noted convention three years later.

The Reverend Miles Selden was appointed rector in 1752. He served as the chaplain of the Second Virginia Convention, which met in the church on 20 March 1775. Here in a short speech, Patrick Henry delivered his famous words, "Give me liberty, or give me death," before some 120 delegates that included Thomas Jefferson and George Washington.

On 17 July 1775, the Third Virginia Convention met in St. John's Church in order to prepare for the war effort of Virginia. In January 1781, the traitor Benedict Arnold, by now a general in the British Army, quartered his troops in the church.

Under the rectorship of the Reverend William F. Lee, the church received its name, St. John's. The following entry is found in the vestry book shortly after Mr. Lee became rector: "At a meeting of the Vestry of Henrico Parish, at the lecture-room of St. John's Church, Richmond, Saturday evening, April 25, 1829..." In the Diocesan Convention journal of that year, the church is entered as St. John's Church, Richmond, Henrico Parish.

The church was known for almost a century by a variety of names: The New Church, The Upper Church, The Richmond Church, The Town Church, The Church on Richmond Hill, Henrico Church on Richmond Hill, The Church, The Old Church, et cetera.

In 1830, St. John's Church was enlarged by an addition to the nave. Several years later, the tower was built. The church continued to prosper under Rev. L. W. Burton, and during his ministry, Weddell Chapel and the Chapel of the Good Shepherd were built.

In 1905, a chancel, organ chamber, vestry room, and other improvements were built on the south side of the old part of the church. The church is now cruciform and points directly to the four points of the compass.

The original box pews, with their backs cut down, are still in the church. In one of them, to the left near the font, stood Patrick Henry when he made his famous address.

The bowl of St. John's baptismal font is a precious relic from Curle's Church. It was found in 1826 and had been used as a mortar for beating hominy. The communion silver, which had been presented in 1722 to the Lower Chapel, Middlesex, found its way to Richmond after the chapel was

Historic St. John's Church as it appears today. Its parish, Henrico, was formed in 1611, making it one of the oldest. Reenactments of the Second Virginia Convention occur weekly during the summer.

abandoned by Episcopalians in 1846. It was purchased by the St. John's vestry and is used occasionally.

The oldest grave in the churchyard is that of Robert Rose, just outside the east doorway. He died in 1751 and during his lifetime had served as rector of St. Anne's Parish, Essex County, and of St. Anne's, Albemarle County. His brother, Charles Rose, was the earliest recorded rector of Yeocomico Church in Westmoreland County.

Today, shaded by magnificent trees and situated in the heart of a very busy city, St. John's Church stands as a connecting link with the earliest civil and ecclesiastical history of our Commonwealth and nation. It bears witness to what the Church of England and the Protestant Episcopal Church have done through the years to instill in the people liberty, brotherly love, and faith.

Consider these words, spoken by the bishop of Southern Virginia, in an address delivered in St. John's Church on its

150th anniversary, 10 June 1891. He is speaking about one of the church's earliest members, the forefather of two former vestry members, Richard Randolph, who had supervised the building of St. John's Church in 1741, and Edmund Randolph, who had represented the church in the first Convention of the Diocese:

A simple, strong true man he must have been; out of his loins sprang three great men. He was the ancestor of Chief Justice Marshall, the great jurist of America. He was the ancestor of Thomas Jefferson, the greatest political thinker of America. He was the ancestor of Robert E. Lee, the greatest soldier of America. The ancestor of these three men lived in this parish. St. John's Church continues to have great and deserved appeal for worshippers and visitors alike, because of its historic fame, its graves and beautiful surroundings.

HUNGARS PARISH CHURCH
NORTHHAMPTON COUNTY

Erected: 1742

Denomination: Anglican

Location: Northampton County of the Eastern Shore on Route 619, 2 miles north of Bridgetown, off of Route 13.

Religious Services: Sundays, 9:30 A.M.
Wednesdays, Eucharist at 9:30 A.M.

This photograph of Hungars Church was taken in the early 1900s. The parish is one of the oldest in the nation, formed in 1632.

The history of the Eastern Shore of Virginia begins with Capt. John Smith's exploration of the Chesapeake Bay in 1608, of which he recorded:

Leaving the Phoenix at Cape Henry, wee crossed the bay to the Eastern Shore, and fell in with the isles called Smith Isles. First people encountered were two grim, stout Savages upon Cape Charles, with long poles, javelings headed with some bone, who boldly demanded who and what we were. After many circumstances, they seemed kind, and directed us to Accomack, the habitation of their Weorwance, where we were kindly treated. This Rex was the comeliest, civill salvage we encountered. His country is pleasant, fertile clay soyle, some small creeks, good harbours for barques, not ships. They spoke the language of Powhatan.

The largest of this group of isles is still known as Smith Island. It would later form a very insignificant part of the property of Mrs. Robert E. Lee, who inherited it through many generations from her ancestor John Custis of "Arlington" in Northampton County, Virginia.

The home of "Rex," whom John Smith met during his 1608 visit, was located on what is now called Old Plantation Creek—so named because the oldest settlement on the Eastern Shore was made on this beautiful tidal inlet, probably on the farm at the head of the creek, also called Old Plantation.

The first settlement of the Eastern Shore occurred in 1614, seven years after the settlement at Jamestown. It was described in 1616 by John Rolfe, who married the Indian princess Pocahontas, as being situated on the coast near Cape Charles. "Accawmacke," an Indian term meaning "the other side place," was given to this area.

In 1634, the Accawmacke region became one of the eight original shires, or counties, established in Virginia. In 1642, the county's "heathen" name was changed to the more suitable English name of Northampton. By 1663, there were enough settlers in the county to warrant dividing it into two: Northampton and Accomac (which retained this spelling until 1940, when the "k" was placed on the end by a resolution of the Virginia General Assembly).

The earliest published mention of the name Hungars appears in the 1625 census, which records that there had been granted to "Sir George Yeardley at Hunger's [sic], 3,700 acres of land by order of court." The grant confirms the previous gift of this land to Sir George Yeardley, the British colonial governor of Virginia, by Debedeavon, "the laughing

[Indian] King of Accomack, upon the occasion of Yeardley's visit to the Eastern Shore in 1621." This gift, as recorded at Northampton Courthouse in 1668, conveyed to Yeardley all of "that neck of land from Wissaponson Creek to Hungars Neck." The site of the Hungars plantation house is still marked by several tombstones of the Yeardley family.

Hungars Parish was formed in 1632, when settlers came to the Eastern Shore to find salt for the colonists at Jamestown. It is one of the oldest parishes in the nation.

The present Hungars Church is believed to have been built as early as 1742. When it was originally built, it was the longest and next to the largest rectangular church in colonial Virginia. The original dimensions of this church were ninety-two feet long and forty-four feet wide. While its width has remained forty-four feet, at present the church is now seventy-four feet long.

Prior to the Revolution, the interior furnishings of Hungars Church were very handsome, all of them brought from England and most, if not all, of them gifts from Queen Anne. Mr. M. C. Howard of Northampton County, near the turn of the nineteenth century, saw a fragment of the chancel draperies: dark crimson velvet of superb quality, with gold embroidery and bullion fringe, all of which had defied time and retained a brilliancy he claims he had never before seen.

There were difficult periods following the Revolution and Disestablishment of the Episcopal Church when Hungars was abandoned. An act of the General Assembly was passed in December 1788 authorizing the appointment of trustees to hold title to the glebes, churches, et cetera, for the use of the Protestant Episcopal Church. From 1788 to 1799, the attack upon the right of the Episcopal Church to hold title to her property continued.

Hungars Parish Church was abandoned after the Disestablishment, but it was restored to service in 1819. The old building was repaired at a cost of $1,400 and consecrated by Bishop Richard Channing Moore.

In 1837, seats were built under the west gallery for the accommodation of African American people. The congregation yielded to the spirit of change, which was rampant at that time, and destroyed most of the remaining colonial features of the church interior. The high colonial pulpit, which stood at the north side of the church near the side door, was moved to the chancel, and later it disappeared from the church.

By the end of 1850, the building was declared unsafe, and a fund was started for rebuilding the church. In 1851 the church vestry decided to take the church down and build a new church on the same site. Fortunately for the

preservation of the historic landmark, an alternative proposal made by Thomas H. Stevenson of Snow Hill, Maryland, was approved. Stevenson carried out the restoration and he inscribed and signed a shingle in the roof stating he had done the work in 1851 for $1,500 and had "sunk a hundred dollars" in the process. His workmanship was excellent.

The brickwork of the rebuilt west gable is the product of a master builder, as it can scarcely be distinguished from that of the original walls, while the care taken in preserving and installing the colonial rubbed brick arches, with their fluted brick-tile keys, over the rebuilt doorways and windows, merits the highest praise.

The following is a list of the clergy who served the Hungars Parish from 1623 until 1803:

Rev. Francis Bolton	1623-30
Rev. William Cotton	1632-45
Rev. John Rosier	1644
Rev. Nathaniel Eaton	1645
Rev. Thomas Palmer	1647-48
Rev. Thomas Higby	1651-56
Rev. Francis Doughty	1655-60
Rev. Isaac Key	1676

The west gable was eventually rebuilt, the brickwork barely distinguishable from the original walls.

Hungars Church in 1930. The original furnishings were gifts from Queen Anne.

Rev. Thomas Teakle	1680
Rev. John Monroe	1692
Rev. Samuel Parker	1695
Rev. Patrick Falconer	1710-18
Rev. James Falconer	1719
Rev. Thomas Dell	1721-29
Rev. John Holbrooke	1729-47
Rev. Henry Barlow	1747-61
Rev. Richard Hewitt	1761-74
Rev. Samuel S. McCroskey	1774-1803

Bishop William Meade mentions in *Old Churches, Ministers, and Families of Virginia* some of the vestrymen for Hungars Church, who served from 1812 to 1857: Peter Bowdoin, Nathaniel Holland, John Addison, John Upshur, John Windee, Littleton Upshur, George Parker, William Satchell, Thomas Satchell, Isaac Smith, John T. Elliott, James Upshur, Abel P. Upshur, Charles West, John Leatherbury, John Ker, and Severn E. Parker.

The 1758 to 1782 vestry book for Hungars Church survives. The current vestry book commences in 1819. The interval between the two is the result of the difficult period that followed the Revolutionary War, in which the Church of Virginia was disestablished and Hungars Church was abandoned.

There are no colonial markers in the churchyard.

AUGUSTA STONE CHURCH
AUGUSTA COUNTY

Erected: 1747

Denomination: Presbyterian

Location: 7 miles north of Staunton on U.S. Route 11 at the hamlet of Fort Defiance

Religious Services: Sundays, 11:00 A.M

Augusta Stone Church (1930) was crafted from local limestone.

THE ORIGINAL LOG BUILDING STOOD IN THE OLD cemetery across the road from the present Augusta Stone Church. The first building was perhaps erected shortly after 1740, the year the congregation was organized. The present church was erected in 1747 and dedicated in 1749. In a colony where brick churches were the rule, pioneers here brought from Pennsylvania their skill in adapting the local limestone to the meeting houses. Tradition has it that the women of the congregation at Timber Ridge Church, between Lexington and Fairfield, used pack horses to bring the sand for the mortar from the nearest stream. If this is true, it was probably the North River, which is only a few miles away. The first portico and the rear wings, which gave the building its T-form, were added in 1922. The building has a gallery and barrel ceiling. Presently, a vaulted ceiling covers the chancel and transept.

In 1714, Governor Spottswood and his gallant band of cavaliers, with their attendants, ascended the Blue Ridge at Rockfish Gap in Albemarle County and became the delighted beholders of the rich and beautiful valley below. He claimed the region for the crown in the course of the expedition to protect this western frontier from encroachments of the French. After its discovery by Governor Spottswood, the region of the Blue Ridge was defined as being a part of Essex County, which had no specific western limits. In 1720, Spotsylvania County was laid off from Essex and named in honor of the governor, and in 1734, Orange County was created to cover the region farther west, which was named for William, Prince of Orange, later King William III of England. In 1738, the General Assembly, which governed the Church of Virginia, created in the parts of Orange west of the Blue Ridge the new counties of Frederick and Augusta, naming them for the Prince of Wales, the son of King George II, and his wife Princess Augusta. Augusta, in the year 1738, became the frontier county and was therefore called West Augusta.

A renowned pioneer of this area was John Lewis, who came to Virginia from Dublin, Ireland, about the year 1720. Some ascribe a Welsh origin and others a Huguenot to the family. John Lewis had four sons. His eldest son, Thomas, was born in Ireland in 1718. Thomas was a vestryman of the early church in Augusta and one of the first delegates to one of the first meetings of the General Assembly. The second was Andrew Lewis, the hero of the Battle of Point Pleasant (10 October 1774 in West Virginia). The third was William, who, like Thomas, was a vestryman in Augusta and afterward settled at Sweet Springs. The fourth was Charles, who was killed by the Indians in the Battle of Point Pleasant.

Although the county of Augusta and the existing parish were organized within the established Church of England, exemption from parish taxes left the way open to dissenters. Early on the region was populated by Scotch-Irish Presbyterians. They had come originally from Northern Ireland by way of New Castle, Delaware. They founded the Donegal Church in Pennsylvania, and under that church they were the first settlers to enter the Cumberland Valley, where they founded and settled many Presbyterian churches. They finally moved south through the Cumberland Valley and settled in Virginia. After arriving in Augusta County, the Presbyterians requested a pastor from the Donegal Presbytery in Pennsylvania.

The Reverend John Craig (1709-74) was sent to Augusta County to lead the new congregation. He was born in County Antrim, Northern Ireland, came to Pennsylvania in 1734, and was licensed to preach in 1737. During the year 1740, he arrived in Augusta County. It was not until six years later, one year before Augusta County was created, that the first election ever held in the county took place. The 1746 vestry election resulted in the choice of James Patton, John Buchanon, John Madison, Patrick Hays, John Christian, Col. John Buchanon, Robert Alexander, Thomas Gordon, James Loehart, John Archer, John Matthews, and John Smith. These were among the most prominent and influential men of the county. This vestry was chosen for the new Anglican parish, and at that time, the first Anglican minister, the Reverend John Hindman, entered Augusta. It was some years later, however, that the first Anglican church was built in Augusta County.

Rev. John Craig had a very large parish covering an area of approximately fifty miles. The church owns Reverend Craig's Bible (London, 1782), his record of baptisms from 1740 to 1749, his autobiography dated 1770, and one published sermon that contains fifty-five divisions. This sermon is based on 2 Sam. 23:5, which reads: "Yea, does not my house stand so with God? For he has made with me an everlasting covenant, ordered in all things and secure for will he not cause to prosper all my help and my desire?"

In 1847, the small stone Session House attached to the north side of the church building was removed and rebuilt in its present location, adjacent to the church. During 1975, the Session House was converted into a charming museum. Here the most treasured heirlooms of this church are housed. Among the historical items on exhibit are John Craig's pulpit Bible; baptismal records; and autobiography;

Augusta Stone Church is now a registered national landmark.

copper communion tokens bearing the initials "J. C.—A. C.," which represent John Craig—Augusta Church; his silver sugar tongs; and study chair, which belonged to the second minister, Dr. William Wilson. The eighteen-piece silver communion service on display here is the largest set of colonial church silver in the state of Virginia. This service was made in London, circa 1764, and consists of three flagons, six goblets, six patens, and three alms basins. The story of this beautiful church silver has been included in many books and articles and, for a time, it was on display at the Virginia Museum of Fine Arts in Richmond.

In 1989 and 1990, Augusta Stone Church celebrated its 250th anniversary with various activities highlighting the celebration. A commemorative quilt was made by church members, on which are displayed various scenes from the life of Augusta Stone, and which includes the names of the present members. Also, a time capsule containing the prayers and handprints of the children of the church was buried on 19 August 1990 and will be opened in the year 2015. Tinkling Spring Presbyterian Church, located in Fishersvlle, Virginia, Augusta Stone's sister church, also celebrated its 250th anniversary. The two congregations, originally one, worshipped together in both sanctuaries during the Sesquibicentennial year in celebration of their long heritage and the service of their first minister, John Craig.

Augusta Stone Church was constructed for the ages. Excellent workmanship and superior quality stone and sand have enabled the building to stand firm. The selfless love and dedication of the generations who have worshipped within the stone walls have made this venerable church truly a house of God.

In over 250 years, Augusta Stone Church has had only eighteen ministers. They are as follows:

Dr. John Craig	1740-74
Dr. William Wilson	1780-13
Dr. Conrad Speece	1813-36
Dr. William Brown	1836-60
Rev. Francis Bowman	1861-68
Dr. I. W. K. Handy	1870-77
Dr. Alexander Sprunt	1879-85
Rev. George L. Bitzer	1885-89
Rev. J. N. VanDevanter	1891-1917
Rev. John B. Gordon	1917-24
Rev. John M. McBryde	1925-52
Dr. J. A. Allison Jr.	1952-59
Rev. R. E. Hildebrandt	1960-62
Rev. L. H. Zbinden Jr.	1963-67
Dr. James R. Kennedy	1968-77
Rev. James M. Hovland	1977-86
Dr. Richard N. Sommers	1987-91
Rev. Gary S. McGrew	1992-

Old Stone Church, as it is now affectionately known, was first remodeled in 1855. The growth of the congregation and the increased enrollment of Augusta Military Academy, whose cadets worshipped in the church from 1865 until the school closed in 1984, made a larger building necessary. Thus, in 1921, transepts were artistically added to the original church building, changing it into its present structure—the form of a cross. The steeple was also added at this time. In 1956, John Craig Hall, the third addition, was built and serves as a fellowship center. The restoration of the sanctuary was initiated and completed in 1968. This remodeling included the renovation, enlargement, and relocation of the Moller pipe organ to the balcony. The high pulpit and sounding board were also added during this restoration.

In 1974, Augusta Stone Church was added to the Virginia and National Landmarks Registers.

BUCK MOUNTAIN CHURCH

EARLYSVILLE (ALBEMARLE COUNTY)

Erected: 1747

Denomination: Anglican

Location: From Charlottesville, take Route 29 North for 8 miles. Turn left onto Route 649 for 1 mile, then left onto Route 606 for another mile. Turn left on Route 743 for 1 1/2 miles. Church is on right in village of Earlysville (approximately 2.7 miles from Charlottesville-Albemarle airport).

Religious Services: Sundays, 10:00 A.M.: first, second, third, and fifth Sundays, Holy Communion; fourth Sunday, Morning Prayer

Buck Mountain Church as photographed in 1986. Notice the bell tower on the right that was destroyed by gale–force winds in 1995.

119

After the separation of Louisa County from Hanover County in 1742, and of the Fredericksville Parish in Louisa from St. Martin's Parish in Hanover, the parish of Fredericksville was enlarged by taking in part of Albemarle lying north and west of the Rivanna River. After a number of years, Fredericksville Parish was divided to create Trinity Parish in Louisa County. Following this division, the parish had no place of worship, except an old mountain chapel where Walker's Church eventually stood. The first meeting of the Fredericksville Parish vestry occurred in 1742.

In 1745, a decision was made to build three frame churches. One was to be constructed in the central part of Louisa County and called the Lower Church, or Trinity Church. Two were to be erected in Albemarle County: one called Middle Church, or Walker's Church, and the other called Buck Mountain Church, located on Buck Mountain Road.

Buck Mountain Church was built in 1747, and its dimensions were thirty feet by sixty feet. After its disestablishment in 1784, the building was used at various times during the years 1801 to 1833 by Baptists and members of other non-Episcopal denominations. The church building was dismantled in 1861 and moved to its present location. The original site of the church is about two miles west of the current building. Although there is nothing indisputably colonial to be seen on the exterior or in the interior of the present building, it is generally believed that the roof trusses and the upright framing members derive from the original church. The floor joists are notched and hand-hewn, as is the building, but if its rafters, joists, and upright members are indeed from the 1747 church building—as primarily believed—then Buck Mountain Church has as much right to be called colonial.

The church derives its name from the striking eminence six miles to the west, and the mountain itself was named apparently for the myriad buck deer encountered there. Fredericksville Parish was probably named for Prince Frederick, father of George III, for whom the town of Fredericksburg (1728) was also named.

There were at one time, two gravestones that marked the site of the first church, but these can no longer be located.

Following is a list of clergy who served Fredericksville Parish from 1747 to 1838. Buck Mountain Church was served in conjunction with other congregations during those time periods.

Rev. _____ Arnold	1747-54 (no known first name)
Rev. Thomas Beckett	1754
Rev. James Maury	1770-1808
Rev. John P. Bauusman	1818-19
Rev. Frederich Hatch	1820-30
Rev. Zachariah Mead	1830-33
Rev. W. C. Jones	1833-38

Some physical changes have occurred at Buck Mountain Church during the last eight years. To the east of the church, a tall bell tower stood for many years enclosed by sides of lattice work. During some gale–force winds in 1995, the bell tower fell and has not been replaced.

During 1996, the church built a new parish hall and dedicated the building to the Reverend Ellen Deese and her husband, Jim. Ellen faithfully served Buck Mountain Church as a priest until her untimely death.

The dimensions of the current church building are sixty feet long and thirty-two feet wide. The new parish hall measures approximately fifty feet by twenty-six feet. A breezeway connects the parish hall to the church, which increases the dimensions to 135 1/2 feet by thirty-two feet.

Buck Mountain Church now serves a very active Episcopal congregation in the Diocese of Virginia.

Buck Mountain Church today. The original building was dismantled and moved to its present location.

PROVIDENCE CHURCH
LOUISA COUNTY

Erected: circa 1747

Denomination: Presbyterian

Location: At the crossroads of Routes 250 and 522 at Gum Spring, proceed west 0.2 mile and turn right onto Route 700. Continue for another 0.2 mile. Turn right at church sign. White frame church can be seen at the end of the wooded lane.

Religious Services: Sundays, 11:00 A.M.

Providence Church is one of five frame churches to survive the colonial period.

P ROVIDENCE PRESBYTERIAN CHURCH, AS IT IS KNOWN today, is one of five frame churches to survive the colonial period. It stands at the end of a wooden lane in Louisa County off Route 250 near Gum Spring. The church lies southeast by northwest, and its dimensions are fifty feet three inches by twenty-six feet four inches. The exact construction date is unknown; however, the church was probably erected by the year 1747 and used as a reading house—a place where people congregated to read the works of Protestant reformer Martin Luther—and shortly thereafter became a Presbyterian meeting house. It was probably named for God's providence, which was felt during the colonial period.

Providence Church is located in Louisa County, which was named after Princess Louisa, daughter of George II and wife of Frederick V, King of Denmark. Louisa County was formed from Hanover County in 1742 and then grew through various acquisitions of land that occurred between 1742 and 1877.

While the settlements of the Scotch-Irish were multiplying in the Valley of the Shenandoah, along the eastern part of the Blue Ridge, and on the waters of the Roanoke, many Presbyterian congregations began to form in Hanover County and in some of the adjacent counties, whose inhabitants were of true English descent and connected with the established church. Reports of organized Presbyterian religious services prevailed in New Jersey, New England, and Pennsylvania, and some parts of Maryland, then spread through Virginia.

In a 1743 letter to the bishop of London, the Reverend Samuel Davies wrote that about four or five persons—heads of families in Hanover County—had dissented from the established church because of doctrines generally delivered from the pulpit. He reported that these families had begun to meet in private homes to listen to readings from books by Martin Luther, who had led the Protestant Reformation in Germany during his lifetime (1483-1546). Mr. Davies assured his lordship that Luther's writings, which included catechisms for the instruction of the common people and a number of fine hymns (including "Ein Feste Burg," which, in English, begins with the line, "A mighty fortress is our God"), were the principal cause of these families leaving the church. In fact, the reading of Luther's works had become so popular that private homes could not contain all the people who attended them. Eventually, these families agreed to build a meeting house.

In another account of the times, the Reverend James Hunt of Montgomery County, Maryland, related to a gentleman in Albemarle County, Virginia (who preserved the narrative and published it in the second volume of the *Evangelical and Literary Magazine,* edited by the Reverend John H. Rice, D.D.), "that in the County of Hanover four gentlemen, of whom his father was one, at the same time became convinced that the Gospel was not preached by the minister of the parish church, and that it was inconsistent with their duty to attend upon his ministrations."

They agreed to meet every Sabbath, alternately, at each other's houses, and spend the time with their families in prayer and reading the scriptures, together with Luther's *Commentary on the Galatians,* an old volume that they had acquired.

According to the article in *Evangelical and Literary Magazine,* cited above,

Mr. Hunt, in his narrative, gives an interesting account of a visit made, by his father and some other gentleman, to Williamsburg, to have an interview with the Governor and Council. He tells us that one of the company, travelling alone, was overtaken and detained by a violent storm, at the house of a poor man on the road. He interested himself in looking over an old volume which he found upon a shelf covered with dust. Upon perusing it, he was amazed to find his own sentiments, as far as he had formed any on religious things, drawn out in appropriate language; and as far as he read, the whole summary met his approbation. Offering to purchase the book, the owner gave it to him. In Williamsburg, he examined the old book again, in company with his friends; they all agreed that it expressed their views on the doctrines of religion. When they appeared before the Governor, they presented this old volume as their creed. Governor Gooch, himself of Scotch origin and education, upon looking at the volume, pronounced the men Presbyterians, as the book was the *Confession of Faith of the Presbyterian Church of Scotland*; and that they were not only tolerated but acknowledged as a part of the established church of the realm.

On Sunday, 6 July 1743, the first sermon from a Presbyterian minister was delivered in Hanover County, Virginia. The minister, William Robinson, had been born near Carlyle, England, and was the son of a Quaker. His scripture lesson or text was taken from Luke 13:3: "I tell you, nay but except ye repent ye shall all likewise perish."

Samuel Morris, a member of the congregation, said, "With us preaching four days successively, the congregation increased from day to day." After four days of preaching, Mr. Robinson departed, and it was rumored that officers of the law were preparing to arrest him as an itinerant. A committee was appointed to put into the hands of Mr. Robinson a considerable sum of money before his departure. Mr. Robinson later appropriated the money to the education of Samuel Davies, an acquaintance with promising talents who, at that time, was studying with a view to the ministry. Unfortunately, Robinson died in 1746, and Samuel Davies did not come to Hanover until April 1747 (his license was dated 14 April 1747). Present at Samuel Davies first service were Gov. William Gooch, John Robinson, John Grymes, John Custis, Philip Lightfoot, Thomas Lee, Lewis Burwell, William Fairfax, John Blair, William

Nelson, and William Dawson, clerk.

The following account describes Davies's ministry:

No mention of Presbyterian history should be attempted without some word of Parson Davies. Born in the colony of Delaware, near Summit's Ridge, on November 3, 1723, of a good Welsh family, he had educational opportunities in a good English school and later was fortunate in having a Welsh minister, Mr. Morgan, gave him training in the classics. Following that, he was put under the tutorage of the Reverend Samuel Blair at Faggs Manor in Pennsylvania.

He was licensed to preach by the New Castle Presbytery on July 30, 1746, and in October of the same year married Sarah Kilpatrick. The following spring he was ordained an Evangelist to preach in Virginia. He, it will be recalled, was the student who was helped by the funds from the Presbyterians in Hanover.

He was licensed to preach in Virginia by the Council of April 14...He settled himself in Hanover, about twelve miles from Richmond, in the neighborhood of Morris's Reading House. Here he maintained himself and family through his period of missionary activity in Virginia.

Mr. Davies was a staunch supporter of the colonists in their trials both with the English government and with the hordes of savage tribes in the West. His sermons, many of them, had definite and direct patriotic appeal, a thing that did not belong to the province of dissenter ministers in the early days. Noteworthy was his appeal to men at Hanover to join Captain Samuel Overton's company, in which his prophetic allusion to Colonel George Washington was made.

Mr. Davies preached in Louisa at old Providence and also, it is said, at old Fork Meeting House. He was successful in his efforts to get ministerial help, which came in the person of John Todd. It was to Todd he entrusted the Presbyterians of Virginia when he went to England in the interest of the New Jersey College, which was one day to become Princeton.

This is the man of whom Henry said in later years, he was the greatest orator he had ever heard, and mayhaps it was his influence that led to Patrick's remarkable career.

Davies went on his mission to England in 1753, and returned in 1755. Again he took up his work and continued until called to be President of the College of New Jersey in 1759. He succeeded the distinguished Reverend Mr. Johnathan Edwards. His services to the college had been largely done, for he was its head for the brief period of two years.

Davies, "the apostle to Virginia," as [the Reverend William Henry] Foote calls him, died Feb. 4, 1761...

A native of Ireland, the Reverend John Todd (1719-93) came to Virginia in 1752 to assist Samuel Davies. He had emigrated to America in 1737 and had attended Princeton University, from which he graduated in 1749.

Todd had a very strong relationship with the Presbyterians in Louisa County. His oath, which was prescribed by law for dissenting ministers, was administered at Williamsburg on 12 April 1752 and, on 12 November 1752, he was installed as minister by Samuel Davies.

In 1755, Todd established his residence in Louisa County, which would remain his home for nearly forty years. During his residence there, he served as the minister of the old Providence Church, the county's oldest house of worship. The building itself is small and simple in all details, much like the dissenters who first sat in its pews. Inside its walls, one detects a deep religious atmosphere, while outside, it stands amidst oak and pine trees, evoking memories of the days when a meeting house was the most important place in community life.

As demonstrated in the following account, John Todd's presence was felt in Louisa County.

He established at his home the first classical school in Louisa, and one that was attended by [James] Monroe, [James] Madison, Col. [John B.] Callis, and others. This school was the forerunner of Hampden-Sydney College, and Mr. Todd was one of its first trustees. It was left to him by the Presbytery to communicate with Mr. [Patrick] Henry and Mr. [James] Madison, inviting them to become members of the Board of Trustees of the newly formed college in 1775.

The Reverend John Todd became interested in Kentucky, where his nephew Col. John Todd had settled. Consequently, he was partially responsible for the founding of Transylvania College in Lexington and gave the college part of his library. He finally moved to Kentucky after residing in Virginia for about forty-two years. His son, also the Reverend John Todd, was licensed to preach at the Cove on 13 September 1800. John Todd Sr. died in 1793.

The parcel of land on which the present Providence Church stands was deeded on 29 June 1753, from planter Arthur Slayden (Slayton) of Goochland County, St. James Northam Parish, to Joseph Shelton and others for five shillings. (The deed can be found on pages 514 and 515 of Deed Book A in the Louisa County Courthouse.)

According to a will written in 1767 and probated two years later, the congregation received two silver cups that are still in use for communion services. The cups bear the initials "J. N." These markings would indicate that they were made by John Neville of London.

Many illustrious ministers have spoken from the church's pulpit, and many Virginia families, including the Sheltons, Richardsons, McCoys, Lacys, Whites, Minors, and Woods, have been devoted members over the years. The congregation remains active today.

DEEP RUN CHURCH

RICHMOND

Erected: 1749
Denomination: Baptist
Location: 10907 Three Chopt Road in Richmond
Religious Services: Sundays, 11:00 A.M.

A photograph of Deep Run Church in 1924. It was known as Hungry Church until 1819, when its name was changed to Deep Run.

EEP RUN CHURCH, WHICH STANDS ABOVE DEEP Run Creek, began as an Episcopal chapel in the Henrico Parish. This parish dates from the year 1611, at which time a settlement was founded at a site now known as Farrar's Island and called the city of Henrico. Henrico, which includes the city and a vast territory beyond, was one of the four great divisions, or corporations, of the colony ordered on 18 November 1618 by the Virginia Company to be established, and likewise, it was one of the original shires created in 1634. It was named in honor of Prince Henry, son of King James I.

At that time, there were, of course, no regulations of parish bounds; subsequently, each corporation, group-settlement, borough, or particular plantation supplied with a church was called a parish. Henrico County was described as extending through the valley on both sides of the James River from the Charles City County line indefinitely westward, and the parish was coterminous with these boundaries. Bristol Parish was created by an act in 1643, and at that time, Henrico Parish embraced the present counties of Henrico, Chesterfield, Powhatan, Cumberland, Buckingham, and a part of Appomattox, in addition to a large area on the north side of the James River west of the falls. In 1720, the Henrico Parish was divided, and St. James Parish in Henrico County was established.

Deep Run is first mentioned in the vestry minutes of Henrico Parish on 2 October 1742:

> On petition of Thomas Fenton and others, it is agreed and ordered that a chapel be built on a hill above Deep Run on land belonging to [illegible], to be 48 feet long and 24 feet wide; to be weatherboarded with fetheredge plank and covered with hart shingles, nailed on—to have three pews, reading desks, pulpit and gallery, to be finished workmanlike in a strong plain manner. And it is agreed that the Vestry do meet at Curl's [sic] Church on the last Saturday in November next to treat with undertakers about building the said chapel.

At this same meeting, ten thousand pounds of tobacco were appropriated toward the building of this chapel.

From this description of the early Richmond Church (St. John's) it would seem the two churches were built on the same general plan, with five windows on each side, a door in the west end, a gallery at the west end, and a small belfry. It may seem strange that the side of Deep Run Church faces the road rather than the front. However, this may be explained by the fact that it was the practice of the early Episcopal Church to position their buildings east to west.

Quoting again from vestry minutes, "November 19, 1744...John Coles and Peter Randolph were appointed to agree with the cheapest workmen they can to finish the chapel to be built at Deep Run."

The chapel was built on an acre of land purchased from John Shoemaker. At a meeting of the vestry, 2 December 1745, John Shoemaker was paid 536 pounds of tobacco for cleaning the arbor and for an acre of land to set the chapel on. "In 1750, the church wardens were ordered to pay John Shoemaker when he acknowledged the deed for the acre of ground on which Deep Run Church stands." For some reason Mr. Shoemaker was reluctant to sign the deed. By the deed dated 1 October 1753 and recorded in the Henrico County Deed Book (1750-57), Bowler Cocke Jr. and Samuel DuVal, church wardens, bought the land on which the chapel was standing from John Shoemaker. Hence the church was built before the deed was signed.

Builders tell us the beams in the sanctuary are fastened together with wooden pegs. From this evidence and the condition of the timbers, they speculate without doubt that it represents the original frame work. If these timbers could speak, what a wealth of history they could reveal.

William Stith was the minister of the parish from 1736 to 1751. He became president of the College of William and Mary in 1752. His salary as minister of the parish was 16,640 pounds of tobacco. However, Deep Run also had lay readers (Readors).

On 4 October 1762, a silver cup and salver, of the same size as used at St. John's Episcopal Church at Churchill, were ordered for Deep Run. Although no record in the vestry minutes states that these were paid for or delivered, it is presumed that the church acquired them.

Between the years of 1764 and 1773, William Street is mentioned in the vestry minutes as being clerk of Deep Run. His salary was 1,789 pounds of tobacco. Other sextons during this period were John Ellis, Joseph Ellis, and Joseph Freeman. Each received 536 pounds of tobacco as yearly salaries.

In 1773, Rev. Miles Seldon served as rector of the parish. At this time, the revolution clouds were gathering. The record is broken, and we find only glimpses of the parish's history until 1785. One of these short mentions is of particular interest. In the *Virginia Magisterial History, Volume III,* we read that "during the Revolutionary War, General Peter Muhlenberg, who was also a preacher, camped at Deep Run

Church and there enrolled men among his forces." It is also reported that Lafayette and his soldiers gathered at Deep Run to discuss plans during the Revolutionary War. Wounded soldiers were cared for in the church building, which was being used as a hospital. We can find no documentation about this, but accept it as true, as having been passed down from generation to generation.

At the first vestry meeting in March 1785, at the courthouse in Richmond, Edmund Randolph and Bowler Cocke were appointed church wardens and instructed to repair the churches. It is evident that Deep Run was one of the churches appointed to Randolph and Cocke (Moore, *History of Henrico Parish,* p. 25). There was no minister. The Reverend John Buchanan was elected by the vestry. He had come to Richmond from Amherst County. "His duty was to preach every other Sunday at Richmond Church and on the intervening Sunday at Curles and Deep Run alternately."

Reverend Buchanan served the Henrico Parish from 1785 to 1822. He was born in Scotland in 1743 and ordained in 1775. For twenty-nine years he was the treasurer of the Diocese and throughout his ministry in Richmond was a leading member of the Convention.

In 1792, the condition of the Henrico Parish was crumbling. Only one vestry meeting was documented between April 1794 and May 1812. During this time the Episcopal Church in Virginia declined, and for several years, churches ceased to hold conventions. Not content with disestablishing the church in 1784, the Virginia legislature, in 1802, confiscated all the property the Episcopal churches had secured before the Revolutionary War.

The confiscated land included glebes and other property. The Episcopal Church lay dormant in a state of collapse for many years. In 1830, the Episcopal Church was small, counting but twelve bishops in twenty dioceses, six hundred clergy, and thirty thousand communicants, mostly confined to the Atlantic Seaboard.

Baptist beginnings in America date back to the establishment of a Baptist church at Providence, Rhode Island, in 1639 by Roger Williams. Williams was a Separatist minister who had founded a new colony dedicated to religious liberty after he had been driven out of the Massachusetts Bay Colony. In the years that followed; severe persecution in New England discouraged any large growth of Baptists, although a sprinkling of churches could be found there prior to the start of the Great Awakening in the late 1720s. The liberal atmosphere of the Pennsylvania Colony allowed the organization of the first association of Baptist churches in America in 1707, when five small congregations organized the Philadelphia Baptist Association. During the Great Awakening, the number of Baptists increased as evangelists made a strong appeal for personal religion. The Baptists gained strength in Virginia, and in 1788, the General Association had been formed and divided into four districts. The Lower District was named Dover.

In 1789, the Baptists sent a petition to the House of Delegates asking that all church land and property purchased before the Revolutionary War be put to public use and that all church buildings be free for people and preachers of every denomination. Also in 1789, there were twenty-one churches reported to the newly formed Dover Association. This organization had quickly grown to twenty-seven by 1791.

The present Deep Run Baptist Church was formerly called Hungry Church, which was named after the church was started by Chickahominy Baptist Church in 1791. Unfortunately, there are no church minutes for the first 139 years of this church. For information, historians refer to the minutes of the Dover Association. An old sign on the property reads, "Built—1742, Remodeled—1888." It's possible that this sign was suspended under a porch, which was removed in 1957, and later relocated when the church was rebuilt (recorded in the Dover minutes of 1888).

Part of the original church building near the entrance was lost to termites. At present, a hardwood floor covers the original floorboards. In 1994, the original weatherboard walls of the colonial church were sided with vinyl.

The first pastor to serve Deep Run Baptist Church was Peter Cottrell, and the congregation at that time consisted of forty-one members. He was unfortunately expelled for "falling into disorder." Two elders served the church until 1798. The name "Hungry," given to the church in 1791, disappeared from the Dover Association records in 1817. During this period of decline in the Episcopal Church, permission was granted to other denominations, mainly the Baptists and Methodists, to use their abandoned church buildings. Soon after, the Deep Run Church was possessed by a Baptist congregation, which changed the name from Hungry to Deep Run. From the minutes of the Dover Association, dated 9 to 11 October 1819, the following was recorded: "The name of the church formerly called Hungry is now known by the name Deep Run."

The Sunday school record found at the Virginia Historical Society explains that Sunday school was adjourned in 1861 because there were so few scholars. This declaration was signed by William DuVal, secretary of the Sunday school. No doubt this was due to the War Between the States. In 1866, we find that the Sunday school was reorganized. In 1893, Deep Run Church was also said to host a mission school.

No signs remain of abuse during the Civil War, as suffered by so many of our colonial buildings. After the war, in 1868, we find that fifty-three names were removed from the membership of Deep Run Church with no record of reason. These members may have been former slaves who left to unite with an African-American church. The following statement is taken from the historical records of the Quioccasin Baptist Church: "History shows that the Deep Run Baptist Church was listing its membership as consisting of 257 Negroes and 244 White." In 1865, Rev. Royal Smith, and a group of African members, pulled out from the Deep Run Baptist Church. This band of people organized and was recognized as the Quioccasin Baptist Church.

In 1919, 3.88 acres of land on the north side of Three Chopt Road was deeded to Deep Run Church by Mr. John T. Jones for cemetery purposes. On 20 January 1920, James Henley became the first person to be buried there. In the early days of Deep Run Church, the deceased members were buried around the church. The location of these graves are a mystery, but some believe that the present educational

building is situated over these graves.

In 1920, the first addition was added to the back of the sanctuary. Six classrooms were constructed at that time. Also in 1920, an extension was attached to the sanctuary, as well as a large vestibule. Deep Run Baptist Church owns an antique—though not colonial—communion set. It was a gift from Mrs. Fannie Higgenbotham, who was active in the church in 1905. The set has since been restored and properly engraved. It consists of two chalices, two plates, and one flagon. These items are currently on display in a cabinet built by Mr. W. L. Jones Sr.

In closing this brief history of Deep Run Church, I would like to offer two rather interesting and amusing anecdotes to the church's history.

In the early 1930s, kerosene lamps were replaced by a Delco Plant to generate electricity. The church was still, however, being heated by a stove in the center of the church. One Sunday during the service, the church caught on fire when the stove overheated. The congregation evacuated the building until the fire was extinguished. With no reservation, the pastor called the people back in, took up his sermon where he left off, and completed the service!

By 1937, the floor of the church was very old. Cracks between the boards and holes that had been cut to accommodate tobacco chewers made the floor very cold. When it

Deep Run Church today. The beams in the sanctuary are fastened together with wooden pegs, which most likely indicates their colonial authenticity.

was proposed that a new floor be installed over the old, a great argument arose. Some of the older members thought it not right to cover the boards that had been trodden by their forefathers. Finally the church voted to put down a new floor. The completed job cost $175.

The following have served Deep Run Baptist Church since its beginning:

Peter Cottrell	1792
Elders Courtney and Webber	1793-98
Elder Bernard Reynolds	1798-1824
Elder Eli Ball	1825-34
Reuben Ford	1841
John Hay	1846
Joseph Rocke	1847
W. G. Thomasson	1849
G. G. Elall	1850-57
H. D. Nuckols	1858
H. Satterwhite	1867-77
E. Harrison	1878
Arthur E. Vox	1880
J. W. Reynolds	1883
J. B. Cook	1885
H. W. Jones	1887
R. W. Cridin	1888
E. Harrison	1891
J. R. Wilkinson	1894
E. T. Poulson	1901
L. L. Gwaltney	1903
J. O. Kirk	1904
L. W. Smith	1905
Samuel Livingston Naff	1905-09
J. A. Clarke	1909
A. L. Shumate	1911
W. Herbert Brannock	1913
W. J. Yeaman	1912
Robert Lord Bausum	1916
S. Roy Orrell	1917
Mr. Sheppard	1918
W. W. Townsend	1921
Noah B. Farris	1924-26
C. J. Ashley	1926
Gordon L. Price	1927
R. Cole Lee	1930
W. Franklin Cale	1932
Arthur W. Rich Jr.	1934
Philip W. Tomlinson	1937
Carl A. Collins	1938
E. Maynard Adams	1940
Woodrow W. Herrin	1942
Harold White	1943
Ira S. Harrell	1945
J. Vernon Brooks	1947
Malcolm M. Hutton	1952
Dr. Ramond B. Brown	1953
Edward G. Lambert	1955
Dr. O. W. Rhodenhizer	1960
Philip Lesley Cumbia	1961

Herbert Raymond Carlton	1980
Matthew Davidson	1981
Edgar Burkholder	1984

In 1984, as the church began another phase of its life, the following prayer was offered:

The torch we carry today—dedication to the worship of God and the proclamation of His gospel—has endured in this church for over two hundred years. It is our obligation and privilege to pass it on to future generations.

The torch we hold was given to us
By other's hands we know;
We hold it high that all may see
Its brightly gleaming glow.
Let us then be true and faithful
As we walk this earthly sod,
That our Lord Christ be exalted
And men may come to worship God.

CATTAIL CHURCH

ST. DAVID'S PARISH CHURCH

KING WILLIAM COUNTY

Erected: 1751

Denomination: Baptist (called Mt. Sinai Baptist)

Location: At the end of Route 606, 1/4 mile south of Route 611. The junction of Route 606 and 611 is 1/2 mile west of Rout 360. The church is approximately 2 1/2 miles south of Aylett and 1 1/2 miles from Central Garage.

Cattail Church as it appeared in the early 1900s. The steeples and buttresses were later additions.

An ACT OF THE GENERAL ASSEMBLY IN 1744 STATED that "by reason of the large extent of the parish of St. Margaret in the counties of King William and Caroline," a petition had been submitted by "the inhabitants of the lower part of the said parish, and of the upper part of St. John's parish in the county of King William that they may be divided from their respective parishes and be united and erected into one distinct and middle parish." The act provided that St. David's Parish embrace that part of King William County lying northwest of the line, from Vicary's plantation to the mouth of Manquin's Creek. The parish was represented in the first convention of the Church of Virginia in 1785.

St. David's Parish was probably named after the patron saint of Wales. There is some doubt as to whether the church was built as the first or the second parish church of St. David's Parish when the parish was formed out of lower St. Margaret's Parish and upper St. John's Parish in 1744. The church is known to most as Cattail Church, from its proximity to the swamp of that name. The construction, begun within the specified time limit by 1748, would have been completed in two or three years. This projection is consistent with the construction date of 1751, found cut in a brick over the west entrance during its remodeling in 1921. There is also a known documentary reference to the church in a patent of 1752.

The church building is rectangular with a wing, and the original dimensions were probably sixty feet by thirty feet. Cattail Church most likely occupies the site of a former chapel of St. John's Parish and would have been the second parish church of St. David's. The church over the years has been extremely altered, having two steeples added, buttresses added to the south and north walls, and the entire building stuccoed. Today, no visible evidence remains inside or out that defines this building as one of Virginia's colonial churches.

Cattail Church was abandoned by the Episcopalians after the Disestablishment of the Church of England, and it became a free church, to be used by any denomination. The old church building was quite overlooked, receiving no upkeep or repairs from those who used it, and finally the roof fell in. The property was then turned over to a black congregation called the Mt. Sinai Baptist Church. The present owners have shortened the church by ten feet at the east end and added buttresses to reinforce the weakened brick walls. Although in the process of neglect and renovation the building has lost its original resemblance, Cattail Church still remains a surviving colonial church in Virginia.

Cattail Church is presently known as Mt. Sinai Baptist Church.

THE RUINS OF LOWER SOUTHWARK CHURCH
SURRY COUNTY

Erected: 1754

Denomination: Anglican

Location: Route 10 about 1/2 mile from the village of Bacon's Castle and 7 miles southeast of Surry Courthouse

The ruins of Lower Southwark Church are quite picturesque.

S URRY COUNTY LIES ON THE SOUTH SIDE OF THE JAMES River, across from Jamestown, where the first English settlement was made in the New World in 1607. It was named for Surrey, the county on the south side of the Thames River, across from London. According to an account by the late Dr. Lyon G. Tyler of Williamsburg, the lands that became Surry County are shown by land grants to have been located in James City County previous to 6 December 1651. Its first justices were appointed in April 1652, as shown by county records. The county was represented by three burgesses in the General Assembly, which met in November 1652.

The county was laid off from James City County, one of the eight original shires then confined to the north side of the river. Surry originally included the present Sussex County, extending southward toward the North Carolina line. Two Anglican parishes were formed in the part of Surry located from north of the Blackwater River to the James River. One of them was Lawne's Creek Parish, founded in 1639 and named after Sir Christopher Lawne, who settled at the mouth of the James River in 1619. The other was Southwark Parish, created by an act of the General Assembly in November 1647.

The founding date of the first Southwark Church is unknown, although it is reasonable to suppose that it may have been built around 1650. Most likely, it is the church mentioned in a deed dated 2 April 1655 from Thomas Woodhouse to Robert Huffard for land known to have been located in the upper part of Southwark Parish. And it was definitely in existence by the time the following court order, dated 23 November 1686, was written: "It is the opinion of the Cort that the old Roade, that went from Southwarke pish [sic] church by the old Church to the Stony Runn is the most conv [convenient] and nearest way and the survey of the Highways therefore ordered to remove the roade and make it that way."

The second Southwark Church stood in the fork of the present highway and the old road to Stony Run, which is now overrun with trees. All of the ruins of this church have been removed, but the outline of its foundation reveals that the church building measured sixty feet by thirty feet and stood inside the churchyard, which measured 108 feet wide by 135 feet long. A number of references in the county records all identified with this second building suggest it was constructed prior to 1673. References also state that a new roof was put on the second church in 1682 and 1683. These latter references involved litigations between the vestry and a contractor over the material to be used. An entry dated 4

July 1682 states that the church wardens of Southwark Parish were granted judgment against John Smith for lumber and material.

Following the Revolutionary War, in 1784, the old Lower Southwark Church suffered a period of abandonment, during which its few remaining members were not permitted to use it, due to the intense popular feeling against England and the English Church. After occasional use of the church by other denominations, Episcopal services were resumed in it, about 1847, on a mission basis and, in 1850, a resident minister, Rev. John C. McCabe, was secured by the new congregation. The Episcopalians withdrew in 1854 because their occupancy was being disputed by other denominations. The Episcopalians erected a modern frame building on a neighboring site and it was consecrated by Bishop John Johns on 29 April 1857 as St. Andrew's Church. Its ruined walls were still standing as late as the Civil War, but have disappeared since that time.

Shortly before Southwark Parish became coterminous with Surry County, through the formation of Sussex County in 1754, two additional brick churches were built by the parish vestry. The first of these named Cypress Church was ordered on 5 April 1743. Cypress Church was located about one and a quarter miles northeast of Dendron, on the north side of the old road to the present Surry Courthouse. As an Episcopal church, the last service was held in 1873 by Bishop William Meade, third bishop of Virginia, who found it abandoned and in need of serious repair. He preached to a congregation of one white parishioner and the former African-American sexton. A photograph of Cypress Church, taken in 1919 by Maj. W. E. MacClenny of Suffolk, was reproduced as an illustration in his book *The Life of James O'Kelly* and shows that the old church was of conventional design.

The second and last church to be built for Southwark Parish is the present-day Lower Southwark Church, which today survives as only a picturesque ruin. It was the only parish church built in Surry County.

An advertisement in the *Virginia Gazette* for 18 April 1751 shows that the new brick Lower Southwark Church, ordered in 1751, occupied the same site as the first Lower Church of Southwark Parish, which had been the mother church of Lawne's Creek Parish prior to the latter's dissolution in 1739. According to Bishop Meade, Lower Southwark Church was built in 1754, which represents a date of completion entirely consistent with this advertisement.

Lower Southwark was a very beautiful rectangular church, with four tall windows on the south side and five on

THE RUINS OF LOWER SOUTHWARK CHURCH

the north. The entrances were located on the south and west sides of the church, which measured seventy-four feet by thirty-four feet along the outside, with walls twenty-one inches thick.

According to George Carrington Mason in his book *Colonial Churches of Tidewater Virginia,* the colonial Lower Southwark Church was burned down soon after the Civil War, in 1868, by former slaves who had been using the church yard as a burying ground and who had set fire to the old church in an attempt to discourage white parishioners from reclaiming their ancient cemetery. While the restoration of our colonial churches is generally desired, it is almost hoped that this one will be left undisturbed, for it makes a beautiful ruin with a variety of trees growing around it, as well as periwinkle, shrubs, and vines.

Bacon's Castle, a residence built about 1650 and fortified in Bacon's Rebellion of 1676, is located near the ruin.

ABINGDON CHURCH
GLOUCESTER COUNTY

Erected: 1755

Denomination: Anglican

Location: East side of Route 17, about 1 mile south of White Marsh and 7 1/2 miles north of Yorktown

Religious Services: Sundays, Holy Eucharist at 8:00 A.M. (Rite I) and 10:30 A.M. (Rite II)

Abingdon Church in 1930. It is thought that the grandmother of George Washington, Mildred Warner, worshipped at the first Abingdon Church.

Gloucester County was laid off from Charles River County (later York County) in 1651. Scholars debate the actual establishment of Abingdon Parish, and recorded dates range from 1650 to 1655. It seems likely that Abingdon Parish was established about 1652, because court records from that year report two parishes, one of which borders Gloucester on the north. The parish lies in the southeastern area of Gloucester County, fronting the York River and Mobjack Bay. It is bounded on the north and west by Ware and Petsworth Parishes. The parish name is believed to be derived from the Robins family, who were early colonists and who came from Abingdon, England.

The foundations of the first Abingdon church building (ca. 1660) are found within its walls, under the south transept of the existing church. The first building, which the Reverend Charles Mann reported "had been enlarged," was supposedly built in the early days of the parish upon ground donated by Col. Augustine Warner, the maternal great-grandfather of George Washington. Here, Mildred Warner, daughter of Colonel Warner, must have worshiped and received her religious training. She married Lawrence Washington of Westmoreland County, Virginia, and was the grandmother of George Washington. This older church was used nearly one hundred years, when it became unsafe and plans were then made to build the present Abingdon Church.

Early records of the parish and county were lost in a series of tragic fires. Bishop William Meade, in his multi-volume work *Old Churches, Ministers, and Families of Virginia,* made the following statement: "In attempting to write articles on Ware and Abingdon Parishes and their churches, I am embarrassed by finding the county and church records almost wholly destroyed up to the year 1830." Many valuable documents were burned at Jamestown in 1676, when Nathaniel Bacon kindled the first fires of rebellion in the colony. At Williamsburg, in 1776, many precious documents were consumed by fire. In 1820, the Clerk's office at Botetourt, which is now called Gloucester, the county's old seat, was burned with its contents. Again, on 2 April 1865, a fire in Richmond destroyed all of Gloucester County records.

In 1608, Capt. John Smith made his first visit to the county now called Gloucester. It is here Pocahontas saved the life of John Smith. Weworocomico, the chief home of Powhatan, is distinctly located on Captain Smith's map, and also on the map of Tyndall; these maps seem to fix the location of this legend to Purton Bay, York River.

The construction of the present church building was begun in 1751 and completed in 1755. There is an inscribed brick in the lower southwest corner of the west wall of the nave that confirms this date ("WB 1755"). The church is in the form of a Latin cross, fronting the west, with the main entrance at that end. The church measures eighty-one feet by seventy-one feet, with walls over two feet thick. According to James Scott Rawlings, the large reredos was installed in 1841. It may have derived from 1755, as it is undoubtedly colonial in design. There is certain difficulty in assuming its originality, however, for the reredos itself extends fifteen feet and the space between the two east windows is only fourteen feet. Rawlings concludes that the reredos may have been moved to Abingdon from another nearby church.

This distinctive pentagonal reredos is accurately described by Mrs. Fielding Lewis Taylor:

It represents the façade of a Greek temple in the bas-relief, about twenty feet in height and extending entirely across the back of the chancel. It is handsomely carved and painted snowy white. Straight across the lintel of the façade runs the first line of the Te Deum, "We praise Thee, O God." The roof of the reredos dividing at the apex, supports a pineapple, both in high relief. Between the four fluted pilasters of the reredos are set four long black tablets, framed and lettered in gold. These contain the Creed, the Lord's Prayer, and the Ten Commandments. Alas! the breath of time has dimmed the beautiful words. The light from the great arched windows [in the head of the cruciform building, on either side of the chancel] shines full upon these four foundation pillars of the Faith once delivered to the saints. The effect of the whole is simple, but beautiful, full of deep spiritual glass.

The original eight-feet wide aisles are gone, but some of the colonial flagstones remain in the vestibules of the church. The original pews are large, with high sides, typical of the colonial period. The pews in the two galleries of the transepts are also authentic. The chancel occupies the east end of the cross. Also, the galleries in the arms of the cross, are still furnished with colonial pews.

During the Civil War, the large box pews were used as horse stalls by Federal troops. In 1867, in the course of repairs, they were replaced with modern pews. In 1897, the building was completely restored. Interestingly, while the church was closed to religious services, the phrase "We praise Thee, O God," remained on the reredos from the

Abingdon Church in the present. The colonial section of its cemetary is quite expansive and well preserved.

Christmas dressing of 1861. When the building was repaired, these words were painted on the reredos in gold.

In 1890, aware of the weak roof, the vestry ordered a thorough investigation of the building. Mr. Joseph Dye Lahendro of Richmond was hired as architect. It soon became known, after initial investigations, that the nineteenth-century wooden floor was also near collapse due to termite damage. Preservation was essential. Like a good mystery, architectural research was aided by clues left during the past centuries. Paint and plaster ghosts—the reuse of eighteenth-century panels and other fabrics, brick foundations, et cetera—left a remarkable image of most important finishing details.

Abingdon owns several silver communion pieces dating to the early part of the eighteenth century. The set of communion silver still in use was made in London in 1702 and was presented to the church, in 1703, by Maj. Lewis Burwell of Carter's Grove. There is also a large paten of 1710 and 1711, fashioned by Alice Sheene and inscribed "ABINGDON PARISH PLATE."

In the colonial section of the cemetery, graves are quite numerous. There are several well-preserved tombs with legible inscriptions and coats-of-arms. Several Burwell tombs were moved in 1911 from "Carter's Creek" and bear dates from 1658 to 1785.

Abingdon Church, on the National Register of Historic Landmarks and the Virginia Landmark Commission, is one of America's finest examples of eighteenth-century architecture.

CHUCKATUCK CHURCH

ST. JOHN'S CHURCH
NANSEMOND COUNTY

Erected: 1756

Denomination: Anglican

Location: On Route 630, approximately 5 miles west of Driver and 1 1/4 miles east of Chuckatuck

Religious Services: Sundays, 8:00 A.M. and 10:30 A.M.

"Chuckatuck" meant "Crooked Creek" to the Nansemond County Indians. Here is the church photographed in 1930.

CHUCKATUCK PARISH ORIGINALLY WAS LAID OUT IN 1642 as the West Parish. It was located on the west side of the Nansemond River, a tidal arm of the James River, dividing the northern part of the county. At the time of its creation, there were the South, East, and West Parishes. The East Parish became known as the Lower Parish.* In 1725, the Lower and Chuckatuck Parishes were united to form Suffolk Parish. In 1744, the Upper Parish was divided, and a section was thereof added to Suffolk Parish. It is believed that the word "Chuckatuck" meant "Crooked Creek" to the Indians of Nansemond County.

Soon after their formation in 1643, church buildings were erected for all three parishes. The earliest recorded reference to these churches is found in a land grant of 28 October 1672 to George and Harvey Billingsley for five hundred acres in Chuckatuck, Nansemond County. The church mentioned in this record seems to have been built for the West, later Chuckatuck, Parish. During May 1940, evidence of this church building was discovered when a grave digger uncovered the massive foundation of a brick tower.

The vestry book, at the beginning of 1749, reveals the existence of a Chuckatuck Church, which is proved by later entries. On 15 November 1751, the vestry met at this church and ordered its replacement with the following resolution: "The vestry having this day come to a Resolution to build a brick church in Chuckatuck near the place where the old one stands." The contract was awarded to Moses Allmand on 20 May 1752. The church building measures 60 1/2 feet by 30 1/2 feet on the outside and is constructed of brick-laid Flemish bond; the walls are nearly two feet thick. The present Chuckatuck Church (now known as St. John's Episcopal Church) can be identified as the later structure of 1756, while the tower foundation clearly belongs to the first church building.

Located high on the south wall near the east end of the present Chuckatuck Church, are the initials "A. H." and "E. H.," which appear with the date of construction. It seems the initials stand for Anthony and Esther Holladay, who had given the land for the building site from their "Holladay's Point Plantation." The aisle of the church is still paved with original flagstones, eighteen inches, of pinkish-brown sandstone.

The old vestry book of the parish begins in the year 1749, during the ministry of Rev. John McKenzie. At his death in 1754, the Reverend John Agnew succeeded. In 1758, the vestry of the Suffolk Parish was dissolved by Act of Assembly, on petitions of the inhabitants of the Lower

Parish. The vestry held in trust for the Lower Parish valuable lands and a cash donation from Richard Bennett, Thomas Tilly, and Richard Bennett Jr. According to the bequests, the poor of Lower Parish were to benefit. The vestry of the United Parishes allowed the Chuckatuck members of their body to colonize the poor of Chuckatuck in Lower Parish, and thus receive the benefit of the Bennett and Tilly bequests.

In 1755, the Assembly passed a law that every person receiving aid from the parish should, "upon the shoulder of the right sleeve, in an open and visible manner, wear a badge with the name of the parish cut either in blue, red or green cloth, and if any poor person neglect or refuse to wear such badge, his or her allowance shall be withdrawn or the offender whipped not exceeding five lashes for each offense." The law was defeated in most parishes but was rigidly enforced in Suffolk Parish.

A colonial vestry book was preserved from Suffolk Parish, which includes the years 1749 to 1784, but then reopens after a lapse of forty years (1784-1825). In 1826, a new vestry was elected that restored Chuckatuck Church to service.** In 1827, the Reverend Mark L. Chevers was chosen as minister. Sometime after 1840, Suffolk Parish was served by the minister of Upper Parish, who resided in Suffolk.

It was not until 1845 that Chuckatuck Church was referred to for the first time as St. John's Church.

According to tradition, Federal forces occupied the church during the Civil War. There are no colonial gravestones in the yard at Chuckatuck Church. The church today is served by the rector of St. Paul's Church in Suffolk.

* See article on Glebe Church, also called Bennett's Creek Church.

** The Glebe Church remained desolate and deserted for another thirty years before enough money was raised to repair it.

Above: St. John's Church and its cemetary as it appears today. In 1940, a grave digger discovered the foundation of a brick tower, which probably belonged to the first Chuckatuck church building.

Opposite: A desolate Chuckatuck Church in 1900. It was in 1845 that the church was first referred to as St. John's.

TIMBER RIDGE HOUSE
ROCKBRIDGE COUNTY

Erected: 1756

Denomination: Presbyterian

Location: Just east of the Route 11 and Interstate 81 (Lexington) exit. 5 miles south of Fairfield and 6 miles north of Lexington on Route 11

Religious Services: Sundays, 11:00 A.M.

Timber Ridge Church, as photographed in 1930, was constructed of native limestone.

TIMBER RIDGE HOUSE RECEIVED ITS NAME FROM ITS surroundings, the mountainous wilderness now known as Rockbridge County. It was situated on the side of a hill, covered with a heavy growth of fine timber, hence its name. The region was settled mainly by Scotch-Irish Presbyterians, who came into the Shenandoah Valley from the Cumberland Valley of Pennsylvania. The Presbyterian Church takes it name from the Greek word for elder, presbuteros, which is found in the New Testament. The Presbyterian form of government first took root in France with the Huguenots. The first Presbyterian National Synod of France met in France in 1559 and adopted a Confession of Faith, which was Calvinistic in theology, and a Book of Discipline, which was Presbyterian in polity. John Knox (1515-72) became the great leader of the Reformation in Scotland, which became the headquarters of Presbyterianism. The Presbyterian Church took root in ten northern counties of Ireland, known as Ulster, during the reign of James I of England.

As early as 1640, a Presbyterian church was formed at Southold, Long Island, by a colony of New Englanders. John Blair, a native of Northern Ireland who was serving as a Presbyterian minister in the Cumberland Valley, made two visits to the Timber Ridge region. He organized four Presbyterian congregations: Forks of James, Timber Ridge, New Providence, and North Mountain, but only the present Timber Ridge House remains.

In 1746, we find the sturdy pioneers building the first log meeting house. It occupied a site about two miles northeast of the present stone Timber Ridge House. It was built of logs and covered with clapboards from the nearby forest. The floor was earth. The seats were split logs, hewn smooth on the top side. The pulpit was built high against the wall. The windows were narrow horizontal openings, a protection against the Indian's arrow.

The log meeting houses at New Providence, Timber Ridge, and Falling Springs were accepted as houses of worship by the court of Augusta, 20 May 1748. The records state, "On motion of Matthew Lyle, yts ordered to be certified that they have built a Presbyterian meeting house at a place known as Timber Ridge." And as the order book informs us that the one at Timber Ridge was in place in February of the same year, it could hardly have been built later than the fall of 1747. There have been statements that the first church was built in 1742, but this is very doubtful. As stated earlier, the congregation of Timber Ridge was organized—or as the Presbyterian record expresses it, "put

into church order"—by the Reverend John Blair of the Presbytery of Donegal, Pennsylvania, while on a visit to the Valley of Virginia early in the year 1746. The logs of the pioneer church were later used to build a house for M. H. Crist and stood until 1906.

A serious rift developed within the Presbyterian Church between the years 1745 and 1758. It was caused by the outdoor, unconventional, revivalistic preaching of George Whitefield (1714-70). He was a British clergyman who made seven trips to America. The conservative faction was known as the "old side" and the progressive as the "new side," or "new lights." The Presbyterian Church was greatly affected by this First Great Awakening, which started about 1735. This was the American counterpart of the contemporary Wesley-Whitefield revival in England. The outstanding Presbyterian leader in this Awakening was Gilbert Tennent, the son of William Tennent, founder and sole faculty member of the Log College. William Tennent opened his school for the training of Presbyterian ministry in a log cabin on the banks of the Heshaminy, in Bucks County, Virginia, about 1735.

Shortly after the organization, Timber Ridge aligned itself with the "New Lights." Thus their ministers came from the Presbyteries of New Castle, New Brunswick, and New York. The congregations of Timber Ridge and the Forks of the James united in extending a call to the Reverend William Dean of New Castle Presbytery. He accepted the call in 1748, but died before he could begin his ministry. In 1753, the Timber Ridge and New Providence congregations united in extending a call to the Reverend John Brown, a graduate of Nassau Hall, Princeton, and a licentiate of New Castle Presbytery. He accepted the call, thus becoming the first regular pastor of Timber Ridge. He continued to minister jointly to Timber Ridge and New Providence until 1767, when he resigned the Timber Ridge pastorate.

A movement was started shortly after the arrival of Rev. John Brown to abandon the old log meeting house and build a more substantial house of worship. James McClung and John Lyle were chosen by the congregation to act as the building committee. The congregation gave freely of their money, time, and labor. The new stone church was completed and dedicated on 3 October 1756. Tradition states that the women helped to build the church. They assisted the men with filling sand bags. They even rode pack horses with bags of sand on their backs. Some of the men, carrying rifles, accompanied them through the forests to protect them from sudden Indian attacks. There is a tablet in the church placed by their descendants in 1904, paying tribute to these

The present Timber Ridge Church and its cemetary, in which many of the first Valley settlers are buried.

admirable women. It reads, "To the memory of the noble women, who with their own hands, helped to build this church, 1756. Erected by their descendants 1904. The dedication of this tablet is so noted in the *Rockbridge County News* dated October 5, 1904."

The church was constructed of native limestone, quarried from the hill, several hundred feet southeast of the church. The original portion of the church is approximately forty-three feet ten inches long and thirty-five feet wide. In 1871, the door next to the cemetery was closed. A front entrance was built to the north end, called a vestibule, which faced the highway.

We find in the second church that the earth served as a floor, as was the case in the original church. Later the floor was created of split logs, hewn smooth and placed upwards. This type of flooring was known as a "puncheon floor." And again, this floor was replaced by sawn boards, hand planed, tongued, and grooved. Logs, with the top side flattened, were used for seating until the Revolutionary War period. These were later replaced by high-backed pews. Difficulties developed when these pews were assigned to the congregation. In 1786, the church settled its disputes by assigning to each fam-

ily the pew where its family log had previously been located.

On 9 July 1755, General Braddock's army was defeated, and this left the Valley vulnerable to Indian attacks. A volunteer company was organized among the Timber Ridge congregation, and Capt. Archibald Alexander was placed in command. The deed to the church was secured by the members of Timber Ridge on 21 November 1759, when Robert Huston deeded, to the trustees of the church, a tract of land thirteen poles square for the sum of five shillings sterling. On 17 July 1763, Cornstalk and his band of Shawnee Indians invaded the little settlement of Kerr's Creek and massacred a number of men, women, and children. Some pioneers escaped this massacre because they were attending a religious meeting at the church. The church was used as a fort during Indian raids because of its massive stone walls.

At Timber Ridge, a school was started by Robert Alexander in 1749 that was to become a university. In 1774, when the Reverend John Brown was teaching the school, it was taken over by the Presbytery. In 1776, it was moved to Mount Pleasant, where it occupied a new building, Liberty Hall, and after only a year there, it was returned to Timber Ridge. In 1780, Liberty Hall Academy was moved from

Timber Ridge to Lexington, where it grew to become Washington and Lee University.

Lexington Presbytery was organized at Timber Ridge in 1786. Rev. John Brown was elected moderator and preached the opening sermon from 2 Cor. 2:16. Of the twelve charter members, the first five ministers and two elders on the following list were present: Rev. John Brown, New Providence; Rev. William Wilson, Good Hope; Rev. William Graham; Rev. Samuel Garrick; Elder John Houston; Elder Michael Dicks; Rev. John Montgomery, Winchester; Rev. Benjamin Erwin, Mossy Creek; Rev. Samuel Shannon; Rev. Moses Hoge; Rev. James McConnel; Rev. Edward Crawford; and Rev. Archibald Scott, Bethel.

Among the Timber Ridge congregation's distinguished members is the father of Sam Houston. President Houston, of Texas, was born nearby. Many distinguished clergymen, professors, and political figures also derive from the Timber Ridge House.

The cornerstone to a wing of the church was laid with a ceremony on 1 July 1900. The vault within the cornerstone is six inches by four inches by ten inches. Within this vault were placed the following:

1. Sermons by Rev. George D. Armstrong, Rev. D. C. Irwin, Rev. Alfred Jones, and Rev. J. H. Davis
2. The last sermon preached at the church before renewal
3. The centennial address by Dr. Henry Ruffner
4. A list of original subscribers to the church in 1756
5. A list of members of Ten Commandments Church in 1900
6. A list of Sunday school officers for the year 1900
7. A list of subscribers to the present improvement
8. Sessional record as far back as kept
9. A church directory for 1900
10. Copies of *Christian Observer, Central Presbyterian, Lexington Gazette,* and *Rockbridge County News*

On 2 December 1900, the historic Timber Ridge House was dedicated with an all-day service. The service conducted was reminiscent of the old Scotch-Irish days in the Valley when each family started early for church and carried their baskets, dinner to be eaten later during the intermission.

In 1819, Timber Ridge House began to conduct services at Fairfield, as a mission church. In 1840, the congregation at Timber Ridge-Fairfield became two separate congregations. From 1840 to 1851, Rev. G. D. Armstrong, D.D., of Washington College, served as minister. In 1851, the church was united with Bethesda. In 1899, Timber Ridge became independent and self-supporting and, since that time, has not united with any other congregation. Near the site of the old Timber Ridge Log Meeting House, there is an old cemetery on a farm that was owned by Mr. H. T. Muse for many years. There was a notice printed in the *Lexington Gazette* dated 4 September 1879. It reads:

The ladies of Old Timber Ridge church contemplate having a dinner at Mackey's School House, near the burying ground of the old church on the 10th inst. The proceeds will be devoted to placing a fence around the old burying ground. This was the former site of the present Timber Ridge Church, and is one of the oldest burying grounds in the county.

Many of the first settlers of the Valley rest in peace at this old burying ground. The old log meeting house ceased as a place of worship in 1756, but many of the members continued to bury their dead there until 1920. The congregation's second cemetery is just east of the church's east wall. It has been remarkable that the Timber Ridge House, as a building or as a congregation, has survived for nearly two hundred and forty years. During its history, many factions were at work among the Presbyterians in the Valley as well as at Timber Ridge. From 1814 to 1856, the Seceders, who later became adherents of the Associate Reformed Presbyterian Church, worshipped at the Timber Ridge House every other Sunday. After 1856, they built their own meeting house near Timber Ridge. Rivalry between the communities of Ten Commandments and Fairfield, as well as the division between the Calvinists at Timber Ridge and elsewhere, was caused in part by some Presbyterians singing songs other than approved metrical translations of David's Psalms. The Associate Reformed Presbyterians finally consented to sing other hymns in worship, in addition to the metrical Psalms.

Only three walls remain of Timber Ridge's colonial meeting house. All of these walls have been greatly repaired over the years. Timber Ridge House has stood for 240 years and is a memorial to the countless men and women who endured so many hardships during the difficult frontier days in Virginia.

Ministers of Timber Ridge Presbyterian Church:

Rev. John Blair	1746
Rev. William Dean	1748-48
Rev. John Brown, D.D.	1753-67
Rev. William Graham	1776-85
Rev. Daniel Blain	1802-14
Rev. Henry Ruffner, D.D.	1819-31
Rev. Allen D. Metcalf	1831-34
Rev. James Paine	1835-38
Rev. George D. Armstrong, D.D.	1838-51
Rev. W. W. Trimble	1851-66
Rev. R. J. Taylor	1866-73
Rev. D. C. Irwin	1873-81
Rev. Alfred Jones, D.D.	1881-99
Rev. Henry Alexander White, D.D.	1890-93
Rev. John H. Davis	1893-98
Rev. J. Layton Mauze	1899-1902
Rev. J. E. Booker	1902-03
Rev. J. A. Trostle	1904-10
Rev. R. L. Kinnard	1910-13
Rev. F. F. Jones	1913-19
Rev. Cochran Preston	1920-21
Rev. J. M. Williams	1922-27
Rev. T. Henry Patterson	1928

AQUIA CHURCH
STAFFORD COUNTY

Erected: 1751; destroyed by fire in 1754, and rebuilt in 1757

Denomination: Protestant Episcopal

Location: On the east side of U.S. Route 1, south of Alexandria, Mount Vernon, and the Pohick Episcopal Church, and 3 miles north of the Stafford County Courthouse. Easy access from Interstate 95 at Route 610 (Garrisonville exit)

Religious Services: Sundays, Holy Communion at 7:30 A.M. (traditional), 9:00 A.M. (contemporary), and 11:15 A.M. (traditional)

Aquia Church, as photographed in 1905, was constructed in the shape of a Greek cross.

Aquia Church, in Overwharton Parish, Stafford County, Virginia, stands on the very early settled land of the New World, the county organization occurring fifty-seven years after the settlement of Jamestown. By the year 1700, there were two parishes in the county: Overwharton, with 318 parishioners, and St. Paul's, with 346. Collectively, these parishioners represented about one-fourth of the county's population.

The Reverend John Frazier was rector of the Overwharton Parish, while in 1710, the Reverend Alexander Scott became rector of St. Paul's parish. The latter clergyman remained in this post nearly twenty-eight years. During Mr. Scott's rectorship—which ended with his death on 2 April 1738, at age fifty-two—the old Potomac Church probably served as the parish church. Bishop William Meade, in *Old Churches, Ministers, and Families of Virginia,* speaks of it as "one of the largest in Virginia." This church was situated near Potomac Creek, six or seven miles from old Aquia.

From a report by Mr. Scott to the bishop of London, as noted by Bishop Meade, it appears that the parish included "six hundred and fifty families, eighty to one hundred communicants in attendance." The communion service, which is in the possession of Aquia Church, and in regular use, is a beautiful memorial to Mr. Scott. The service consists of a flagon, chalice, and a paten—all crafted in London by Thomas Farren. The service bears the inscription: "The gift of the Rev. Mr. Alexander Scott, A.M., late minister of this parish Anno 1739." It was evidently purchased with money bequeathed for the purpose, as the pieces are dated a year after Mr. Scott's death. The communion silver has passed through some of the country's most trying times, and was buried for safety during each of three great wars: the Revolutionary War, the War of 1812, and the War Between the States.

Mr. Scott was succeeded by the Reverend John Moncure, who was a native of Scotland, but a descendant of the Huguenots. He received his holy orders from the bishop of London. He had been curate to Mr. Scott before becoming his successor. His rectorship spanned twenty-six years, during which time Aquia Church was built. After the second church building was completed in 1757, the names of the minister and vestry were painted on the gallery: the minister was Reverend Moncure, and the members of the vestry were Peter Houseman, John Mercer, John Lee, Mott Donithan, Henry Tyler, William Mountjoy, Benjamin Strother, Thomas Fitzhugh, and John Peyton.

Records of the House of Burgesses in 1757 mention that

Aquia Church is presently thought to be haunted.

Mourning Richards in 1751 built a large brick church near Aquia Creek for an agreed price of 110,900 pounds of tobacco. The church is built in the form of a Greek cross, with two tiers of windows set in very thick walls. There are three double-door entrances—one in each arm of the cross, with the altar in its east end. Against the reredos of the white woodwork are four arched panels in black, inscribed in English script with the Ten Commandments, the Apostles' Creed, and the Lord's Prayer. At the southeastern re-entrant angle stands the original "three decker" pulpit, with its great sounding board.

When Bishop Meade visited the church in 1839, he found that the building had been neglected and that the grounds were overgrown. When he returned in 1856, however, just before the publication of his popular book *Old Churches, Ministers, and Families of Virginia,* a transformation had taken place; the building had been repaired and the congregation had grown very active.

During the Civil War, the church, like so many other colonial churches, was damaged by soldiers. The colonial Bible was discarded into the nearby woods and, while found later, it was never returned to the parish. The magnificent pulpit was almost dismantled and sold by Sidney Smith Lee, a brother of Gen. Robert E. Lee, and other members of the Aquia vestry in 1869 because the rector was infirm and could not ascend the steps. Fortunately for the pulpit, Colonel Lee died before the project could be consummated.

There are a number of colonial graves in the churchyard, ranging from 1733 to 1773.

It is worth noting that one of the vestrymen in 1757, Mott Donithan, was the great-great-great-great–grandfather of Pres. Harry S Truman. His name is inscribed on a panel in the front of the west gallery, along with the name of the rector, John Moncure, and the names of the other nine vestrymen and the two wardens, who comprised the vestry of twelve. Over the south door are the names of Mourning Richards, who undertook the building contract, and William Copein, the mason.

George Mason (1725-92), author of the Bill of Rights of Virginia, was a warm friend of Mr. Moncure, as well as a kinsman of the clergyman's wife. His beautiful home, Gunston Hall, overlooks the Potomac and is one of the many colonial plantation houses still standing in the Northern Neck.

Aquia Church remains one of Virginia's most outstanding churches. With its beauty and grace, it stands in majesty for all to see and appreciate.

BUCKINGHAM CHURCH
TILLOTSON PARISH CHURCH OR CHAPEL (BEFORE 1771)
GOLD HILL, BUCKINGHAM COUNTY

Erected: 1758

Denomination: Baptist

Location: On the east side of Route 15, at Gold Hill, approximately 8 1/2 miles south from the James River Bridge at Bremo Bluff and 6.8 miles north of Dillwyn

Religious Services: Sundays, 11:15 A.M.

Buckingham Baptist Church today. Its churchyard includes the grave markers of Civil War soldiers.

This photograph shows the original structure of Buckingham Baptist Church, which dates to 1771.

IT WAS LONG BELIEVED THAT BUCKINGHAM COUNTY WAS named for one of the English dukes of Buckingham. More probable is the theory that it was called after "Buckingham," a tract owned by Archibald Cary on Willis's Creek, which was located within the county at the time of its formation. This tract appears on the Fry-Jefferson Map of 1751, and it is mentioned in documents dating to 1761, the actual year of the county's creation.

In 1757, St. Anne's Parish in Albemarle County was divided into two separate parishes. That portion of the county north of the James River retained the name St. Anne's, while the region south of the river became known as Tillotson Parish, named for John Tillotson (1650-94), archbishop of Canterbury and a noted theologian. Albemarle County split in 1761, and that section comprising Tillotson Parish was designated as Buckingham County.

The original building, a thirty feet by sixty feet rectangular wood frame structure with a hipped roof (the southwest wing of the present building), was probably erected about 1758 or soon after the Tillotson Parish was formed.

Before 1771, all Baptists in Virginia were members of the Sandy Creek Baptist Association, which held their meetings in North Carolina. Buckingham Baptist was the first Baptist church in Buckingham County. The church later joined with eleven other Virginia Baptist churches to form the General Association of the Separate Baptists in Virginia.

Buckingham Church is believed to have been originally organized as a church of England, built by orders of King George III, who was the last British monarch to rule the American colonies. The king is said to have planned the church, built at the head of "Borden's Creek," for an Episcopal congregation. Legend has it that a leaden image of this king stood in front of the church during colonial times, and that it was melted down and molded into bullets used by the patriots during the Revolutionary War.

The origins of Buckingham Church are credited to the missionary efforts of Christopher Clarke from Spotsylvania County, who visited the area late in 1770. During that time, he organized in Buckingham County a branch congregation of the Lower Spotsylvania Baptist Church, which is now known as Wallers Church in the Goshen Association. On 7 May 1771, the Buckingham branch was made an independent church, and Rane Chastain Jr. and William Johnson were sent as delegates to a gathering of the First Separate Baptist Association held at Craigs Meeting House in Orange County, Virginia. In 1772, Rane Chastain was ordained the first pastor of the new church. Needless to say, Buckingham Church was seeing its early years out during a time of distressed religious conditions in Virginia.

Despite the discrimination and persecution of the non-Anglican dissenters, the movement for colonial independence continued. Records for Buckingham Church are very limited due to a fire that also destroyed the Buckingham County Courthouse in 1859. Since the official records are gone, several legends have been handed down from generation to generation. One story has it that bodies were buried under the church to prevent their being molested by Indians. This is unlikely, however; historians doubt the presence of Native Americans in Buckingham County at the time the church was built (1750-71).

A room off to the north side of the chancel was constructed over the graves of Capt. and Mrs. John Flood Sr., Royal Navy (1694-1770s). A memorial was erected by Eleanor Flood Schoellkoft and Bolling Byrd Flood, which states that the Captain and Mrs. Flood were colonial ancestors of a Virginia family line that includes the Honorable Henry De La Warr Flood, member U.S. Congress (1900-21); Mrs. Richard Evelyn Byrd; and Judge Joel West Flood, Fifth Judicial Circuit of Virginia (1940-64). It is an established fact, however, that there exist other graves beneath the original portion of the church.

The original or southwest wing of this structure, which was erected about 1758 as a church for the newly formed Tillotson Parish, measures thirty feet by sixty feet. During the spring of 1970, the remodeling of Buckingham Church was completed. This building project had commenced at a "groundbreaking" ceremony held on Sunday, 25 July 1965. The new addition was joined to the original building on the same front plane and duplicated in size and design the original structure. The old addition was taken down and there now exist separate front entrances for each section of the church building. These sections don a pyramid-shaped roof covered with Buckingham slate. The addition increased the outside dimensions of the church to sixty feet by eighty-four feet.

A very interesting painting now hangs in the library of this church. It is an oil painting of the original structure of Tillotson Parish/Buckingham Church. The painting was beautifully rendered by Susie S. Adams in 1971. The early congregation entered the church by rock steps on the south side of the building, while the slaves entered from wooden steps on the west side. At one point during the life of this church, a stove was located in the center of the chapel to warm the congregation. Evidence of the stove remains, as a round hole (now covered) could be seen in the ceiling of the sanctuary. The floor and structural parts of the gallery are probably colonial, if not original. For many years the Sunday service attendance was greatly increased by the presence of slaves who came to worship at Buckingham Church.

Earliest available records of the church date back to the year 1826 and indicate that a majority of slaves in the church area were enrolled members. There were at least two Negro deacons in membership. Separate rolls were kept for men and women, as well as for black and white members. According to these rolls, the Negro membership exceeded the white and, as might be expected, the females outnumbered the males. Thus when the Negro members left the congregation to form their own church or churches at the end of the Civil War, the exodus was reflected in a sudden and significant decrease in the reported membership of the mother church.

Such a reduction was indicated in the 1870 and 1871 report of the church to the July 1871 James River Association meeting, when the current roll was listed as 129, after the deduction of 384 members during the reporting period. It can be assumed that within or closely following this period, nearby Baptist Union Church, and perhaps other Negro congregations established in the area, were composed of former members of Buckingham Church.

The church at present owns a photostat copy of the min-
utes of Buckingham Baptist Church from 18 March 1826 to 14 June 1851. According to the minutes of the Tillotson Parish, the Episcopal Church retained control of the church building, and a minister was assigned to the church until 1788. An act of the General Assembly was passed in December 1788 authorizing the appointment of trustees to hold title to the glebes, churches, et cetera, for the use of the Protestant Episcopal Church. From 1788 to 1799, the attack upon the right of the Episcopal Church to hold title to its property continued; petition after petition flooded the Virginia General Assembly until, wearied of the strife and desirous of putting an end to the dissension, the Assembly on 22 January 1799 repealed every law that in any way favored the Protestant Episcopal in Virginia, totally disestablishing it. Thus did the Commonwealth of Virginia completely divorce itself from that Church to which it had been wedded since 1619. The Baptists could not legally have acquired the building until 1799 (a state law was in effect at that time dealing with abandoned property). During this period of time, all the churches in Virginia suffered depressed conditions between 1799 and 1812. Even annual conventions were discontinued for several years.

The minutes of Buckingham Church prove that a Baptist congregation was in place in March 1826. In the minutes of September 1836, a resolution was adopted "to add a 16 foot wide shed to the north side of our meeting house and to seal the old and new parts with plank." In the minutes of 20 May 1826, Buckingham Church was referred to as the "baptist church of Christ, called Buckingham."

The churchyard is spacious and well kept, but most of the property in front of the church is consumed by a large cemetery. There are no colonial markers in the large yard, however; the oldest stones remain for soldiers who died during the War Between the States.

Buckingham Church celebrated its bicentennial anniversary on 9 May 1971. The new Chastain-Taylor Annex was dedicated during this time, which was named for two former pastors, Rane Chastain and William H. Taylor. In April 1772, Reverend Chastain was ordained and chosen as the pastor of Buckingham Church. He served the people of Buckingham and Cumberland Counties for over fifty-three years. Reverend Taylor was the minister from 1847 to 1889. His service of forty-two years has been unsurpassed since the inception of Buckingham Church. A portrait of Reverend Taylor hangs in the front hallway of the church, near the entrance to the annex.

Buckingham Baptist Church is presumed to be the oldest church building in the county. It stands today as an monument to Chastain and Taylor and the countless others who have devoted strong moral and spiritual leadership during the past 225 years.

The ministers who have served Buckingham Baptist Church follow: Rane Chastain, Pondexter F. Smith, William Moore, William H. Taylor, W. C. Foster, J. W. Reams, Reuben Baker Boatwright, G. H. Cole, W. H. Lawson, R. W. Bagwell, H. W. Connelly, Norman F. Jacobs, W. T. Henderson, Winfrey W. Davis, E. Rives Ferguson, Edgar L. Patton, Paul R. Gilliam, Carlton Milstead Jr., Billy E. Griffin, John E. Mann Sr., and Richard Long.

ST. PAUL'S CHURCH
KING GEORGE COUNTY

Erected: 1766

Denomination: Anglican

Location: Owens, Virginia, off Route 218 in King George County

Religious Services: Sundays, 9:00 A.M.
First and third Sundays, Holy Communion
Second, fourth, and fifth Sundays, Morning Prayer
Homecoming, first Sunday in August at 10:00 A.M.

Tours by appointment

St. Paul's Church was once in ruins. This photograph was taken in 1905.

S T. PAUL'S CHURCH IS LOCATED IN THE NORTHERN Neck of Virginia, ten miles north of the Rappahannock River and only a few miles south of the Potomac River. St. Paul's is one of four Episcopal churches in King George County, one being Lamb's Creek (1769), another colonial church of Virginia. In 1720, King George County was laid off from Richmond on a narrow strip along the Potomac. In 1776, the boundaries of Stafford and King George were changed to make both counties border on both rivers, thereby transferring St. Paul's Parish to King George County, on the Potomac side, with Hanover Parish on the Rappahannock side.

Formerly, there were two parishes in King George, Hanover and Brunswick Parishes, lying along the Rappahannock, the latter of which reached the falls at Fredericksburg. In 1732, Brunswick Parish was formed from Hanover Parish. The Muddy Creek Church of Brunswick Parish was succeeded by the present Lamb's Creek Church of King George County. For many years during the nineteenth century, Lamb's Creek and St. Paul's shared one minister as a United Church.

Regarding St. Paul's Church's age, there is some doubt as to the exact date that the present building came into existence. There are parish records that go back as far as 1716. It was during the ministry of William Stuart that the present building was built. Bishop William Meade claims the date 1766, but others believe it to be older.

The Reverend David Stuart, the first rector of the parish, was a direct descendant of the royal house of Stuart, came to America from Scotland in 1715, and was soon given charge of St. Paul's Parish. At that time, the church building was located several miles from its present site. His son, Rev. William Stuart, was another rector. He was a saintly man; his goodness and eloquence and lovable personality helped to strengthen and beautify the spirit of the parish. With the passing of Reverend Stuart, St. Paul's fell on very hard times. For some reason, his successor, John Parsons, who was to officiate as deacon, was never ordained to the priesthood. A few years after Mr. Parsons's death, the church was in ruins, and, as a vestryman wrote sadly, "The life of the church is almost gone." Only the walls remained. Bishop Meade's account of his visitation in 1812 is a vivid picture of the desolation that had come to a once prosperous church. He writes:

St. Paul's was then in ruins. The roof was ready to fall, and not a window, door, pew or timber remained below. Nevertheless, notice was given that we should preach there. A rude temporary pulpit or stand was raised in one angle of the cross, and from that we performed service and addressed the people. On the night before the meeting a heavy rain had fallen, and the water was in small pools here and there where the floor once was, so that it was difficult to find a dry spot on which the attendants might stand.

A few years later the Legislature turned the ruins of the church over to the citizens of the county. Funds collected from the sale of glebe lands, after the Disestablishment of the Episcopal Church, were in a fund available for educational purposes; the Legislature then permitted the building to be repaired and converted for use, both as a church and an educational institution. For a while, there was an academy sharing the church with the parishioners. Methodists and Baptists accepted invitations to preach at the academy.

This arrangement at St. Paul's did not prosper. After a time, the academy was neglected and the church became inconvenient for the purposes of worship. In 1830, after the Legislature had returned the property to the Episcopal Church, St. Paul's was restored to its original use.

The building is a large cruciform structure in Georgian style. The brick is laid in Flemish bond, with headers matching the stretchers in type and color. There are two tiers of windows; those of the upper tier that light the three galleries are headed with semicircular brick arches. A high wine-glass pulpit stands in the back of the chancel, in front of which the communion rail forms a semicircle.

There is an interesting story that was told during the time St. Paul's Church stood in ruins. A woman had spent her entire life near the church, having been the property of a family that was part of the congregation. She used to go regularly every Sunday and sit among the ruins. Someone asked her, "Why do you sit in the ruins every Sunday?" She replied, "It does me more good to sit here and think over the old prayers' than to go-a-praying in any of the newer church of other denominations."

St. Paul's stands today, as it did for over two centuries ago, unchanged in form, unaltered in construction, with the same bricks in its walls that the very first builders erected. As mentioned previously, the shape is cruciform; three parts of the cross make up the place of worship, while the fourth is a spacious vestry room. Three flights of stairs lead up to a gallery, which runs around three whole sides of the building, and affords itself room for a congregation.

Several treasures remain in the possession of the church,

St. Paul's Church today remains unchanged.

including a plate which bears the inscription, "Given by Henry Fitzhugh of Stafford County, St. Paul's Parish, Gent., for the use of the Church." There is a prayer book, presented in 1830 by Miss Jane Parke, a descendant of the first rector, and a large Bible, the gift of the well-beloved Rev. William Stuart, inscribed with his name and the date 1769.

The names of the early vestrymen include Richard Bernard, John Hooe, Richard Foote, Henry Fitzhugh, John Stewart, Thomas Pratt, Samuel Washington, Laurence Washington, Andrew Grant, Robert Stith, Thomas Short, Henry S. Ashton, Charles Massey, Rice W. Hooe, Robert Chelsey, Langhorne Dade, and Benjamin Grymes.

Today, St. Paul's stands as a landmark, a proud possession of King George County.

THE FALLS CHURCH
FALLS CHURCH, FAIRFAX COUNTY

Erected: 1767-1769

Denomination: Anglican

Location: South Washington and East Fairfax Streets

Religious Services: Sundays, Holy Communion at 8:00 A.M. and 12:00 M.
(at the historic church); Morning Prayer at 9:00 A.M. and 10:45 A.M. (in
the new sanctuary)*
 Wednesdays, Holy Communion and Healing Service at 12 M.

*First Sundays and third Sundays (with five in the month), Holy
Communion.

An older photograph of Falls Church, which was named for the nearby Little Falls of the Potomac River.

FALLS CHURCH WAS NAMED FOR THE LITTLE FALLS OF the Potomac River, which are only a few miles away. The Falls Church occupies over four acres of land. During colonial times, it was referred to as "The Anglican Church."

Truro Parish, formed in 1732, was named for the borough of Truro in Cornwall, England. The borough was the shipping port for the tin and copper mined in Cornwall. Truro Parish originally included The Falls Church and Pohick Church, both of which were served by the same rector and vestry. In 1765, Truro Parish was divided, and the upper half was organized as Fairfax Parish, including Alexandria and Falls Church. The predecessor of the existing church was a frame structure built about 1734, soon after Truro Parish had been formed from the upper part of Hamilton Parish. The builder was Col. Richard Blackburn of Ripon Lodge. The deed of the land on which the church stood was recorded in the Fairfax Courthouse in 1745, a decade after it was built. In 1750, the church was enlarged to accommodate the growing congregation. A vestry meeting of Truro Parish was held at The Falls Church on 28 March 1763 with the following members present: Henry Gunnell, William Payne Jr., John West, Charles Broadwater, Thomas Wrenn, Abraham Barnes, Daniel McCarty, Robert Boggers, and George Washington. They met to examine the building, which was in a deteriorating state and in need of repairs. It was the opinion of the vestry that the old church was rotten and unfit for repair, and a new church should be built at the same location.

During the existence of Truro Parish, The Falls Church listed on its vestry rolls the names of Capt. Augustine Washington, his son George Washington, George Mason, George William Fairfax, and Capt. Henry Fairfax. A portion of Braddock's ill-starred army is said to have once encamped in the yard, and the present church building was used in the Revolutionary War as the company recruiting headquarters of Col. Charles Broadwater, one of Fairfax County's first patriots.

The existing Falls Church was originally constructed, in the years 1767 to 1769, from plans submitted by James Wren for both Christ Church (Alexandria) and The Falls Church. George Washington also used the plans for his drawing for Pohick Church, near Mount Vernon. Falls Church was completed several years before Christ Church. In 1787, The Falls Church was abandoned by the Episcopalians. This was a time of general deterioration for the Anglican Church because of its association with England and English tyranny. Bishop William Meade wrote, "it has been used by any who were disposed to occupy it as a place of worship; and the doors and windows being opened itself standing on the common

highway, it has been entered at pleasure by travelers on the road and animals of every kind." During the War Between the States, many a suffering, dying soldier found merciful shelter and medical care within the holy walls of this church. Like most of Virginia's colonial churches, The Falls Church was also used as a stable for horses during the Civil War. In 1865, the Federal government appropriated a sum of $1,300 to The Falls Church for repairs.

The Falls Church is built of dark red brick. The church's exterior measurements are sixty feet by forty feet. Although galleries were specified for The Falls Church, none were ever built. After a visit to The Falls Church in 1827, Bishop Meade writes the following: "It is a large oblong building, and, like that near Mt. Vernon, has two rows of windows, being doubtless designed for galleries all around, though none were ever put there."

It is commonly known that George Washington and George Mason were among Truro Parish's distinguished vestrymen. According to James Scott Rawlings (*Virginia's Colonial Churches: An Architectural Guide*), however, one author suggests that the Anglican hymnodist and author of the National Anthem, Francis Scott Key, also served The Falls Church upon occasion as a lay reader, but this is not authenticated.

One of the first ministers of Fairfax Parish, according to vestry records, was the Reverend Townshend Dade, who was ordained by the bishop of London in 1765, and assumed his duties about a year later. It is probable that he was the son of either Mr. Townshend Dade, who appears on the list of the first vestry, or Mr. Baldwin Dade, who was a vestryman at a later date and owner in part of the land on which Alexandria was built. Reverend Dade resigned after alleged misconduct and neglect of his congregation. The Reverend David Griffith, a chaplain in the Army and former minister of Shelburne Parish became minister in October 1780. The Reverend Bryan Fairfax succeeded him in 1790. He was ordained deacon in 1786 by Bishop Seabury. At the resignation of Reverend Fairfax, the Reverend Thomas Davis was chosen. He continued until 1806, when he moved to Hungar's Parish on the Eastern Shore, where he died.

The following account is from Spark's *Life of Washington:*

After the French War, while in retirement at Mount Vernon, Washington took a lively interest in Church affairs, regularly attending public worship, and being at different times a vestryman in two parishes.

The following list of votes for vestrymen in Fairfax parish and Truro parish is copied from a paper in

Falls Church as it appears today. Its construction is based on plans drawn by James Wren; this same design was used for Christ Church, Alexandria, and Pohick Church in Lorton.

Washington's handwriting, and shows that he was chosen a vestryman in each of those parishes. How long he continued in that station, I have no means of determining. The place of worship in Fairfax parish was at Alexandria; in Truro parish, at Pohick; the former ten, the latter seven, miles from Mount Vernon.

The vestry chosen for Fairfax Parish, on 28 March 1765, follows, with the number of votes for each:

John West	340
Charles Alexander	309
William Payne	304
John Dalton	281
George Washington	274
Charles Broadwater	260
George Johnston	254
Townshend Dade	252
Richard Sandford	247
William Adams	244
John Posey	222
Daniel French	221

The vestry chosen for Truro Parish, on 22 July 1765, follows, with the number of votes for each:

George Mason	282
Edward Payne	277
George Washington	259
John Posey	259
Daniel McCarty	246
George William Fairfax	235
Alexander Henderson	231
William Gardner	218
Tomison Ellzey	209
Thomas W. Coffer	189
William Lynton	172
Thomas Ford	170

The Falls Church has been thoroughly restored. It has a very active and strong congregation of over two thousand parishioners. One author says, "Some of our Colonial churches may seem to be over-praised and overcited in relation to their sister Colonial churches. It is the other way round with the Falls Church."

LAMB'S CREEK CHURCH

KING GEORGE COUNTY

Erected: 1769-70

Denomination: Anglican

Location: On Route 607, 1/2 mile northwest of the Route 3 and Route 607 junction

Religious Services: Homecoming service is held on the last Sunday in August at 10 A.M.

The Lamb's Creek Association supports restoration and preservation. The church is used for occasional baptisms and weddings. Tours are available by appointment.

Lamb's Creek Church remains virtually unchanged today.

L AMB'S CREEK CHURCH TAKES ITS NAME FROM THE waterway that runs about a half-mile east of the building. It is believed to have been built in 1769 by John Ariss, who later constructed the colonial church Little Fork, near Rixeyville in Culpeper County in 1776. The dimensions of Lamb's Creek are seventy-nine feet eleven inches by thirty-three feet eleven inches.

When it was completed, Lamb's Creek Church replaced Muddy Creek Church as the Brunswick Parish meeting place. In use in 1710, Muddy Creek Church stood in the western part of King George County, where Muddy Creek separates King George County from Stafford County. It became the first Brunswick Parish church in 1732, after Brunswick Parish was formed from the upper part of Hanover Parish.

According to the account of former rector Dr. George McLaren Brydon and Mary Goodwin, the Brunswick Parish was active until 1797. In that year, a lay delegate from the parish attended the Diocesan Convention, but the organized parish ceased to exist thereafter, and Lamb's Creek Church was abandoned.

After the Disestablishment, Lamb's Creek Church was partially restored in 1825. It continued to be active until the Civil War. As with many colonial churches in Virginia, Lamb's Creek Church was occupied by Federal troops during the War Between the States. Soldiers used the church as a stable, and its interior was destroyed.

The church was not restored to service until 1906 and was not repaired until 1908, when the Reverend Byrd Thorton Turner, the rector of the parish and a Confederate veteran, managed to obtain eight hundred dollars as indemnity from the Federal government.* A new floor and a new roof were also added during the rectorate of Reverend Turner. During its restoration, prompted by the Virginia Tricentennial in 1907, the church received a new roof, a new door, and new windows, and services resumed. The square pews, reredos, and pulpit from the colonial period either were ruined or disappeared between 1862 and 1906, when only occasional Baptist services were held in the church. There are no colonial gravestones in the church yard.

During 1911, Dr. George McLaren Brydon became rector of the Episcopal churches in King George County and served for three years. Under his rectorship, a vestry was organized, and this action kept Lamb's Creek active as a parish church. Most members of the congregation were very poor and some were illiterate. Dr. Brydon's successor failed to maintain the work, and once again the church became idle. Soon after

that, Lamb's Creek was placed under the charge of the rector of St. John's Church in Hanover Parish, also in King George County.

Lamb's Creek Church is presently inactive, although it still has in its possession a Bible printed in 1716, known as the "Vinegar" edition, and a prayer book printed in 1739. Both items were obtained from Muddy Creek Church. The solid walnut cross that hangs above the altar was made by William D. Taylor, a local craftsman whose daughter was active in the restoration of Lamb's Creek Church, and placed there in 1979.

The yearly homecoming service held at Lamb's Creek Church was initiated in 1908. It is held on the last Sunday in August.

Because Lamb's Creek Church is a fine example of colonial architecture, many people would like to see it completely renovated one day, although concern has always been expressed about whether another Episcopal church could be supported in King George County, which already has three.**

* Reverend Turner was the father of Nancy Byrd Turner, a poet whose many works included a celebration of Charles Lindbergh's flight to Paris called "The Ballad of Lucky Lindbergh."

** Additional information about Lamb's Creek Church can be obtained by contacting the rector of St. John's Episcopal Church in King George County, Virginia.

Lamb's Creek Church in 1930. Its restoration was prompted by the Virginia Tricentennial in 1907 when $800 was granted by the Federal government for damages suffered during the Civil War.

FINCASTLE CHURCH

BOTETOURT PARISH CHURCH
TAZEWELL COUNTY

Erected: 1772
Denomination: Presbyterian
Location: Fincastle, Virginia
Religious Services: Sundays, 11:00 a.m.

Fincastle Church and its churchyard, which is nicknamed "God's acre."

B OTETOURT COUNTY WAS FORMED IN 1770 FROM Augusta County. The act creating Botetourt County likewise created Botetourt Parish, which was coterminous with the county. To give some idea of the extent of the boundaries of the county, the following paragraph from the act is interesting:

And whereas the people situated on the waters of the Mississippi, in the said County of Botetourt, will be very remote from their courthouse and must necessarily become a separate county as soon as their numbers are sufficient, which will probably happen in a short time. Be it further enacted, by the aforesaid,

That the inhabitants of that part of te said County of Botetourt which lies on said waters, shall be exempted from the payment of levies, to be laid by the said County Court for the purpose of building a courthouse and prison for the said County.

Until 1772, Botetourt County and Botetourt Parish included all of Southwest Virginia west of Botetourt County. In 1772, Botetourt County was divided into two counties. The county of Fincastle was carved from Botetourt, and within its boundaries lay all of Southwest Virginia, except the present counties of Botetourt, Roanoke, and Craig. No parish was created when Fincastle was formed.

An act for dividing the county of Botetourt into two counties read as follows:

That from and after the first day of December next, the said County of Botetourt shall be divided into two distinct counties, that is to say, all that part of the said county within a line, to run up the east side of New river to the mouth of Culberson's creek, thence a direct line to the Catawba road where it crosses the dividing ridge, between the north fork of Roanoke and the waters of New river, thence with the top of the ridge to the bend where it turns eastwardly, thence a south course crossing Little River to the top of the Blue Ridge mountains, shall be established as one distinct county and called and know by the name of Fincastle and all that other part thereof which lies to the east and north of the said line shall be one other county and retain the name of Botetourt.

Fincastle County had a short existence. By act dated October 1776, it was entirely divided into three counties, namely Washington, Montgomery, and Kentucky. By the same act, the parishes of Washington, Montgomery, and Kentucky were created. Since no parish was established when Fincastle County was formed, these three new parishes recognized Botetourt Parish as the mother parish. From Botetourt County were subsequently created Greenbrier, 1778; Roanoke, 1835; and Craig, 1851.

Botetourt County was named for Norborne Berkeley, Lord Botetourt, governor of Virginia in 1768. The older parish was named for the county. The other parish in the county was named for the Reverend John W. Woodville of Culpeper.

The first settlers in Botetourt were chiefly Scotch-Irish Presbyterians. They obeyed the Virginia laws in regard to church affairs, but at the same time, worshipped according to their own faith and doctrine. Before churches were established, they worshipped in houses registered and designated for that purpose. In 1754, Robert Montgomery and Patrick Shirky entered a suitable tract of land on Sinking Spring Creek for the use of the congregation, thus showing that the community was interested in its own form of worship and was willing to provide for its religious needs. This became the meeting place for the Presbyterian congregation that later succeeded the established church at Fincastle.

The Reverend John Craig was perhaps one of the earliest dissenting ministers to visit this area. In the spring of 1749, on a trip to Roanoke, he baptized several people at Looney's Mill Creek.

From 1760-1770 there were more regular visits from ministers appointed by the Presbytery and more definite reports about the congregations. In 1762 Rev. Mr. Craig was appointed for one Sabbath at Roanoke and one at Catawba. In 1763 Rev. Mr. Black was recommended for one Sabbath at Roanoke and one at Catawba. In 1766 Rev. Mr. Todd was to administer the sacrament at Roanoke in Augusta County after Rev. Mr. Brown had examined persons for the sacrament and had ordained the leaders. About this time Rev. James Campbell was a supply in the congregation. In 1767 Rev. Mr. Leak was appointed for two months at Forks of James and also two months at Roanoke. In 1768 Rev. Craig conducted six services at Craig's Creek.

In 1770, the parish of Botetourt was organized and vestrymen appointed. On 15 November 1771, it was ordered that the trustees of the county land lay off and convey to the vestry of Botetourt Parish an acre of land for the use of the said parish at a place they considered convenient. Rev. Adam Smyth became rector of the Botetourt Parish soon after its organization. He was parish minister for all Botetourt, as it was originally laid off, from 1774 to 1776. When Washington and Montgomery Counties were organized in 1777, the parish was divided, and in June of that year, the vestry of Botetourt was dissolved by Act of Assembly.

In 1778, Rev. Edward Crawford was called to the Sinking Spring and Spreading Spring congregations. While serving in this capacity, he organized the Presbyterian church at Fincastle. The congregation used the Episcopal church that was not in use at that time. The established church was without support since the majority of the locals were Presbyterians.

According to Vernon Davis, authority on the architecture of colonial churches, it is difficult and perhaps impossible to be certain as to the extent of the original fabric surviving in the present church, now Fincastle Presbyterian Church. It would seem likely that the colonial structure was forty-five feet four inches (east to west) by twenty-five feet four inches (south to north). The church now measures forty-four by fifty-one feet.

Bishop William Meade, in the second volume of his *Old Churches, Ministers, and Families*, says,

> In Botetourt Parish (for all the new parishes were called by the same name with the counties) we find that the Rev. Adam Smith was the minister in the years 1774 and 1776...We know of no other but the Rev. Samuel Gray, who appears on the journal of 1796, and who died in the parish poor-house, the miserable victim of drink. In Fincastle there was an Episcopal church on the spot where the Presbyterian church now stands. A new church being built there, the Presbyterians worshipped in it, and were perhaps most active in its erection. By an act of the Legislature, the lot of ground on which it stood was given to that denomination.

There is very limited architectural evidence available regarding this structure. The architectural expert Rose reports,

> One can only say that parts of the east, north, and west walls probably derive from the colonial structure and that parts of the 1818 southern extensions of the east and west walls may derive from the masonry of the original south wall, one can only guess as to the disposition of the original openings, it seems likely that the rectangular colonial Botetourt Parish Church had the usual west and south doorways and that the 1818 Presbyterian re-arrangements resulted in a square looking building with only an eastern doorway.

We can learn nothing of the character of the early church buildings. Mr. W. A. Glasgow writes, "The *walls* of the present buildig represent the building standing there in 1832 ...In 1849 and 1850 the church was remodelled, removing

the session house, fitting up the walls of the old with the present front, and constructing the interior anew, with galleries and approved pulpit and sittings, putting the whole into a handsome church."

The brick building, as it stood in 1832, was square, the roof coming to a point in the center, upon which was a belfry. It was wrapped around one of the pillars when not in use. In the rear of the church, on the outside, can now be seen the marks of three windows that were in the old building.

The Presbyterian church of Fincastle was probably organized by the Reverend Edward Crawford about the year 1795. At least it is known that Mr. Crawford resided about this period in the county of Botetourt and was regularly employed for a portion of his time in preaching to the Presbyterians of Fincastle. The first ruling elders chosen by the church, and no doubt ordained by Mr. Crawford, were Nicholas Carper and James Delzell. But little is now known of Mr. Crawford's gifts and success as a preacher, nor is it certainly known how long he continued to excercise his ministry among the people of Fincastle and other portions of the county. It appears from reliable sources that Mr. Robert Logan, after a brief period of trial, was settled as stated supply of the congregation, about 15 December 1800.

Mr. Glasgow recorded the following:

> Early in 1770 the county-seat of Botetourt county ws fixed on a tract of forty-five acres presented by Israel Christian, provided the court-house and public prison were built on it. Under this deed from Christian to the county court, the court had the land laid off into lots; some appropriated to the courthouse and prison, some sold, but an eligible lot was set apart to the church. The church lot was built on by Episcopal Church (Church of England), over which there was installed a rector; the church had also a glebe. It is said that one or more rectors were buried under the church building, and that one rectore especially was, in life, a jolly fellow. Soon after the Act of Religious Freedom, passed in 1785, the church was unoccupied. Doubtless it was felt that the act was unfavorable to the Anglican Church, and the tithes being stricken out, the church was without support. The community being largely dissenters, chiefly Presbyterians, the church was opened for service by them. Mr. William Anderson, with his friends, held charge of the church for worship, and from these beginnings the church has been held and occupied to the present day.

The churchyard has long been known as "God's acre." The earliest graves are unmarked. Several of the stones are believed to be dated prior to the Revolutionary War. The oldest marker still readable belongs to Patsey Harvey, who died in 1795. The wife of Governor Giles, Martha Peyton Giles rests in this cemetery as well. She was born in 1777 and died in July 1808.

After the year 1976, the reredos (an ornamental screen behind the altar), pulpit, and railing—all copied from an early plan that may have existed before the church's renovation in 1840—were installed. The pulpit is an enlarged copy of an earlier one, which was probably removed in 1840 and given to an African-American congregation in Fincastle. That church later passed it on to the town hall.

The ministers who served Fincastle Presbyterian Church, from 1795 to 1972, are as follows:

Rev. Edward Crawford	1795-1800
Rev. Robert Logan	1800-28
Rev. John M. Fulton	1829-34
Rev. Jeptha Harrison	1835-37
Rev. Stephen T. Cocke	1837-45
Rev. Henry H. Paine	1845-56
Rev. John S. Grasty, D.D.	1856-67
Rev. John H. Bocock, D.D.	1867-70
Rev. R. R. Houston	1871-90
Rev. P. C. Clark	1891-97
Rev. J. C. Shive	1897-99
Rev. J. M. Holladay	1899-1904
Rev. Thomas Mowbray	1904-10
Rev. Junius Batte	1917-18
Rev. J. C. Clark	1923-25
Rev. James Armstrong	1926-41
Rev. John Morgan	1941-42
Rev. David H. Coblentz	1944-51
Rev. J. T. Hayter Jr.	1954-60
Rev. Edgar L. Mayse	1960-67
Rev. William C. Carperton	1968-72
Rev. William P. Shackelford	1972-

Two chalices, a paten, and a flagon are still in use at St. Mark's Episcopal Church, the second Botetourt Parish Church. They probably derive from about 1774 and 1775. The bell now in use at Fincastle Church was cast by J. Welbank of Philadelphia in 1829.

Drastic alterations, repairs, and enlargements during 1818 and 1849 have caused the Botetourt Parish Church to lose most of its colonial authenticity.

CHRIST CHURCH

ALEXANDRIA

Erected: 1767-1773

Denomination: Anglican

Location: North Washington and Cameron Streets

Religious Services: Sundays, Holy Eucharist at 8:00 A.M. (Rite I with organ music) and 9:00 A.M. (Rite II family service with sermon and choir), Morning Prayer at 11:15 A.M. (Rite I), and Holy Eucharist at 5:00 P.M. (Rite II, no music)
First and fifth Sundays, Holy Eucharist at 11:15 A.M.
First Sundays, Evensong at 5:00 P.M.
Second and fourth Sundays, Laying on of Hands for Healing at 5:00 P.M.
Wednesdays, Holy Eucharist at 7:15 A.M. (Rite II in the chapel), 12:05 P.M. (with laying on of hands for healing), and 6:15 P.M. (in the round in McMurray Commons)

An early photograph of Christ Church, which was designed by James Wren.

From its establishment in 1773, Christ Church has been a central landmark in Alexandria. Though at the time of its construction the church actually stood outside the city limits, today it is a premier focal point of Old Town. It is visited by more than seventy-five thousand tourists each year as they retrace the beginnings of our nation. A recent survey of Episcopal parishes in the United States lists Christ Church, Alexandria, as the eighteenth largest.

Christ Church was one of the first buildings in the United States to be designated a National Historic Landmark. Because of George Washington's close association with the church, it has been called the Church of George Washington (although the Revolutionary War general was active on the vestry of three Anglican churches in Fairfax County: Pohick Church, Falls Church, and Christ Church in Alexandria).

Fairfax Parish was formed on 1 February 1765 from Truro Parish and included an Upper Church (The Falls Church) and a Lower Church that was in Alexandria. On 28 March 1765, Col. George Washington, then thirty-three years old, was elected to be one of the parish's vestrymen. In colonial days, the government of Virginia was largely controlled by the vestry of the parish, as it held in a generous measure the power of civil authority.

Among the first acts of the vestry was the repairing of the two old churches in the parish at a cost of thirty-two thousand pounds of tobacco. In 1766, the vestry decided to build two new church buildings, one at Falls Church near the older existing church and another in Alexandria that was to encompass twenty-four thousand square feet.

In 1767, work began on the church in Alexandria. The property was given by John Alexandria, one of the landholders who developed the expansion of the town. The site was then densely wooded, but it is now open and in the heart of the city, which grew so rapidly that the country's founding fathers considered Alexandria as the location of the nation's Capital. The plans for the church were drawn by James Wren, a reputed descendant of Sir Christopher Wren, an architect who designed many famous London churches. These plans were used later by George Washington in drafting his design of Pohick Church.

The contract was awarded to James Parsons for six hundred pounds, a large sum of money at that time. In 1772, construction of the church came to a standstill. Col. John Carlyle agreed to complete Parsons's unfinished contract for an additional sum of £220. One year later, the church was placed in the hands of the vestry, who regarded it as finished in a "workmanlike manner." That same day Colonel Wash-

George Washington and Robert E. Lee owned pews in Christ Church, as photographed here in 1930.

ington purchased the pew that was known as Number 5.

Originally, the church in Alexandria was considered the twin of Pohick Church in Lorton, but architectural changes were made, and the two churches soon grew apart in appearance. The gallery at Christ Church was added in 1787, the west aisle in 1811, and the tower and steeple at the west end in 1818. In 1810, an organ was introduced and, in 1812, the chimneys were built, making foot stoves no longer necessary.

With the change of appearance came the change of name. For nearly fifty years after its founding in 1765, the building had been referred to as the Episcopal Church, but, on 9 June 1814, the church was officially consecrated by Bishop Thomas Claggett of Maryland with the name of Christ Church.

During the colonial period, which spans 1600 to 1775, there were no bishops in the colonies and, therefore, no confirmations. The first confirmation at Christ Church was recorded in 1813 by Bishop Richard C. Moore, the second bishop of Virginia. It was probably his first official act as bishop of Virginia. Dr. David Griffith, the chaplain of the Revolutionary days, was the first bishop-elect of the Diocese, but due to a lack of funds, he never made the journey to London for ordination.

The colonial portion of the church measures fifty feet north to south by sixty feet east to west, similar to the Meeting House located on South Fairfax Street. Although the galleries were not added until 1785, the two tiers of windows are original. The stone that trimmed the windows and the corners of the church's doorways came from the Aquia Creek quarries in Stafford County. The original juniper shingles of the church's hipped roof have been replaced by slate. The doors and doorways are probably original. The reredos, or tablets, are slightly larger to embrace the large Palladian window, which had six fluted pilasters instead of the four plain ones on the stone interior. There is an inscription at the bottom of the left tablet which reads, "Whatsoever ye would that men should do unto you, even so do unto them: for this is the law and the prophets."

After the Revolution, Washington attended services regularly at Christ Church instead of Pohick Church, which would have been closer to his Mount Vernon home. Washington's family traveled the ten miles north from Mount Vernon in a gold and green coach drawn by four horses. Their family Bible was given to the church in 1804 by General Washington's adopted son, George Washington Parke Custis.

An organ was installed in Christ Church in 1810, but it is now on display at the Smithsonian Institute in Washington, D.C. Also, in 1818, a beautiful chandelier of hand-wrought brass and glass, which hangs under the rear gallery, was bought in London and installed in the church.

Gen. Robert E. Lee spent his boyhood in Fairfax Parish.

He was confirmed by Bishop John Johns at Christ Church in 1853. The chancel rail bears a silver marker showing where Robert E. Lee was confirmed. General Lee's pew (Number 46) is marked with his autograph in silver, as is General Washington's (Numbers 5 and 60).

During the Civil War, Alexandria, Virginia, was occupied by Federal troops, but Christ Church, unlike most of the other colonial churches, was used for church services with a chaplain in charge and escaped damage. During that period, the nameplate on Washington's pew and the parish register from 1765 to 1860 were both stolen. The vestry book from 1765 to 1842, however, was kept safe at a bank in Alexandria.

The large churchyard served as a cemetery from 1767 to 1815, but after 1800, only parishioners were allowed to be buried there. Exceptions were made in 1834 and in 1879 for thirty-seven Confederate soldiers who had died in a local Federal prison during the war. The oldest grave stone is dated 1771. It is believed that the gates and walls of the churchyard were erected sometime between 1885 and 1890.

Subsequent to George Washington's presidency, most U.S. presidents have embraced the tradition of visiting Christ Church on a Sunday near Washington's birthday during their terms in office. During the dark days of the Second World War, Pres. Franklin D. Roosevelt and British Prime Minister Winston Churchill came to Christ Church to worship together on the World Day of Prayer. Pres. and Mrs. Ronald Reagan worshipped in Christ Church on 21 February 1982, the day before the 250th anniversary of the birth of George Washington.

There have been many distinguished ministers who have served this parish. The first rector was Townsend Dade, and after his death in 1778, he was succeeded by David Griffith, who had served as a chaplain in the Continental Army and was a close friend of General Washington. Bryan Fairfax (later Lord Fairfax) served as rector in 1790. He was succeeded by Thomas Davis, who served from 1791 to 1811 and who, in 1799, conducted the funeral services for George Washington.

From 1811 to 1813, William Meade was rector. In 1841, he became the third bishop of Virginia and served in that post until 1862. Bishop Meade is the author of the now-famous, two-volume reference titled *Old Churches, Ministers, and Families of Virginia.*

In 1860, Cornelius Walker became rector and, at the outbreak of the Civil War, he became a chaplain in the Confederate Army.

For generations Christ Church has been a source of consolation, peace, and joy to her sons and daughters. It has a firmly established place in the history of our nation. After 222 years, Christ Church continues to play a central role in the life of Alexandria.

Christ Church today enjoys historic attention, although initially it stood outside the city limits of Alexandria.

HICKORY NECK CHURCH

BLISLAND PARISH

TOANO, JAMES CITY COUNTY

Erected: 1773-1774

Denomination: Anglican

Location: On the east side of Route 60, about 3/4 mile south of the junction of Routes 60 and 168 and 1 mile north of Toano in James City County

Religious Services: Sundays, Holy Eucharist at 8:00 A.M. (Rite I), 9:00 A.M. (Rite II), and 11:15 A.M. (Rite II)
Wednesdays, Eucharist at 7:00 A.M.

Hickory Neck Church was severely damaged during the Civil War, but restored in 1915. Here it is photographed in 1930.

The history of Hickory Neck Church, Blisland Parish, was written by Martha W. McCartney of the Hickory Neck Historical Committee in 1992. Her work is beautifully written and extensively researched.

BLISLAND PARISH WAS ESTABLISHED SOMETIME PRIOR to October 1653, when it was mentioned in a patent for land in the upper reaches of the York River, in what was then York County. By that date, colonists in substantial numbers had moved into the territory along the banks of the Pamunkey and Mattaponi Rivers and had claimed and seated land on the upper side of the York River. Blisland Parish's vast, sprawling territory extended from the mouth of Skimino Creek, westward for an indefinite distance. Its northern limits were the York and Mattaponi Rivers, and its southern boundary line followed the old Rickahock trail that ran up the ridge-back of the James/York peninsula, abutting nearby Wilmington Parish. Blisland Parish appears to have been coterminous with the territory that in 1654 was designated New Kent County, which was carved from the western part of York County. Although the origin of Blisland (or Blissland) Parish's name is uncertain, it may have been the inspiration of a prominent New Kent County settler who had immigrated from Blissland Parish in Bodmin, Cornwall in England, where his father was archdeacon. Bishop William Meade reported in 1857 that the name Blisland was common in England and that it meant "happy land."

A relatively short time after Blisland Parish was formed, it was reduced in size, for in 1655, Stratton Major Parish (then in New Kent County, later in King and Queen County) was created from its northeastern territory. In 1679, Blisland's size was reduced again when St. Peter's Parish was established; the original Blisland Parish was widespread, extending indefinitely to the west and northwest, taking in the land that eventually became the modern New Kent, Hanover, and King William Counties.

Historical records indicate that in 1680 the Reverend Thomas Taylor was the rector of Blisland Parish. The growth of old New Kent County is evidenced by the fact that in 1702 it had 1,245 tithables within its boundaries, almost half of whom were living in the Blisland Parish area. By 1714, New Kent held 1,852 tithables and three parishes: Blisland, St. Peter's, and St. Paul's, which had been formed from St. Peter's.

Although the location of Blisland Parish's first church is uncertain, it was likely situated in the eastern (or lower) section of the territory, which logically would have seen its earliest settlement, being the most densely populated area. By 1703, Upper Church (commonly known as the Brick Church or Warranty—Warrany, Warreneye—Church) had been built at the head of Warrany Creek, near the road to New Kent Courthouse. Blisland Parish's surviving vestry records, which open in 1721, reveal that a Lower Church also was in existence and imply that it was of frame construction. Blisland's vestry usually met once or twice a year, in the spring and fall, and alternated their meetings between the Upper and Lower Churches, except for the times it met in one of the local taverns or a private home.

When Rev. Daniel Taylor, the rector of Blisland Parish from 1704 to 1729, responded to the bishop of London's questionnaire in 1724, he reported that his parish was thirty miles long and consisted of two churches. He said that he had 136 families who attended fairly regularly and an average of sixty to seventy communicants.

It was likely the enlargement of Blisland Parish, in both size and population, and the arrival of a well-qualified and highly esteemed priest that led the vestry to build a new Lower Church, the house of worship that eventually became known as Hickory Neck. In November 1731, the vestry agreed to begin setting aside part of its annual levies toward the construction of the proposed church, a plan it re-endorsed the following year. Finally, in October 1733, when the vestry convened at the parish's old Lower Church, its members agreed that a new structure should "be built of Brick in the Lower part of this parish sixty foot Long & 26 foot wide within the Walles, the farther Dementions to be as the Vestry shall agree with the workmen."

On 11 December 1733, when the vestry of Blisland Parish met at Lower Church, it was agreed that "a church be built of Brick for the Lower part of this Parish of Blisland on Mrs. Holdcrofts Land on the Maine Road below ye Late Plantation of Mrs. Weldys on part of the Land where Mrs. Holdcroft Now Lives, being an Acre of Land given by Mrs. Holdcroft for that use."

Under the leadership of the Reverend Price Davies, the congregation of Blisland Parish's Lower Church apparently grew to the point that it needed more space in which to conduct worship services, for in November 1773, the vestry set aside funds toward the construction of an addition in 1734. They also ordered the churchwardens to find workmen to create the church addition and to make some repairs to the existing Blisland Parish Church. In March 1774, the churchwardens advertised for a builder to undertake the church expansion project. The texts of the advertisements that appeared in the *Virginia Gazettes* published by Purdie and Dixon and by Rind were almost identical:

To be let to the Lowest Bidder on Monday the 21st of this Instant [March] at Hickory Neck Church in Blisland Parish, James City County. A BRICK addition to the said church, the Dimension[s] of which are to be agreed on that Day: and great Part of the Money will be paid to the Undertaker, who is to give Bond and Security for the Performance of his Contract to the Churchwardens.

Perhaps the most significant item in the 13 March 1774 advertisement is the use of the name "Hickory Neck Church" to identify Blisland Parish's Lower Church, the first such printed reference to the church by that name. At a vestry meeting that was held in October 1774, Col. Burwell Bassett, one of Blisland Parish's churchwardens and George Washington's brother-in-law, donated a generous sum toward the "addition to the lower church."

Blisland Parish vestry records for 1775 contain a contract awarded to the two men who were hired to build a twenty-four feet addition onto the parish's Upper Church (Warrany). This document gives us some idea of what occurred at Hickory Neck when a new transept was added onto the original part of the church. The addition to Blisland Parish's Upper Church was to be twenty-four feet in length and the same width as the older part of the church, and it was to include two windows per exterior wall. These changes were identical to those made at the Lower Church when it was enlarged in 1774. The brick-walled yard surrounding the Upper Church was partially dismantled to accommodate its new transept, but it was not reattached to the addition (as it was at the Lower Church); instead, it was lengthened by eight feet. Since graves were situated close to the walls of the Upper Church, the men who agreed to construct the addition were cautioned to lay the foundation "as low as the Graves (where they Interfere)." The pulpit of the Upper Church was to be moved from south to north, as was done at the Lower Church in 1774, when a north transept was added. The V specified that the pulpit was to be "fixed according to the Rev. Mr. Thacker's direction," and the communion table was to be moved and fitted with new rails and banisters. Like the older section of Upper Church, its new transept was to wear a compass (or barrel) ceiling that was covered with planks and roofed with cypress shingles. The interior walls of the enlarged church were to be lathed, plastered, and then whitewashed, just like the walls at the Lower Church.

Vestry records for the late 1770s suggest that life in Blisland Parish carried on much as it had before the Lower Church was expanded.

In 1825, the old nave and chancel in the original 1734 building were demolished and the southern end of Hickory Neck's north transept, built in 1774, was extended approximately ten feet. A new window was added to each of its side walls, making three windows per wall, and the building's original windows were lengthened by one foot. When the end of the church was bricked up, an entrance door and a fireplace were built.

Scars on the exterior of Hickory Neck provide graphic evidence of the modifications that were made when the church was converted into a school house. In 1834, the rec-

tor of Bruton Parish reported that although Hickory Neck no longer sent representatives to the Diocesan Convention, Episcopal services had been held in the ancient colonial church one Sunday a month ever since its "reconstruction as a school building." He also indicated that various denominations held worship services there from time to time.

Although the General Assembly in 1825 had authorized the conversion of Hickory Neck Church into a primary school for the use of local inhabitants, by the 1840s, it had become an academy or institution where secondary education was offered. Robert Morris, a James City County school teacher, who lived near Croaker, wrote in his diary that on 13 September 1845, he went to Hickory Neck Academy, where he "heard letters read from applicants." Morris, who conducted classes in a small schoolhouse that was located near his home, also served as a trustee of the Hickory Neck School Society; during the early 1850s, he was a James City County school commissioner. His diary indicates that during 1844 and 1845, he attended "union" or ecumenical worship services held at several local churches, including the Chickahominy Baptist Church, the Methodist Chapel, Olive Branch Church, and Hickory Neck. On 18 May 1845, Morris reported that he walked to Hickory Neck, where he heard the conclusion of a Mr. Henshall's sermon.

According to the recollections of one local resident, who was born right after the Civil War, Hickory Neck fared very badly, as it was used as a camp site by both armies. He said that the building's pulpit and flooring were torn up and used for fuel and that one of its walls was damaged. The church reportedly was surrounded by a brick wall, within which were old, broken tombstones that had been vandalized. The road to New Kent extended along the west side of the church's walled yard, whereas the road to Ware Creek ran on its south side. The two roads reportedly forked directly in front of the church. Thanks to Hickory Neck's ruinous condition, the building stood vacant for nearly a decade.

The Reverend E. Ruffin Jones of Bruton Parish began personally campaigning for Hickory Neck Church's restoration to be used as an Episcopal house of worship. On 12 March 1912, the General Assembly passed an act by which the James City County School Board was authorized to convey the church lot to the trustees of the Hickory Neck Protestant Episcopal Church. On 8 August, the School Board executed a deed that conveyed the Hickory Neck Academy lot, which was one acre in size, to Hickory Neck's trustees: J. G. Carlton, W. Walker Ware, and D. Wesley Marston.

In June 1913, Reverend Ruffin sponsored the publication of a fundraising pamphlet in which he appealed for donations to repair and remodel the church "to what extent is necessary to make it fit as a house of worship." He said that out of the one thousand dollars needed to restore the church to useable condition, about three hundred dollars already had been raised locally and another two hundred dollars was expected to be forthcoming. He said that "the country about the old church is developing rapidly, and we trust that every one to whom this paper comes will help to rehabilitate this old landmark not only as a historic witness to our faith but as a House of Prayer for a growing community."

In repsonse to Rev. E. Ruffin Jones's efforts, regular wor-

A photograph of the present Hickory Neck Church, which was changed to All Saints Church then renamed Hickory Neck.

ship services resumed at Hickory Neck Church in 1915. It was during that summer that the vestry hired G. P. Sweeney to build a sacristy, or robing room, at the north end of the church and a small covered porch at its entrance. Fragments of the tombstone of Col. Lawrence Taliaferro (1721-48) of Snow Hill in Spotsylvania County were then embedded in the cement flooring of the new porch.

In 1953, Bishop George Gunn asked the congregation of Hickory Neck to select a name for the church that had an obvious religious association. Therefore, when the bishop performed his annual visitation on All Saints Day 1953, Hickory Neck Church was formally renamed All Saints. However, local sentiment for the church's traditional name persisted and, in June 1972, Bishop David Rose, in response to a petition from the congregation, restored the name Hickory Neck. Later in the year, Hickory Neck was added to the Virginia Landmarks Register. This was followed in 1973 by

the inclusion of Hickory Neck Church in the National Register of Historic Places, a designation that is reserved for America's most important historic sites. A year later, the church commemorated the bicentennial of Hickory Neck's 1774 north transept with a program that somewhat resembled the 1934 celebration. At that time, archaeological tests were performed and an interpretive drawing was prepared that depicts the various components of the 1734/1774 church and its 1742 yard; also shown on that drawing are the porch and sacristy additions from 1917.

During the 1970s, the Hankins family donated an adjacent parcel of land to Hickory Neck for the enhancement of the church's grounds. In 1978, the church's trustees sold its old parish house on Depot Street and two years later built a new one on the donated land. The new parish house, which became available for use in 1980, currently serves as a Sunday school building and activity center.

THE MEETING HOUSE
THE OLD PRESBYTERIAN MEETING HOUSE
ALEXANDRIA

Erected: 1774

Denomination: Presbyterian

Location: 317 South Fairfax Street in Old Alexandria

Religious Services: Sundays—fall, winter, and spring—8:30 A.M. and 11:00 A.M.; summer, 10:00 A.M.

The Old Presbyterian Meeting House in 1930. The meeting house was destoyed by fired in 1835, but was restored the next year.

I
N THE HISTORIC SECTION OF ALEXANDRIA STANDS THE OLD Presbyterian Meeting House, which still remains of considerable interest to many people.

The population of Alexandria in its early days was composed largely of Scottish merchants and sea captains who had settled here. Consequently, Presbyterianism was established even before the incorporation of the town, and previous to the granting, in 1760, of a charter under the Toleration Act from the Governor's Council of the colony of Virginia.

After this date, the Presbyterians held their meetings in the upper room of Alexandria's new Town House (so named instead of Town Hall), which was located on the southwest corner of Cameron and Fairfax Streets. The Reverend David Thom, a native of Scotland, officiated.

In 1767, John Parsons undertook a project to build a "church at Alexandria." In 1772, John Carlyle took over the project. Mr. Carlyle was a Presbyterian and very much interested in formulating the plans for the erection of a church of his own.

The most desired location for the meeting house was on Fairfax Street between Duke and Wolfe Streets. For the sum of one shilling sterling, Richard and Eleanor Arrell, natives of Pennsylvania, conveyed two lots in this vicinity (numbers 90 and 91 in the plat of Alexandria, town of Fairfax County and colony of Virginia) by deed executed 12 July 1773, to the congregation's pastor, the Reverend William Thom, trustee, and successive Presbyterian ministers of the church. With the aid of a lottery, this project was completed in 1774.

Mr. Thom, the son of the Reverend David Thom, was ordained in 1772 by the Synod of Philadelphia, which was meeting at Carlyle, Pennsylvania.

He was still a young man when he died of an epidemic fever in 1780 and was succeeded by Parson Keith, who came to Alexandria from New Jersey. After Keith's death in 1789, the Reverend Dr. James Muir became the minister of the Presbyterian church in Alexandria. As a chaplain of the Masonic Lodge in Alexandria, he assisted Dr. Elisha Cullen Dick at the funeral of George Washington. During the latter years of Dr. Muir's ministry it became necessary for him to secure an assistant at the Presbyterian Meeting House.

Strong opinions as to the choice of the assistant resulted in the breaking off from communion of thirty-three men and thirty women, leaving the congregation of the First Presbyterian Church (as it was thereafter called) with a membership of sixty-two persons. On 28 June 1818, the Reverend Dr. Elias Harrison was installed as co-pastor with Dr. Muir, who presided at the installation ceremony and was assisted by the Reverend Dr. William Balch of Georgetown and the Reverend Colin McIvor of North Carolina. From this date forward, the church's membership continued to increase, and for many years it was one of the most prosperous churches in Alexandria.

The seceding party formed the Second Presbyterian Church and opened a meeting house on the east side of Fairfax Street between Prince and Duke Streets. This meeting house was known as St. Margaret's Chapel after the name of a woman who was prominent in making the move. This chapel had been occupied for about nine years by the people of Christ Church who had supported the cause of the Reverend William Gibson and who eventually built St. Paul's Church in 1817. The Presbyterian seceders purchased the little chapel from them for $4,500 and occupied it until they built the Second Presbyterian Church on the corner of Prince and St. Asaph Streets in 1822.

During Dr. Harrison's ministry, the original meeting house was destroyed by a fire that was caused by a very destructive electric storm on Sunday, 26 July 1835. The storm also destroyed the old bell whose musical notes had inspired many to respond to its call over the years.

The church was rebuilt in 1836, with alterations to the original design that involved the unfortunate destruction of many graves. The construction of a bell tower on the west end in 1843 and the addition of the eastern end in 1853 are the most significant of the many structural changes.

The church's original size of approximately sixty feet by fifty feet is the same as Christ Church, built in 1767 a few blocks to the northwest, at North Washington and Cameron Streets. The walls of The Meeting House are two feet thick. The present roof trusses date back to 1837, when the church was restored to service after the fire. The 1843 tower measures nearly sixteen feet (north and south) and fourteen feet (east and west). The present organ was installed in 1849. The old manse, or parsonage, now called the Flounder House, was built in 1787 and is still in use.

A child's memory, dating several years before the Civil War, supplies some interesting items concerning the old church:

It was a long way from most of our homes, for the town had grown in another direction, but the ringing of the bell generally found us on the way to Sunday School, where the classes were arranged according to age and sex in the galleries of the church—girls on the north side and boys on the south. It was my fortune to be in the class of Miss Lizzie McNight. Miss McNight taught us the [Isaac] Watt's Child's Catechism.

*The Meeting House in the present. Its yard contains a tomb of an
unknown soldier of the American Revolution, which was made a patriotic
shrine.*

After a ministry that spanned forty-five years, Dr. Harrison passed away in February 1862. He was seventy-three
years old. His venerable form and dignified presence were
well remembered by many who had received from him the
baptismal rite. During the last year of his life he was unable
to perform the ceremony of matrimony and, in many instances, to bury those of his congregation who were interred outside the city limits at Ivy Hill Cemetery. His mortal remains
rest in the Presbyterian Cemetery, among many of those
departed friends who had known, love, and revered him.

After Dr. Harrison's death, the members of the congrega-
tion gradually scattered to other churches. During the Civil
War, both Union and Confederate armies used The Meeting
House as a hospital.

At the close of the Civil War, few members of the old congregation remained. The church continued under the Northern Assembly with ministers from that section. The Second

Presbyterian Church, which belonged to the Southern Assembly, became more popular. Finally, as it seemed impossible for the little congregation on Fairfax Street to support a minister, the church closed its doors in 1886.

The old churchyard, located between the church and the parsonage, was used as a burial ground from the time the deed to the property was granted, as you can see from a stone erected to the memory of Archibald Thomson, who died 15 July 1772.* The burial ground also contains a tomb of the unknown soldier of the American Revolution, "known only to God," who died in 1821; his grave was made a patriotic shrine in 1929 by several organizations. His remains were discovered in the uniform of the Continental Army.

The present church, as rebuilt in 1836, covers the graves of a considerable number of people. Among them: Dr. Muir; Capt. John Harper and his son, Edward Harper; and other members of the Harper family. When the mural tablet was placed on the wall of the restored church, it testified that Dr. Muir was buried under the pulpit, which formerly had that position. His table gravestone was then removed to the northwest corner of the lot beside the tombs of his wife and children. It is here that the last interment was made—that of Miss Mary Muir, who died about 1862.

Numerous Scots are buried in the graveyard, including Hepburns, Logans, Lindsays, Douglases, Hunters, Muirs, Ramsays, Carlyles, Alisons, Balfours, Cranstons, Kincaids, and Kennedys. There are also several Germans, such as the Bogues, Brocchuses, and Ludwigs, and even the Swiss Cazenoves. The character of the inscriptions on their headstones is, as a rule, dignified and expressive of a hope of a blessed immortality.

A few inscriptions show the tendency to play upon words, as was customary in those days. The most unique example of this is found on the stone of the Reverend Dr. James Muir's young child, who died in 1791, shortly after a visit to her mother's family in Bermuda. The inscription reads:

> *Elizabeth Muir, infant daughter of Rev. James Muir—*
> *Sleep, sweet babe,*
> *Summer Isles she saw, o'er the ocean she flew,*
> *But Columbia brought her to slumber here.*

A memorial tablet on the north wall, which survived the fire of 1835, still records the worth of Dr. Muir, a beloved pastor, while another on the south wall was placed there by some surviving members of the old congregation to the memory of the Reverend Dr. Elias Harrison and his faithful associate, Robert Bell, who served the old church for more than fifty years and entered into eternal rest on 16 July 1885.

Today, the old church stands as a monument to the many departed citizens of Alexandria who reared and maintained it for so many years—citizens whose worth effected so much for the prosperity of Alexandria.

---

* Although the deed for the church property wasn't granted until 1773, thirty-two members received recognition as an organized church in 1772.

POHICK CHURCH
TRURO PARISH
FAIRFAX COUNTY

Erected: 1769-1774

Denomination: Anglican

Location: South side of Route 1, near Lorton and Mount Vernon

Religious Services: Sundays, September to May, Holy Eucharist at 7:45 A.M.
(Rite I traditional), 9:00 A.M. (Rite II contemporary), and 11:15 A.M. (Rite I
and II alternating)
Sundays, June to August, Holy Eucharist at 8:00 A.M. (Rite I traditional) and
10:00 A.M. (Rite II contemporary)
Wednesdays, Holy Eucharist and Laying on of Hands at 7:30 P.M.

Open daily 9:00 P.M. to 4:30 P.M.

George Washington attended Pohick Church, pictured here in 1930, and served the vestry of Truro Parish.

Pohick Church is not only one of the most impressive colonial churches in Virginia, but it stands out as one of the nation's greatest historic landmarks. It shares the honor with Christ Church, Alexandria, of being intimately associated with the religious life and worship of George Washington. It was also the parish church of another notable figure of the American Revolution: George Mason of Gunston Hall, author of the Virginia Declaration of Rights.

Fortunately for the history of Truro Parish, in which Pohick Church is located, the late Rev. Dr. Philip Slaughter, historiographer of the Diocese of Virginia, recovered the old parish's vestry book in 1887 from someone living in the northern part of the country, for a fee of twenty dollars. The book had been lost to the public eye for so long that even Bishop William Meade said he could "hear no tidings" of it and was constrained to construct his sketch of the parish from such facts and traditions as he could gather from other sources and from his own rich personal knowledge.

After the recovery of the vestry book, it was possible for the first time to authenticate the parish's history by its own records, which are continuous from 1732 to 1785, when the civil functions of the vestries were devolved by law upon the Overseers of the Poor.* The book also contains a record of the proceedings of the Overseers of the Poor from 1787 to 1802; this record includes the names of many people who served on the vestry of the church.

The first church building stood on the south side of Pohick Creek, several miles from Gunston Hall. It was a wood-frame building, built around 1700, most likely as a chapel or as the upper church of Overwharton Parish.** The word "Pohick" is related to the Dogue Indian word for hickory.

The vestry appointed the Reverend Charles Green, M.D., as the first regular rector of Truro Parish on 13 August 1737. A few months later, on 3 October, the vestry appropriated 16,729 pounds of tobacco for Dr. Green's salary. From 1760 to 1765, Dr. Green was the only Episcopal minister in Fairfax County. He ministered alternately at three churches, situated at a distance of about nine, ten, and eighteen miles, respectively, from Mount Vernon, George Washington's home. This schedule allowed Dr. Green to preach seventeen or eighteen times a year at Pohick Church.

On 14 January 1767, it was ordered that the Reverend Lee Massey—a man of "moral character and unexceptionable life and conversation"—be received in the parish as minister. He was allowed the annual sum of four thousand pounds of tobacco in lieu of a glebe until one was purchased.

An agreement was made between the vestry of Truro Parish and Daniel French of Fairfax to build a larger church on 7 April 1769.*** The present church measures sixty-six feet by forty-five feet, with walls that are two feet thick, as specified in this building agreement. The plans also called for the altar piece to be twenty feet high and fifteen feet wide and designed with wainscot after the Ionic order. In addition, the Apostles' Creed, the Lord's Prayer, and the Ten Commandments were to be neatly painted on the altar piece in black letters. The floor of the communion place was to be raised twenty inches higher than the floor of the house, and the communion table of black walnut was to be built of a proper size. In exchange for building the new Pohick Church, the vestry agreed to pay Daniel French the sum of 875 pounds, which was the currency used in colonial Virginia.

There were some differences of opinion between two friends over the selection of the site for the second church. George Mason felt that the church should be built at the site of the old church, near his home of Gunston Hall, because of the burials there, but this location was not convenient to all the members of the parish. After George Washington made a survey of the parish, mapping out the residences of each member of the congregation, the vestry chose the present site as being the most convenient. In addition to Mason and Washington, other members of the building committee included Edward Payne, Daniel McCarthy, and George William Fairfax. The new church was completed in 1774, five years after it was begun.

At its meeting on 5 June 1772, the vestry ordered that several pews be sold for the benefit of the parish. They were purchased by the following people at the following prices: Pews 3 and 4 to George Washington for fourteen pounds, eleven shillings, and eight pence each. Pew 5 to Thomas Withers Coffer for fourteen pounds, thirteen shillings. Pew 13 to Martin Cockburn for fifteen pounds, ten shillings. Pew 14, next to the rector's pew, to Daniel McCarthy for fifteen pounds, ten shillings. Pew 21, next to the communion table, to George William Fairfax for sixteen pounds. Pews 22 and 23 to Alexander Henderson for twenty-six pounds, ten shillings total. Pew 28, one of the center pews, also to George Washington for an additional sixteen pounds. Pew 29, another center pew, to Lund Washington for thirteen pounds, ten shillings. Pew 31, also in the center, to Harrison Manley for fifteen pounds, ten shillings. In addition to these sales, the vestry ordered that Pew 15, adjoining the north wall of the church and next to the pulpit, be reserved for the parish rector.****

General Washington resigned from the vestry of Truro Parish in 1782, and shortly afterwards the Reverend Lee Massey ceased to conduct services there, owing he said, to physical disability. 25 April 1785 seems to mark the date that Washington left Pohick Church to begin his habitual attendance at Christ Church, Alexandria. (It is interesting to note that while George Washington was a parishioner at Pohick Church, he frequently stood as a sponsor at the baptism of infants.)

After the Disestablishment, services at Pohick were only occasionally held until 1836. Methodists are said to have used the church during that time. The Parson Mason Locke Weems, who told so many stories about Washington, including the legend about the hatchet and the cherry tree, conducted services for a time at Pohick.

During the War Between the States, Pohick Church did not escape the destruction of Union troops. They used the interior of the building as a stable and the exterior for target practice. They also stripped the interior, removing the altarpiece, pulpit, canopy, and other items—everything except for the cornice—for souvenirs.

Services resumed in 1874, and a major restoration of its colonial interior began in 1890, with smaller restoration projects continuing to this day. The large font located in the cross aisle is said to have come from the first Pohick Church. The brass chandeliers allegedly were obtained from an eighteenth-century French church.

Many unmarked graves are located at Pohick Church, some of them from the colonial period. In 1925, the vice-regent of the Mount Vernon Ladies Association of the Union for Connecticut sponsored the erection of a commemorative stone in a wall at the southwest corner of the churchyard that reads: "To the unknown dead of Pohick Church." This monument attracts reverent interest.

Pohick Church today has an active congregation of 882 baptized members.

* The Overseers of the Poor succeeded the parish vestry in the administration of relief to the poor in the county. In some instances the vestry would turn over civil functions to the Overseers, such as the sale of parish glebe lands confiscated under the Act of 1802, and the invested proceeds were partly appropriated to the construction of new county buildings.

** Overwharton Parish (created in 1689 or earlier) was first known as the Upper Parish. It was known from 1664 to 1702 as Stafford Parish, and, from 1702 to the present, it has been called Overwharton Parish (see the chapter on Aquia Church). It has been written that there have been only two Pohick Churches, but some believe that the present building is the third church. If there were three churches, the second building became part of Hamilton Parish in 1730 and of Truro Parish in 1732.

*** At least six names are associated with the construction of Pohick Church, which lasted from 1769 to 1774. These names include George Washington, George Mason, William Fairfax, Daniel McCarthy, Edward Payne, and Daniel French of Rose Hill who was the builder. William Copein

who also worked at Aquia Church was the mason. At Christ Church in Alexandria, where Washington served on the vestry, building there had begun two years before. The design for that building, drawn by James Wren, evidently was used by Washington as the plan that he drafted for Pohick Church.

**** One historical footnote: the new Christ Church in Alexandria was completed about the same time as the second Pohick Church. George Washington also bought Pew 5 in Christ Church for thirty-six pounds, ten shillings, on the day after that church was turned over to the vestry by the builders. This pew was later used by Gen. Robert E. Lee and continues to attract many visitors to Christ Church.

Pohick Church survived being raided for souvenirs and being used for target practice by Union soldiers during the Civil War.

LITTLE FORK CHURCH

CULPEPER COUNTY

Erected: 1776

Denomination: Anglican

Location: Off Route 29, 8 miles north of Culpeper, Virginia. Church sits at the junction of Route 624 and 726.

Religious Services: Sundays, Morning Prayer at 8:00 A.M.; Holy Eucharist at 9:30 A.M.

This present brick structure replaced the original Little Fork Church in 1776.

THIS COLONIAL CHURCH IN CULPEPER COUNTY WAS SO named because it is located near the fork of the Rappahannock and Hazel Rivers. At one time, there was another colonial church, built near the fork of the Rappahannock and Rapidan Rivers, called the Great Fork Church, but the Little Fork is the only colonial church in the entire area to have survived. The present structure was erected in 1776.

Little Fork Church is located in St. Mark's Parish, which was originally in Spotsylvania and part of St. George's Parish. On 21 May 1730, the vestry book for St. Mark's listed twelve able and discreet persons as vestrymen: Goodrich Lightfoot, Henry Field, Francis Huntley, William Peyton, James Barber (now Barbour), Robert Slaughter, John Finlason, Francis Slaughter, Thomas Staunton, Benjamin Cave, Robert Green, and Samuel Ball. Robert and Francis Slaughter were the first church wardens.

Three houses of worship are recognized as being in use before the division of the parish: a church at Germanna and two chapels. At the March 1731 vestry meeting, the church at Germanna was ordered to be repaired and the roof tarred, while the chapels, Little Fork Chapel and the Mountain Chapel, were ordered to be swept and kept clean.

In 1732, the vestry built a new Mountain Chapel at the two springs on the Germanna Road at a cost of thirty-six thousand weight of tobacco. In 1735, a chapel was ordered between Shaw's Mountain and the Devil's Run. In 1743, an addition of twenty-four feet was ordered at the Little Fork Church.

In 1750, a chapel was ordered to be built at the Little Fork, where an old chapel had once stood. In 1752, the site of this new chapel was changed to a spot of land named Freeman's old field, and it was to be called a church rather than a chapel. In 1760, an addition measuring thirty-two feet by twenty-two feet was ordered to be built onto the Little Fork Church. In 1771, another addition of the same dimensions was ordered for the church. A year later, an eight-room glebe house measuring forty-eight feet by thirty-two feet was ordered at the cost of 35,900 weight of tobacco.

This initial Little Fork Church was replaced in 1776 by the present brick structure, which was built in late Georgian style. With its hipped roof, continuous cornice, and six arched windows on a single level on the south side, the design is very similar to that of Lamb's Creek Church in King William County. The church is somewhat long, measuring more than eighty-three feet by thirty-three feet in diameter, with windows more than eight feet in height. Like two other colonial churches in Virginia—Falls Church and Pohick Church—the Little Fork Church was built with south doorways that are used as the principal entrance.

During the War Between the States, the Little Fork Church was used by the Federal troops as a stable for their mounts. The church was repaired in 1871. In 1892, the Methodists sued unsuccessfully for possession of the building. Their use of the name "Oak Shade" for Little Fork is unwarranted and should be disallowed as having neither historical precedent nor legal basis. Between 1892 and 1894, more repairs were made to the Little Fork Church. The Methodists continued to borrow and use the church until they purchased a more modern building at Rixeyville some time ago.

According to Bishop William Meade, from 1740 until 1772, the rector of St. Mark's Parish was the Reverend John Thompson. He was a native of Scotland who had received a degree at the University of Edinburgh and had received his priest's orders from the bishop of St. David's in the Chapel of St. James in the palace royal of St. James of Westminster. He came to St. Mark's Parish in 1740 at the recommendation of Sir William Gooch, governor of Virginia.

In that year, former Governor Spotswood died. Two years later, Lady Spotswood, his widow, who lived in the mansion at Germanna, married the Reverend John Thompson. There was much opposition to this marriage, and an entire reconciliation of all parties was not effected until many years later, by the intervention of the Reverend Robert Rose, the friend and executor of Governor Spotswood. Mr. Thompson had two children by this marriage: Ann Thompson, who was born at Germanna in 1744 and who married Francis Thornton of Fall Hill, near Fredericksburg, and a son, William Thompson.

Soon after the resuscitation of the Church of Virginia, a new church called St. Stephen's, at Culpeper Courthouse, was established within the bounds of St. Mark's Parish. For many years, Little Fork Church was served by the rector of St. Stephen's Episcopal Church.

Restoration of Little Fork Church began in 1976, and the church was rededicated on 21 October 1979. The congregation at Little Fork has now formed its own independent church within the Diocese of Virginia and is served by its own priest.

Although there are no graves in the well-maintained churchyard, the grounds contain a marble monument that was erected in 1904 to the memory of the Little Fork Rangers, Company D of the Fourth Virginia Cavalry.

THE OLD CHAPEL
CLARKE COUNTY

Erected: 1791

Denomination: Anglican

Location: 3 miles south of Berryville at the intersection of Virginia Route 255 and U.S. Route 340

Religious Services: Second Sunday in September and Easter Sunday

The Old Chapel, "the oldest Episcopal Church west of the Blue Ridge," in 1910.

CUNNINGHAM CHAPEL PARISH, ESTABLISHED IN 1866, was named for one of the earliest houses of worship in the Shenandoah Valley. Once a part of Frederick County, created in 1738, the parish was comprised of the congregation of Christ Church at Millwood in Clarke County, which was transferred from Frederick Parish. This chapel, located within the boundaries of the parish, is first named in a 1752 court order, which directs the building of a road from "the Chapel at James Cunningham's to the Chapel at Robert McCoy's [McKay's] Spring." The court records further show that James Cunningham was licensed to keep a tavern at his home on a hill just north of the chapel.

Among the first things the vestry of Frederick did after its reorganization in 1787 was to adopt measures for the building of a stone chapel. The stone chapel was intended to replace the original Cunningham Chapel, which had failed through the disagreement of the people and vestry just before the Revolution.

Two acres of ground, previously owned by Col. Nathaniel Burwell, was given by Col. Hugh Nelson.* Construction of the chapel began in 1790, and it was completed the following year. A plaque at the church reads, "Old Chapel— Dedicated to the Memory of Colonel Nathaniel Burwell of Carter Hall, Clarke County, Virginia, who gave this site 1789 for the 'Old Chapel' and adjoining burying ground. Born at 'Carter's Grove,' near Williamsburg, Virginia. Born April 15, 1750, and died at Carter's Hall on March 29, 1814."

Eventually, this chapel grew too small for its increasing congregation, and its location was no longer convenient for many members of the church. In 1834, a decision was made to build another larger church in a more central location. The new church, called Christ Church, was to be built in the village of Millwood, three miles from the chapel, on land opposite the entrance to Carter Hall (the mansion built by Nathaniel Burwell in the 1790s). Once Christ Church was built, the "Old Chapel" would have secondary status to the new church.

However, such was the attachment of many people to The Old Chapel that funds for Christ Church could not be obtained, except on condition that services would be held on alternating Sundays at the chapel. As the years passed by, however, services at The Old Chapel became less frequent, until they were reduced to an annual pilgrimage on some summer Sabbath, plus the occasional service held for servants and the funerals that were held for tenants.

The first clergyman to conduct services at The Old Chapel was the Reverend Alexander Balmaine, who had been a chaplain in the Army during the Revolution. During the last years of his life, he was assisted by the Reverend William Meade, who would later become the third bishop of Virginia in 1841.

Meade was a native of White Post, a village located about six miles from The Old Chapel. (Meade Memorial Church, located in White Post, is named in his honor.) He served as rector of The Old Chapel for twenty-five years preceding the construction of Christ Church at Millwood. He is perhaps best known as the author of the book *Old Churches, Ministers, and Families of Virginia.*

On one occasion in the early 1800s, the Reverend Mason Parson Locke Weems, who originated the fable of George Washington and the cherry tree, preached from the wooden-canopied pulpit of The Old Chapel.

Among those buried at the well-maintained Old Chapel cemetery is Edmund Randolph (1753-1813), a distinguished lawyer who served as aide-de-camp to Gen. George Washington during the Revolutionary War and then later became governor of Virginia. Randolph was educated at William and Mary College in Williamsburg soon after Thomas Jefferson, Gov. John Page, and other notable Virginians. He later joined his uncle Peyton Randolph, Governor Page, Judge Edmund Pendleton, and others in defending the church and religion.** Randolph was often employed by church vestries as their counsel. The later days of Randolph's life were spent mostly at the home of his son-in-law, Bennett Taylor of Frederick County. He died at Carter Hall, the home of Colonel Burwell.

The cemetery record lists only four eighteenth-century graves. One belongs to Winnifred Waller Calmes, who died 6 October 1751, the wife of Maj. Marquis Guillame de Calmes II, a member of the first Frederick Parish vestry. Two others belong to children of Col. Nathaniel Burwell and his wife, Lucy: Susanna Grymes Burwell, who died on 19 October 1793, and Mann Page Burwell, who died on 5 August 1794. The fourth belongs to Maria Holker, who died on 3 June 1794; she was the daughter of John Holker, French consul general to the United States during the Revolutionary War.

Also buried at the cemetery is Mary Nelson Meade, wife of the Right Reverend William Meade, third bishop of Virginia. She was born in 1792 to Philip and Sarah Burwell Nelson of "Long Branch." She married in 1812 and died only five years later on 3 July 1817. Her first cousin Thomasia Nelson became Bishop Meade's second wife.

During the Civil War, in September 1864, Federal troops tore down a portion of the stone wall around the church and

The Old Chapel today holds a lot of memories and the affection of past parishioners.

ran a road through the cemetery.

The burial ground also holds the remains of eighteen Confederate soldiers. Memorial services for these soldiers have been held at the cemetery every summer since 1866. In addition, the cemetery serves as the final resting place of several slaves.

According to the accounts of adults who had attended services as children, The Old Chapel was intolerably cold during the winter, and the good Bishop Meade was not unwilling that people should "endure hardness" as a good discipline.

Other childhood recollections included the melancholy swing of the old c-spring carriages, as they rolled through the mud, nearly axle deep, while saintly mothers sang the good old hymns and psalms of the collection of that day. One favorite hymn was "Children of the Heavenly King, as We Journey Let Us Sing."

There were also fond memories about Robin, the courteous old black sexton, who had a little stand by the right-hand side of the south door as you entered. There, he kept a pail of cool water from the chapel spring and a nice clean gourd, for the refreshment of those who had come many miles to church.

Inside The Old Chapel today, the pulpit and sounding board, as well as the high-back pews remain in excellent condition. A lady from one of the earlier congregations once said that "the large middle pew held the magnates of the land." She refers to the benches that run across the house from the east to the west doors.

The first Frederick Parish vestry, elected in 1744, was comprised of Samuel Earle, James Wood, Thomas Ruther-ford, Morgan Morgan, Marquis Calmes, Jacob Hite, John Hardin, and Andrew Campbell. The vestry elected after the Revolutionary War, in 1787, included John Woodcock, John Peyton, Thomas Byrd, Isaac Hite Jr., Nathan-iel Burwell, Warner Washington Jr., John Page, Gen. Thomas Parker, Matthew Page, Philip Nelson, Robert Carter Burwell, Fairfax Washington, Henry St. John Tucker, Alfred Powell, George Norris, Philip Burwell, Nathaniel Burwell Jr., Obed Waite, Dabney Carr, Joseph Baldwin, Richard Briarly, Daniel Lee, William B. Page, John W. Page, Strother Jones, Col. R. K. Meade, George F. Norton, Edward Smith, John Thruston, Raleigh Colston, Girard Briscoe, and Maj. Thomas Massey.

Every year on the second Sunday in September, a morning prayer service is held at The Old Chapel and, occasionally, The Old Chapel is used for weddings and funeral services.

Both the chapel and the cemetery are maintained by the Trustees of the Burwell Cemetery, Inc., in Boyce, Virginia. There is also a caretaker who resides on the grounds behind the cemetery.

* Colonels Burwell and Nelson were military officers, landowners, and very active in the Episcopal Church in Frederick County. A Burwell burial ground is still maintained near the site of Old Chapel.

** The act of the General Assembly was passed in 1788 authorizing the appointment of trustees to hold title to the glebes, churches, et cetera, for the use of the Protestant Episcopal Church. From 1788 to 1799 the attack upon the right of the Episcopal Church to hold title to its property continued; petition after petition flooded the Assembly until, wearied of the strife and desirous of putting an end to the dissension, the Assembly, on 22 January 1799, repealed every law that in any way favored the Protestant Episcopal Church in Virginia—as the former established church of Virginia was called—totally disestablishing it.

THE SACRED VESSELS

THE SACRED VESSELS OF JAMESTOWN CHURCH

SEVERAL OF THE SACRED VESSELS OF JAMESTOWN ARE STILL preserved. The large London chalice and matching paten were given to the Jamestown Church by Francis Moryson in 1661. Moryson was at that time acting governor of the colony. Each piece bears the inscription "Mixe not holy things with profane." The maker of this service, whose mark was "T. W.," was also the maker of a celebrated cup owned by the Blacksmiths' Company, London, 1655, and subsequently purchased for 378 pounds.

Bruton Parish Church in Williamsburg, Virginia, owns several pieces of Jamestown silver. The large London paten of 1691 and 1692 is engraved with the arms of Governor Andros of Virginia. According to Bruton Parish vestry records from 1694, "His excellency Sir Edmund Andros, Knight, was pleased to give Bruton Parish a large silver server." It was used to serve the Eucharistic bread. The alms basin of 1739 and 1740, by Thomas Farren of London, is also from the Jamestown Church. This was given to Bruton Parish Church in 1758 after the Jamestown Church fell into disuse and abandoned.

Above: The communion service used in the old church at Jamestown. It is now kept Bruton Parish Church in Williamsburg, where it is displayed during Garden Week and used only on special occasions.

Left: The sacred vessels of Jamestown (1661). The inscriptions read, "For the use of James City Parish Church," and "Mixe not holy things with profane." Photographed by Hans E. Lorenz, courtesy of Colonial Williamsburg.

Opposite top: The sacred vessels of St. Mary's Church are the second oldest in the country. This set is in the possession of St. John's Church in Hampton and is still used.

Opposite bottom: Here the silver is photographed in 1915 with the prayer book that was used at the first communion service in America (1607).

THE SACRED VESSELS OF ST. MARY'S CHURCH
SMITH'S HUNDRED (1618-1619)

S MITH'S HUNDRED IS USUALLY CONSIDERED TO HAVE BEEN founded in Charles City County, the society's lands including 100,000 acres between Weyanoke and the mouth of the Chickahominy River, but the location recorded for the first settlement—and hence, almost certainly, for the church—was at Dancing Point, just west of the Chickahominy, in a section included in James City County for a century afterward. Smith's Hundred was named after Sir Thomas Smith, treasurer of the Virginia Company. The name was changed to "Southampton Hundred" in 1620 in honor of the earl of Southampton, Shakespeare's patron and a prominent patron of the colony as well. The church at Smith's Hundred, probably a simple wooden structure, was founded by Mrs. Mary Robinson of London, England, whose will dated 23 February 1617 to 1618 gave two hundred pounds "toward the helpe of the poor people in Virginia, towardes the building of a church and redceinge them to the knowledge of God's word."

The church was endowed especially with the hope of converting the Indians, but the settlement was almost completely destroyed by them in the great massacre of 1622. The settlement was then abandoned and the surviving colonists transferred to a new site, while the silver vessels were given to Sir George Yeardley, commander of the Hundred, and later governor of the colony, and he in turn took them to Jamestown. Following his death, the set was delivered to the court at James City in 1628 by his widow and later given to the parish church of Elizabeth City on the Southampton River, also named for the earl of Southampton.

The silver communion vessels remain in the possession of St. John's Church in Hampton, Virginia, and are used frequently during Lent and Advent seasons, as well as for weddings and confirmations by the bishop.

The only other English communion set in the United States that is older than these are a chalice and paten made in London in 1611 and owned by St. Peter's Church in Perth Amboy, New Jersey. St. Peter's Church was not founded until 1698 to 1699, and its communion silver was imported at that time, eighty years after the St. Mary's silver came to America.

THE RIGHT REVEREND WILLIAM MEADE, D.D. (1789-1862)

THIRD BISHOP OF VIRGINIA (1841-1864)

BISHOP MEADE HAS BEEN CALLED A VIRGINIAN OF Virginians. His immigrant ancestor was Andrew Meade of County Kerry, Ireland, who came to America near the end of the seventeenth century. Andrew's son, David Meade, married Susanna Everard, daughter of Sir Richard Everard, governor of North Carolina, and Susanna, his wife, who was a daughter of Richard Kidder Bishop of Bath and Wells. Seven children resulted from this marriage and the fourth was Richard Kidder Meade, who first married Jane Randolph of Curles, who died soon after, and second, Mary, daughter of Benjamin and Bettie (Fitzhugh) Grymes. Their fifth child was William Meade, born 11 November 1789 in what is now Clarke County, Virginia.

Col. Richard Meade, the Bishop's father, was educated in England. During the Revolutionary War, he attained the rank of colonel on the staff of Gen. George Washington, whose friendship he enjoyed until the death of the general.

Bishop Meade entered Princeton College at the young age of seventeen. He graduated two years later with high honors. His devotion to the sacred ministry had already been formed. He pursued his theological studies under the guidance of Rev. Walter Addison of Maryland, whose parish was nearly opposite Alexandria. Later he read divinity at Princeton as a graduate student.

Early on a Sunday morning, 24 February 1811, Meade was ordained deacon at Bruton Parish Church in Williamsburg, Virginia, by Bishop James Madison, the first bishop of Virginia. This was the last ordination performed by Madison and the only time he and Meade ever met except when, as a very small child, Meade was confirmed by Madison in Winchester. This ordination was one of the turning points in the history of the Church in Virginia. He was born to leadership. He had remarkable power as a preacher and possessed wonderful influence over others while possessing great control of himself. His confirmation and farewell addresses were simple yet elegant. He was almost ascetic in his own manner of life, as he had little patience with self-indulgence, moral inconsistency, and religious insincerity. In genius, wisdom, and character, he stood in the first rank. Men trusted Bishop Meade, and he led them to high and righteous ends. It has been said

that Bishop Moore was an Ezra, but Bishop Meade was the Nehemiah of the Restoration, who built walls and planted the towers of our Jerusalem on sure foundations. The degree of Doctor of Divinity was conferred upon Bishop Meade in 1827 by the College of William and Mary. His early ministry was devoted to affording religious instruction to the slave population and the problems presented by slavery pressed heavily upon his mind.

He will always be remembered as an author. His two-volume *Old Churches, Ministers, and Families of Virginia* is a valuable contribution to the history of Virginia.

The highest testimony of his character lay in the affection of his people throughout his Diocese. He set an example for

Opposite page: William Meade, D.D., the third bishop of Virginia, 1841-1862.

Above: An 1857 illustration by Bishop Meade of Aquia Church in Stafford County. The bishop sketched many of the colonial churches.

Left: The church ruins at Jamestown.

Below: St. Luke's, The Old Brick Church, in Isle of Wight County.

Above: Bruton Parish Church in Colonial Williamsburg.

Below: Christ Church in Lancaster County.

other bishops to follow. By the testimony of many who came under his personal influence, he was one of the greatest characters in our history. Bishop Thomas Atkinson of North Carolina, who represented almost an opposite type of character and of churchmanship, never spoke of Bishop Meade without the strongest expressions of admiration and reverence. Bishop Atkinson said he had never met a man who was so devoted to truth and duty, in devotion to his Maker and his Redeemer.

The Reverend Dr. Churchill J. Gibson gives us the following reminiscence of his last illness. "It was my privilege to stand at his bedside until he became unconscious, and to witness his last interview with Gen. Robert E. Lee." Visitors had been forbidden by the doctors, but when the General was announced as having called, the Bishop roused himself, and said,

> "I must see him for a few minutes." The General was brought in by Bishop Johns and, grasping warmly the extended hand, he said, "Bishop, how do you feel?" "I am almost gone, but I wanted to see you once more..."
>
> He then made inquiries about the members of his family, Mrs. Lee by name, the daughter of his

much-loved cousin of Arlington, and put several earnest, eager questions about public affairs and the state of the army. He then said, "God bless you! God bless you, Robert, and fit you for your high and responsible position. I can't call you General, I have heard your catechism so often." "Yes, Bishop," said the General, as he stooped over him and pressed his hand tenderly (and I think I saw a tear drop). Again the dying Bishop shook his hand warmly and said, "Heaven bless you! Heaven bless you and give you wisdom for your important and arduous duties." The General then withdrew.

Bishop Meade died on 14 March 1862. He was taken away in love and mercy that his eyes might not see the desolations of his Diocese and the sufferings of the people whom he so dearly loved.

Bishop Meade has been called the "Founder of the Theological Seminary of Virginia," and this title is inscribed on his tomb. He is buried at the "Little God's Acre," Seminar Hill, in Alexandra, Virginia.

After the Civil War, Rev. Joseph Ravenscroft Jones, rector of Cunningham Parish, collected enough money to build the Bishop Meade Memorial Church at White Post in Clarke County, Virginia. The cornerstone was laid in 1872. On a tablet in the church, the following inscription is found:

*Founder of this Church and
its faithful and beloved
pastor for 27 years*

The church stands today as a tribute to this wonderful man, and my intensive study of Bishop Meade has been an inspiration to my own ministry for Christ.

Above: Bishop Meade is buried at Seminary Hill Cemetery at the Protestant Episcopal Theological Seminary in Alexandria, Virginia

Below: Wren Chapel, the College of William and Mary, in Williamsburg.

THE CHRISTIAN PHILOSOPHY OF PATRICK HENRY

CERTAINLY ANY STUDY OF REVOLUTIONARY AMERICA would not be complete without an analysis of the life and religious beliefs of Patrick Henry (1736-99). He is remembered most for his words, "Give me liberty, or give me death," which were spoken in 1775 before the Virginia Provincial Convention, held at St. John's Episcopal Church in Richmond, Virginia.

Henry was born on 29 May 1736 in Hanover, Virginia. He attended public school only briefly, but was taught by his father, who had a good education. The religious convictions of Patrick Henry had extraordinary depth. Henry's guiding principle, in both his political and private life, was his idea of what course of action would best fulfill his Christian obligations. When he was a young man, he once said of the Bible, "This book is worth all the books that ever were printed." In Henry's opinion, the real test of an individual's life was in whether or not the person had conducted himself in accordance with God's plan for the individual's life. Patrick Henry once stated, "I think religion of infinitely higher importance than politics," and therefore his Christian reputation and strong religious beliefs greatly influenced his political decisions.

Henry's biographers agree that he was basically a man devoted to family life. Had he not been deeply religious, his family correspondence surely would have revealed the fact. This was not the case, however, for his letters to his family demonstrate a steady and fervent Christian feeling. A typical example of this can be found in a letter Henry wrote to his sister in Kentucky upon receiving news of her husband's death—a cruel death at the hands of an Indian raiding party:

> We cannot see the reason of these dispensations now, but we may be assured they are directed by wisdom and mercy. This is one of the occasions that calls your and my attention back to the many precious lessons of piety given us by our honored parents, whose lives were indeed a constant lesson and worthy of imitation. This is one of the trying scenes, in which the Christian is eminently superior to all others and finds a refuge that no misfortunes can take away...Perhaps I

may never see you in this world—oh, may we meet in that heaven to which the merits of Jesus will carry those who love and serve him.

In writing to his daughter shortly before her marriage, Henry advised her to study outstanding sermons of the day because "a woman devoid of rational ideas of religion has no security for her virtues; it is sacrificed to her passions, whose voice, not that of God, is her only governing principle." Nothing in his family correspondence indicated that religion was anything less than of primary concern.

There are many illustrations of Henry's devotion to the Christian life in his public as well as in his private career. George Morgan insists that no public record can be found of an instance wherein Henry cursed or swore. This biographer also asserts that Henry, who did not have a reputation for liberality in financial matters, paid for the printing of and circulated at his own expense copies of Joseph Butler's *Analogy of Christianity* and Soame Jenyn's *Internal Evidence of Christ*. The first lawsuit that Henry argued before the House of Burgesses involved, fittingly enough, an attempt to unseat a representative who had allegedly exerted undue influence upon the electorate by expenditure of enormous sums on campaign liquors.

Additional evidence of Patrick Henry's Christian steadfastness was indicated by the fact that almost all of his speeches demonstrated the overwhelming influence of a vigorous Christian spirit. Allusions to the Scriptures abounded throughout. In speaking, for example, of the tendency of the aristocracy to retain a sentimental attachment for the British, he declared, "The flesh pots of Egypt are still savory to degenerate palates." On many occasions during the Revolutionary War, he reminded the hard-pressed Virginia militia that they should pray for divine intervention and that "the same God whose power divided the Red Sea for the deliverance of Israel, still reigned in all of his glory, unchanged and unchangeable..." In scarcely a single one of his public speeches did Patrick Henry fail to reaffirm his faith in an omnipotent and ever-accessible God. At the Constitutional Ratification Convention of Virginia in Richmond, he stated, "I see beings of a higher order anxious concerning our deci-

sion!" In the great bulk of his speeches to the common people, Henry was ever prodding—ever goading—the deep
faith that lay beneath the breast of the American frontiers-
man. This evidently was the way in which to strike a re-
sponsive chord in the masses of colonial America, for it was
the masses, not the aristocracy, who made Patrick Henry the
leader of colonial Virginia.

Often bitter differences of opinions will occur among
equally devout Christians as to just what course of action
God has outlined for a nation or for a people. In determining with any precision the religious viewpoint of a person
and in understanding that person's personal philosophy, one
would find helpful an understanding of the influence that
various divergent doctrines have had on the individual.

Patrick Henry was christened and remained throughout
his life a member of the Episcopal church. His father, John
Henry, and uncle, Rev. Patrick Henry, both Episcopalians,
had great influence on Henry. His uncle was, in fact, a lead-

*Scotchtown was Patrick Henry's home during his most active years in
the American Revolution. Scotchtown was built circa 1719 by Charles
Chiswell of Williamsburg. It is among the oldest surviving plantation
houses in Virginia. Patrick Henry, his first wife Sarah Shelton, and their
six children were living at Scotchtown by April 1771. From Scothtown he
traveled to the First Continental Congress in Philadelphia in 1774. Also
from here he rode to St. John's Church in Richmond where he delivered
his famous "Liberty or Death" speech at the Second Virginia Convention
on 23 March 1775.*

ing member of the Anglican clergy in Virginia. Henry admitted the great influence of this man on his thinking, stating that his uncle taught him

> to be true and just in all my dealings. To bear no malice nor hatred in my heart. To keep my hands from plucking and stealing; not to covet other men's goods, but to learn and labor truly to get my own living in that state of life into which it shall please God to call me.

Although Henry became a firm opponent of the establishment of the Church in Virginia, the fact that he remained a member demonstrates that he must have shared many of its beliefs, at least in regard to his own personal life.* A man of Patrick Henry's religious fervor would certainly not have remained in a church with which he could find no common ground.

Despite the fact that he remained an Episcopalian, Patrick Henry was even more greatly influenced by the frontier democracy and the Calvinistic doctrines of the Presbyterian Church. On many occasions, Henry demonstrated the spirit of the Calvinists in his own intimately personal life and certainly in his idea of the way a Christian should conduct himself in political service. This Presbyterian influence, undoubtedly, came to Patrick Henry through his mother. Bishop William Meade cites evidence to the effect that his mother viewed Patrick's religious training as a serious matter. Another biographer produced a letter of a contemporary of Mrs. Henry, who stated, "Never did I know a Christian character equal to hers." While Patrick Henry was still a boy, Mrs. Henry became a devout member of the Presbyterian Church, as did her father. Every Sunday, Mrs. Henry and Patrick attended the Presbyterian church in a light carriage known as a double gig, and on their return from the services, she would make her son give the text and a summary of the sermon. The influence of this early Presbyterian training on Henry is clear and unmistakable, particularly in his political life. He, on many occasions, voiced his deep respect for the Presbyterian Church and his admiration of the oratorical ability of several of the Presbyterian divines who were

spreading their ideal of Calvinism throughout the Virginia backcountry.

The Episcopalian and Presbyterian Churches were not, however, the only groups to leave their imprint upon the thinking of Patrick Henry. He was always a devoted friend of the Baptists. Meade cites a "systematic persecution" of the Baptist groups near Henry's boyhood home. Despite these persecutions, the Baptists experienced great growth in the Piedmont region of Virginia during this period, and Patrick Henry, on many occasions, represented Baptist groups in court when they ran afoul of the Virginia laws perpetuating the established Anglican Church. The Baptists are perhaps the only group that Henry ever represented without charge in his long career as a lawyer. In recognition of his service, they passed a resolution on 12 August 1776, greeting his election as governor with "unspeakable pleasure." William Wirt Henry quotes from a Baptist Church history of the period to the effect that "the Baptist found in Henry an unwavering friend. May his name descend to posterity with unsullied honor."

Nor was this the end of Henry's contacts among the various church denominations. In his letters, he expressed great admiration for various Methodist pastors who were conducting revivals in Louisa County during his youth, and he was apparently always on good terms with various Quaker leaders. Many Quakers lived in Louisa County during Henry's boyhood. Doubtlessly, he had many opportunities for contact with them, for despite their pacifist sentiments, the Quaker leaders in Philadelphia greeted Patrick Henry's appearance at the First Continental Congress with great enthusiasm. The wide range of doctrinal influences upon Henry in his early years partly explains the depth of his religious convictions.

Henry's lifelong membership in the Episcopal church is, for example, very evident in his personal dealings with others. He had none of the condemnation of the Calvinist in his social relationships. But in this respect he was strikingly reminiscent of American statesman John C. Calhoun, for Calhoun had the same intermingling of stern Presbyterian Calvinism and liberal episcopacy. Like Calhoun, Patrick Henry could fit himself into neither the Jeffersonian nor the

Hamiltonian view of man and government, but exhibited a peculiar mixture of both. Patrick Henry was not unlike the Baptist friends in their officially stated determination to love all Christians as brethren. He was ever vigilant and ever watchful for the opportunity to advance the cause of freedom of Christian worship.

The first appearance of Patrick Henry to give him state-wide recognition and prominence was in his role as defense lawyer in the celebrated "Parson's Cause Case." The legislature of Virginia had passed legislation that would have enabled the clergy of the established Anglican or Episcopal Church of the colony to be paid in coin at the rate of two pence per pound of tobacco as being necessitated by a tobacco shortage due to drought and by the corresponding rise in the price of tobacco, which would, therefore, have worked a hardship on the parishioners if they had been forced to meet the salary payments in tobacco. The king, upon plea of the clergy, had disallowed the act. Thus, lower courts had been forced to declare it null and void. It remained only for the clergy to sue for damages resulting from having been paid their yearly salary on the two-pence scale. The case in Louisa County had attracted great attention. Patrick Henry was at this time a relatively unknown country lawyer, yet he managed to sway the jury with his eloquence to the extent that it brought in a verdict of one-penny damages for the clergy—a decided blow to their pocketbooks. In other words, Henry influenced the jury to give the clergy only half of what they had originally had been allowed by the two-pence law, but which they had objected to since it fell short of what they had been receiving prior to the two-pence legislation.

Henry cited two reasons why the court should find only one-penny damages and thereby uphold the spirit of the Two-Penny Act. First, the king, by disallowing the act, had broken the compact between crown and subject. Henry maintained that government was a conditional compact, composed of twin dependent covenants—the government of the king promising protection on the one hand, and the people pledging obedience and support on the other. As the Two-Penny Act had been a good law and designed for the general welfare, the disallowance was an instance of misrule;

therefore, the king had departed from his role as the father of his people and had degenerated into a tyrant. The people, then, were released from their obligation to follow his order regarding the act. At this point Patrick Henry heard the first murmurs of "treason!" from a Virginia audience.

Second, the clergy had failed to serve the purpose for which they were ordained and, therefore, should be punished. By their refusal to acquiesce to a law designed to meet the general welfare of the public, they had counteracted the aims and purposes of their organization. As a result, instead of the respect due to them as useful members of the state, they should be considered as enemies of the people. In the case before the court, then, they should, instead of being awarded damages, be punished. Henry proceeded to attack the Anglican clergy with vigor. He asked, "Do they manifest their zeal in the cause of religion and humanity by practising the mild and benevolent precepts of the Gospel of Jesus?" and replied, "Oh, no, gentlemen!...These rapacious harpes would, were their powers equal to their will, snatch from the...widow and her orphan children their last milch cow!" He continued his allegory in a violent tone and concluded by saying, "they would snatch...the last bed, nay, the last blanket from the lying-in woman!"

The parsons labeled Henry's speech as violent demagoguery designed to win popularity with the people; yet, an examination of Henry's statements before and after this time show him to be a firm and unyielding foe of the establishment of religion. Henry concluded the case in hand by declaring that the issue was whether or not they would be free and make their own laws, or whether or not they would rivet the bonds of slavery by deciding for the parsons. This insistence on self-government in local matters was to be the beacon that Henry held forth through the Revolution.

The case itself accentuated a revolt against establishment that Samuel Chitwood had begun with the great Presbyterian and Calvinistic revival of Patrick Henry's youth and which culminated in the American Revolution. John Miller maintained that revolution and disestablishment were inseparable forces in the Southern colonies. He pointed out that it was the Presbyterian Church that taught the moral righteousness of rebellion against a dictator. Patrick Henry became the acknowledged leader of both disestablishment and rebellion.

As was so often to be the case, Patrick Henry was the leader of a ground swell of popular sentiment among the people of Virginia in this demand for disestablishment. Chitwood finds that the Anglican clergy was replete with "low ethical standards." The aristocracy, or at least a large portion of them, supported the church and continued their persecution of the Baptists, Presbyterians, and other minority groups up until the very eve of the American Revolution. These common people were innately religious. They responded to the emotionalism and followed the ruggedness of the Calvinistic doctrines. The Episcopalians were, at the same time, becoming more convinced that the Anglican Church formed the "most genteel pathway to Heaven" and that the other groups were "low and vulgar." This spirit of disestablishment was growing also in the Northern colonies, under the guidance of Samuel Adams—the same Samuel Adams who was to join with Patrick Henry in pushing the American Revolution into fruition.

Several reasons are evident for Henry's avowal of disestablishment. Undoubtedly, he opposed the admixture of church and state. He stated, "In my weak judgment, a government is strong when it applies to the most important end of all government—the rights and privileges of the people." To Patrick Henry the foremost right of the people was religious liberty. As he stated at the Constitutional Ratification Convention in Richmond in June 1788, "The great and direct end of government is liberty. Secure our liberty and privileges and the end of government is answered." He demanded protection of religious freedom by a constitutional amendment before Virginia should ratify the Constitution. After the Convention had ratified the document over his protests, he had persuaded them to stipulate among the conditions of ratification the provision that "liberty of conscience...cannot be cancelled, abridged, restrained, or modified by any authority of the United States." He went on to persuade the Convention to refer amendments to the national Congress for ratification. One of these would protect conscientious objectors, and another stated:

That religion or the duty which we owe to our Creator, and the manner of discharging it, can be directed only by reason and conviction, not by force of violence, and therefore all men have an equal, natural, and unalienable right to the free exercise of religion according to the dictates of conscience, and that no particular religious sect or society ought to be favored or established by law in preference to others.

This statement was in part an almost exact duplication of the sixteenth article of the Virginia Bill of Rights, which some of his biographers credit to the authorship of Patrick Henry. These statements were the mere culmination of a long struggle by Henry for religious freedom for all of the various Christian groups within the Old Dominion. As a boy, he must have listened to backwoods pastors proclaim a favorite tenet of the Presbyterian Church, which stated that

God alone is Lord of the conscience, and hath left it free from the doctrines and commandments of men; and that the rights of private judgment, in all matters that respect religion, are universal and inalienable.

The Baptists heralded the election of Henry as governor of Virginia in 1776. He replied to their congratulations in the following letter:

I am happy to find a catholic spirit prevailing in our country, and that those religious distinctions, which formerly produced some heats, are now forgotten. Happy must every friend to virtue and America feel himself to perceive, that the only contest among us, at this critical and important period, is who shall be foremost to preserve our religious and civil liberties. My earnest wish is that Christian charity, forbearance, and love may unite all different persuasions as brethren...

In addition to his innate love of liberty, Patrick Henry cited other reasons for desiring freedom of religious conscience. He said that "Virginia suffered from slavery and lack of religious freedom." He went on to compare the slow growth of Virginia's population in comparison with that of Pennsylvania and concluded that "a general toleration of Religion appears to me the best means of peopling our country." This would also, he felt, increase industry and home-manufactured products and would provide for Virginia the "means of becoming the most prosperous" state on the continent, for "the free exercise of religion hath stacked the Northern part of the Continent with inhabitants...A Calvinist, a Lutheran, a Quaker, who hath felt these inconveniences in Europe, sails not to Virginia, where they are felt perhaps in a [greater degree]."

Nor was Patrick Henry sympathetic with the cries of the Episcopal clergy that they were being persecuted because they had fought against wickedness and vice. He proclaimed, "Reprehension seldom is the duty of a minister. A good life is the best lecture." If the clergy of the established church had merely censured those who were wicked in accordance with their duty, they would not be under attack. For he held that "if it happens that a life is so wicked as to become notoriously offensive,...such a man ceases to be popular. For I dare, affirm, that vice never in any country was held in reverence for its own sake, and so far as a man is openly wicked, he is unpopular." Henry concluded that if a minister were being censured merely for doing his duty, the minister would be upheld by all sensible men. This was not the case in regard to the clergy of the established church.

Henry could not sanction a government that persecuted Christians in order to further an established church which the people felt had become more licentious with each passing day. The government of the king was not serving its purpose when it had encroached upon religious liberty in order to perpetuate the Anglican Church, for Henry held that "liberty ought to be the direct end of your government...Liberty, the greatest of all earthly blessings—give us that precious jewel, and you may take everything else." Undoubtedly the evils of an established church preyed heavily upon the mind of the men who led Virginia into the path of Revolution against the divinely ordained king of the British Empire! The Revolution brought to America a new form of government—a government wherein all men might worship God according to the dictates of their own consciences.

Henry's retreat from public affairs was broken only once during the eight years of his retirement. He was enraged at Thomas Paine's *Age of Reason* and wrote an entire book refuting Paine's agnosticism. Before publication of this book, however, Patrick Henry read Bishop Richard Watson's *Apology for the Bible,* which he considered superior to his own effort in replying to Paine. Henry contented himself, therefore, with circulating the bishop's book (at Henry's own expense) among his friends and neighbors.

As was evidenced by his reaction to Paine's publication, Henry's religious motivation had not altered during his retirement, nor had the depth of his convictions lessened. Visitors to the Henry home reported his diligent study of the Bible, and his letters also indicated a continued devotion to Christianity. He wrote his daughter in 1796 that "amongst all the handsome things I hear said of you, what gives me the greatest pleasure is to be told of your piety and steady virtue." During this period, too, it became Henry's custom to spend the entire day in fasting and prayer before partaking of communion.

Patrick Henry was not a Federalist, but neither was he Jeffersonian in his political viewpoint. True, Henry and Jefferson agreed as to the necessity of separation of the powers of the government and as to the general greater safety of power resting in the state governments, but here the similarity in viewpoints ended. In their basic concepts of life, the two men were poles apart. Indeed, the wonder is that they were able to work together in harmony for so many years during the America Revolution, not that they parted company in 1799.

The principal ideals and beliefs of Patrick Henry and Thomas Jefferson present a striking contrast. The French Revolution was merely the method by which the basic differences of the two men were brought to public attention. This revolution had been in one aspect a revolt not only against the established government, but also against established religion—and therefore Christianity. Milner states that there were several classifications of Deists. He quotes one source that describes the Deists as follows:

Red Hill, the last home and burial place of Patrick Henry. The house was destroyed by fire in 1919. In 1957, the Patrick Henry Memorial Foundation reconstructed only the original portion, using the measured illustrations drawn before the fire.

The Deists are a class of people whose distinguishing character is not to profess any particular form or system of religion, but only to acknowledge the existence of a God, and to follow the law of Nature, rejecting revelation and opposing Christianity...

Thomas Jefferson might feel that "the liberty of the whole earth" was dependent on the success of the French Revolution and might proclaim that "never was such a prize won with so little loss of innocent blood"; however, to Patrick Henry, France was doomed to failure because of her repudiation of Christianity. Henry was firm in his belief that Christian "righteousness alone can exalt them as a nation."

In addition to his fervent support of the French revolutionaries, as a triumph for Democratic government throughout the world, Thomas Jefferson undoubtedly supported a bulk of their theory, and none of their statements or actions seemed to be of repugnance to him. The Unitarian Church in America had counted Jefferson as one of its early members, and they were closely akin to the Deists in their repudiation of formal Christianity in favor of the "God of Reason." The Unitarians were firm in their pronouncement of the

trustworthiness of human facilities, and their competency, when duly trained and freed from prejudice, to receive moral and religious, no less than scientific truths. In pursuance of this principle, they have carried to the fartherest [sic] point yet reached by any denomination the Protestant belief in the right of private judgment and reverence for the individual conscience. They do not hesitate to bring all theological systems and the sacred writings of both Jews and Christians to this test.

This viewpoint was inconceivable to a man trained as Patrick Henry had been to believe that man was incapable of recognizing truth or true goodness except by the redemptive grace of God, and that "the image of God was utterly defaced in man, and he and his posterity of nature became enemies of God, slaves to Satan and servants unto sin..."

That this belief in the "God of Reason" had a great influence on Jefferson was apparent. He wrote a young admirer as early as 10 August 1787, advising him to "fix the existence of a God...Read the Bible then, as you would read Tacitus or Livy..." He urged the youth to inquire into the veracity of the miracles recorded in the Bible as "the pretension is entitled to your inquiry, because millions believe it," and had reassured the boy, "Do not be frightened from this by any fear of its consequences. If it ends in the belief that there is no god, you will find incitements to virtue" through observing the value of a good life in others.

Patrick Henry firmly believed the Bible to be "worth all of the books ever written." He believed, as he had told the Hanover volunteers, that God tested his people to determine their steadfastness and that the "God whose power divided the Red Sea...for the deliverance of Israel" from Egypt "still reigned in all of his Glory, unchanged and unchangeable..."

Jefferson might agree with Thomas Paine that "man was a rational animal," but Henry could never overlook Paine's infidelity, despite the writer's contribution to the American Revolution. Patrick Henry maintained that "the depraved nature of man is well known." Greed of the individual was the reason Patrick Henry had insisted on strong state governments that could be controlled by the people—not because of a Jeffersonian faith in the masses. Henry believed that only an appeal to individual "self-love" could exercise effective control over all men, who were by nature evil. He had feared the centralized government he had foreseen in the Constitution, and he had proclaimed years earlier that "taxation without Representation is Tyranny" because man, motivated by "self-love," could not be given unfettered power over other people.

Patrick Henry, in his final appearance on a public platform, had reiterated the same premises under which he had operated throughout his life. He had once warned the people of the type of government that they were creating, but now that the government was created, he stated that they must abide by it or change it. If it should oppress them, he reminded them, there was still the "Right of Rebellion," the same right that they had exercised against the king of England. Patrick Henry was not a Federalist; he could not support their consolidation of power into the hands of the national government. However, he would trust in God and the people to keep alive the spirit of independence they had always possessed. As alarming as consolidation, however, was the spirit of disobedience to law, and far worse was the spirit of Deism. Patrick Henry could support neither the domestic nor the foreign policy of either party. He was old and infirm; therefore, he had refused to enter once more into public service. However, the spirit of Deism had begun to grow, and there was no longer any other choice, except to return to the service of his country. Henry, faced with governmental policies of the Federalists and with Jeffersonian sanction of French Deism, which he bitterly opposed, made his decision with deliberate certainty. Patrick Henry was neither Federalist nor Jeffersonian, but, as always, his God came first.

Henry returned to his Red Hill plantation after addressing the people of Virginia at the Charlotte Courthouse, exhausted by his trip and confined to bed. He was unable to attend the election in which he was reelected to the Virginia Legislature held on the first Monday in April. The results were clear—the people of Virginia had returned Patrick Henry once more to the service of the state. Patrick Henry was unable to answer their call, however, for on 6 June 1799, he died.

His last words were spoken to his family physician, an old friend who was not a Christian. "Observe," he instructed the doctor, "how great a reality and benefit religion is to a man who is about to die." This dying statement summed up in unmistakable terms the overpowering influence of his Christian beliefs—beliefs that lay not far beneath the surface of his every action and deed throughout his long and varied career.

Those beliefs surfaced again in the legacy that Patrick Henry left to his children. In his will, he had written, after having disposed of his not inconsiderable estate, the following words: "This is all of the inheritance I can give to my dear family. The religion of Christ can give them one which will make them rich indeed."

There was also a final bequest to the American people, for with his will, Patrick Henry had left a copy of the Stamp Act Resolutions, on the back of which he had written the following copy:

> Whether this will prove a blessing or a curse, will depend upon the use our people make of the blessing which a gracious God hath bestowed on us. If they are wise, they will be great and happy. If they are of a contrary character, they will be miserable. Righteousness alone can exalt them as a nation. Reader!, whosoever thou art, remember this: and in thy sphere practice virtue thyself, and encourage it in others!

Throughout his long and varied career, Patrick Henry remained true to his religious and political convictions. He was ever loyal to his country, but first and foremost, Patrick Henry was faithful to his God. During those hard and difficult years of the colonial period, Henry possessed impressive depth and steadfastness in his Christian convictions.

William Wirt of Richmond, Virginia, the accomplished biographer of Patrick Henry, beautifully describes Mr. Henry:

> He retired, loaded with honors, public and professional; and carried with him the admiration, the gratitude, the confidence, and the love of his country. No man had ever passed through so long a life of public service with a reputation more perfectly unspotted. On every great subject of public interest, the part which he had taken was open, decided, manly; his country saw his motivates, heard his reasons, approved his conduct, rested upon his virtue, and his vigour. For more than thirty years, he had now stood before that country, open to scrutiny and the censure of the invidious, yet he retired, not only without spot or blemish, but with all his laurels blooming full and fresh upon him. Although Patrick Henry began life in the school of poverty, in his later years he enjoyed an independence which resulted partly from a remunerative profession, and partly from judicious purchases of lands. His conversation was remarkably pure and chaste, and he was never heard to make the name of his maker, God, in vain.

Gen. Henry Lee also leaves a lasting impression of Henry, with these words from the conclusion of his touching obituary:

> As long as our rivers flow and mountains stand so long will your excellence and worth be the theme of our homage and endearments; and Virginia, bearing in mind, her loss, will say to rising generations, imitate Henry.

It has been said of Patrick Henry that he was Shakespeare and Garrick** combined. Just imagine the wonderful talents of those two men united in the same individual, and transferred from scenes of fiction to the business of real life, and you will have found some conception of the eloquence of Patrick Henry.

In the cemetary at Red Hill, Patrick Henry is buried next to his second wife, Dorothea Dandridge Henry. The inscription on the stone reads, "His fame his best epitaph."

As Thomas Jefferson's distant cousin, the Virginia states-man John Randolph of Roanoke, once wrote, Patrick Henry "was a man, take him for all in all, we ne'er shall look upon his likes again."

* As the non-Anglican sects grew, a revolt also rose against the estab-lishment of the Episcopal Church. Patrick Henry had an increased distaste for the government of the English king, whom the Anglicans held to be supreme and whose government supported the Church. The supremacy of the king is stated among the last six articles of the thirty-nine articles of faith of the Episcopal Church.

** David Garrick (1717-79) ranks among the greatest British actors. He did much to revive interest in Shakespeare, winning fame in 1741 playing Richard III.

COLONIAL CLERGY IN VIRGINIA

FROM 1607 TO 1785

A

Agnew, John: Minister of Suffolk Parish, Nansemond County, 1754-75.

Agnew, Andrew: ordained for Virginia, 19 June 1709.

Agar

Agur, William: Minister, Nottoway Parish, Southampton County, 1773-75.

Alexander, John: Minister, Sittenburne Parish, (Old) Rappahannock County, prior to 1732.

Alford, George: Minister of Lynnhaven Parish, Princess Anne County, 1658.

Allards, Thomas (Allardis): ordained for Virginia, 27 September 1699.

Allett, Thomas: King's bounty to Virginia, 8 April 1718.

Almoner, John (Armourier): in North-ampton County prior to 1651.

Anderson, Christopher.

Anderson, Charles: Minister, Westover Parish, Charles City County, 1692-1718.

Andrews, John: Minister of Cameron Parish, 1754-57; preached in Truro Parish, Fairfax County, 1765.

Andrews, ———: King's bounty to Virginia, 13 September 1700.

Andrews, Rev. Mr.: died 1721.

Andrews, William: in St. Mary's Parish, Essex (later Caroline) County, 1702.

Andrews, Robert, M.A.: Rector of York-Hampton Parish, 1785; Chaplain of a Virginia regiment during Revolution.

Andrews, William: in Nottoway Parish, Southampton County, 1776.

Armourier, John: (See Almoner).

Arnold, ———: Minister of Fredericks-ville Parish, Albemarle County, 1747-54.

Avon

Aven

Avens, Archibald: Minister, Cameron

Parish, 1767.

Avery, Isaac: licensed for Virginia, 18 October 1769.

Ayers, ———: said to have built a church at West Pike Run, now Washing-ton County, Pennsylvania, then Youhgio-gheny County, Virginia, 1777.

Aylmer, Justinian: Minister, Elizabeth City Parish, 1645-67; Minister of James City, 1671.

B

Bagge, John: Minister of Hanover Parish, King George County, 1714; Minister of Sittenburne Parish, Richmond County, 1716; Minister of St. Anne's Parish, Essex County, 1717-25.

Bailye, Thomas: (See Bayley).

Baker, Thomas: applied for Kingston Parish, 1770.

Balfour, William: Minister, Upper Parish, Nansemond County, 1744-45.

Ball, John: Minister of Varina (Henrico) Parish, 1680-84; Minister of St. Peter's Parish, New Kent County, 1685-87, and officiated, 1689.

Balmaine, Alexander: Minister of Augu-sta Parish, Augusta County, 1773-75; Chaplain of 13th Virginia Regiment dur-ing Revolution; Rector of Frederick Parish, Frederick County, 1785-1820.

Banister, John: in Charles City County, 1678.

Barclay, Henry: King's bounty to Virginia, 5 December 1737; joint translator of Liturgy into Mohawk.

Barclay, John: Minister, Cumberland Parish, Lunenburg County, 1756-57.

Bargrave, Thomas (Bargar): came to Virginia, 1619; Minister of Henricopolis.

Barlow, Henry: officiated in Warwi-

squeake Parish, Isle of Wight County, 1726; Minister of Lynnhaven Parish, Prin-cess Anne County, 1729-47; Minister of Hungar's Parish, Northampton County, 1747-61.

Barnard, ———: came to Virginia, 1716; settled by Governor Spotswood in a parish near Williamsburg.

Barnett, John: Minister of St. Thomas' Parish, Orange County, 1771-74.

Barrett, Robert: Minister of St. Martin's Parish, Hanover and Louisa Counties, 1754-87; preached in Fredericksville Parish, Albemarle County.

Barrett, John: cast away off Isle of Wight; King's bounty to Virginia, 3 March 1723-24.

Barrow, ———: King's bounty to Virginia, 11 August 1702.

Bastock, ———.

Basken, James: ordained for Virginia, 16 July 1700.

Bayley, Thomas (Baylye, Bailey): Minister of Newport Parish, Isle of Wight County, 1724; applied for Warwisqueake Parish, 1727; sent by Governor Gooch to Lynnhaven Parish, 1728.

Betty

Beatty, John: Minister, St. Andrew's Parish, Brunswick County, 1733-50.

Beckett, Thomas.

Beckett, J.: Minister, St. James' Parish, Goochland County, 1727; Minister, St. Mark's Parish, Culpeper County, 1733-38; officiated in Fredericksville Parish, 1754.

Bell, John: Minister of Christ Church Parish, Lancaster County, 1711-43; offici-ated in St. Stephen's Parish, Northumber-land County, 1723.

Bennett, Thomas: Minister, Nansemond County; head of Independent congregation.

Bennett, William: Minister at Edward Bennett's Plantation at Warwisqueake.

Berkeley, John: officiated in Cornwall Parish, Charlotte County, 1755-62; perhaps at Jamestown, 1758.

Bertram, John: in Lancaster County, 1690.

Bertrand, John: Minister, (Old) Rappahannock County; perhaps in Lancaster County.

Bewsher, Joseph (Bewsker): declined call to Henrico Parish, 1752.

Black, William: Minister of Accomac Parish, Accomac County, 1709-24.

Blackamore, Arthur: master of grammar school, William and Mary College, 1710-16.

Blacknall, John: in St. Stephen's Parish, Northumberland County, 1726; Minister of Kingston Parish, Gloucester (now Matthews) County, 1740-47.

Blackwell, Robert: King's bounty to Virginia, 15 June 1772.

Blagrove, Benjamin: Minister of Southwark Parish, Surry County, 1774-76; Minister of Martin's Brandon Parish, Prince George County, 1785-87; Minister of Westover Parish, Charles City County, 1787; Minister of St. Peter's Parish, New Kent County, 1789; Chaplain of General Assembly, 1783.

Blair, James: Minister of Varina (Henrico) Parish, 1685-94; Minister of Jamestown, 1694-1710; Rector of Bruton Parish, 1710-43; Governor of Colony, 1740-41.

Bland, William: Minister of James City Parish, 1767-77; Rector of St. Paul's Church, Norfolk, 1789-90.

Blewer, Thomas (Blewit, Bluitt, Bluett): in Richmond County, 1742.

Blomfield

Blumfield, Joseph: officiated in St. Paul's Parish, Hanover County, 1736; preached in Truro Parish, 1737.

Boisseau, James: Minister of St. John's Parish, King and Queen (later King William) County, 1692-93.

Bolton, Francis: Minister of Elizabeth City Parish, Elizabeth City County, 1621-23; Minister of Hungar's Parish, Northampton County, 1623-30; at Jamestown, 1630.

Bolton, John: in Westmoreland County, 1694.

Boucher, Jonathan: Minister, Hanover Parish, King George County, 1762-63;

Minister, St. Mary's Parish, Carolina County, 1764-70.

Bowker, James: Minister of Kingston Parish, 1690-91; Minister of St. Peter's Parish, New Kent County, 1698-1703.

Bowker, Ralph: Minister of St. Stephen's Parish, King and Queen County, 1702-14; brother of James (above).

Boyd, Andrew: ordained for Virginia, 19 June 1709.

Brace, John: licensed for Virginia (Elizabeth Parish [sic]), 1 March 1775.

Bracewell, Robert: chosen to House of Burgesses from Isle of Wight, 1653.

Bracken, John, D.D.: Rector of Bruton Parish, 1773-1818; President of Convention of the Diocese, 1789 and 1812-13; Bishop of Virginia, 1812.

Braidfoot, John: Minister, Portsmouth Parish, 1774-84; Chaplain during Revolution.

Brander, John

Brandler, John

Brandon, John: all three same man; Minister of Russell Parish, Bedford County, 1774-76.

Breechin, James (Brochin): Minister of Cople Parish, Westmoreland County, 1702 and 1714; first Minister of St. Paul's Parish, Hanover County, 1704.

Bridges, Charles: posibly in St. Martin's Parish, Hanover County.

Brockenbrough, ———: York County in 1773.

Brodie, William (Brody): Minister, St. Peter's Parish, New Kent County, 1710-20.

Brogden, William: King's bounty to Virginia, 11 September 1735.

Bromscale, ———: preached in St. Peter's Parish, New Kent County, 1720 (probably from neighboring parish).

Brooke, Clement (Samuel): Minister of Overwharton Parish, Stafford County, 1774-76.

Brooke, Zachariah: Minister of St. Peter's Parish, New Kent County, 1721; Minister of St. Paul's Parish, Hanover County, 1721-36; preached in Goochland and Powhatan Counties; Minister of Dale Parish, Henrico (later Chesterfield) County, 1737-38; Minister of King William Parish, Manakintown, 1737-38.

Bruce, John: King's bounty to Virginia, 7 March 1775.

Brunskill, John Sr. (Brunkell): Minister of Wilmington Parish, James City and Charles City Counties, 1723; Minister, St.

Margaret's Parish, Caroline County, 1738-58.

Brumskill, John

Brunskill, John Jr.: in Hamilton Parish, Prince William (Fauquier after 1759) County, 1754-58.

Brunskill, John: Minister of Raleigh Parish, Amelia County, 1754-76; *probably* Minister, Cumberland Parish, Lunenburg County, 1748.

Buchan, Robert: in Amherst Parish, Amherst County, 1780; in Overwharton Parish, Stafford County, 1785

Buchanan, John, A.M., D.D.: Minister, Lexington Parish, Amherst County, 1780; Assistant, Henrico Parish, 1785, and Rector, 1785-1822.

Buck, Richard (Bucke): second Minister at Jamestown; married John Rolfe and Pocahontas, 5 April 1614.

Buckhan, William: licensed for Virginia, 17 April 1763.

Burges, Henry John: Minister, Newport Parish, Isle of Wight County, 1770-76; Minister of Suffolk Parish, Nansemond County, 1778; ministered Southwark Parish, Surry County, 1785; Rector of Nottoway Parish, Southampton County, 1795.

Burges, Thomas (Burgess): Minister of Nottoway Parish, Southampton County, 1754-58; father of Henry John (above).

Burnaby, Andrew, D.D.: licensed for Virginia, 7 April 1759.

Burnet, John

Burnet, Thomas: same as above; Minister, Lawne's Creek Parish, Surry County, 1702; in Richmond County, 1742.

Burtell, James: perhaps same as James Bushell.

Bushell, James: Minister of Weyanoke Parish, Charles City County, 1702.

Butler, Amory (Almeric): in (Old) Rappahannock County, 1671.

Butler, Edward: ordained for Virginia, February 1704-05.

Butler, Samuel: ministered in Newport Parish, Isle of Wight County, 1780.

Butler, Thomas: Denbigh Parish, Warwick County.

Butler, William: in Washington Parish, Westmoreland County, 1678-80; brother of Amory Butler (above).

C

Cairon, John: Minister of King William Parish, Manakintown, Henrico (later

Powhatan) County, 1710-15.

Calvert, Sampson: Minister, Elizabeth City Parish, Norfolk County, 1649.

Cameron, John, D.D.: Minister, St. James' Parish, Mecklenburg County, 1770-84; Bristol Parish, Dinwiddie County, 1784-93; Rector, Nottoway Parish, Southampton County, 1793; Rector of Cumberland Parish, Lunenburg County, 1806-15.

Camm, John: Minister of Newport Parish, Isle of Wight County, 1745; President, William and Mary College, 1771-77; Rector, York-Hampton Parish, 1749-71 and 1774-79; Rector, Bruton Parish, 1771-76.

Camp, Ichabod: Minister of St. Anne's Parish, Albemarle County, 1751-53; Minister, Amherst Parish, Amherst County, 1773-76.

Campbell, Alexander: King's bounty to Virginia, 30 December 1725.

Campbell, Alexander: licensed for Virginia, 21 January 1745.

Campbell, Archibald: Minister, Washington Parish, Westmoreland County, 1754-74.

Campbell, Isaac: licensed for Virginia, 6 July 1747.

Campbell, James: King's bounty to Virginia, 17 January 1721-22.

Campbell, John: licensed for Virginia (Stratton Major Parish), 6 June 1773.

Cant, ———: King's bounty (Leeward Islands), 29 June 1692.

Cant, Andrew: in Virginia, 1696.

Cargill, John: Minister, Southwark Parish, Surry County, 1708-23.

Carnegie, John (Kerneguy): Minister of St. Mary's White Chapel Parish, Lancaster County, 1702.

Carr, John: Minister, St. Peter's Parish, New Kent County, 1684.

Carr, Robert: Minister of Stratton Major Parish, King and Queen County, 1680-86.

Carson, Jean: in King William County, 1714.

Carter, Jesse: applied for St. James' Southam Parish, Powhatan County, 1773; Minister, Drysdale Parish, King and Queen and Caroline Counties, 1778-85.

Cawthren, William: King's bounty to Virginia, 30 December 1725.

Chaplin, Robert: resigned a parish, 1740.

Chapman, John: King's bounty to Virginia, 10 April 1719.

Chicheley, William: King's bounty to Virginia, 24 September 1729.

Crystall

Christall, Henry: Minister of St. Stephen's Parish, Northumberland County, 1742-43.

Cisse, ———.

Clack, James: Minister of Ware Parish, Gloucester County, 1679-1723.

Clarke, ———: had a parish, 1729.

Clay, Charles: Minister, St. Anne's Parish, Albemarle County, 1769-85; Minister of Manchester Parish, Chesterfield County, 1785-86.

Clayton, Daniel: misspelling of Daniel Taylor Sr.

Clayton, John: Minister at Jamestown, 1684-86.

Clephane, David (Clepham): King's bounty to Virginia, 28 March 1710.

Clough, John: Minister of Jamestown, 1676; Minister of Southwark Parish, Surry County, 1680; possibly same as John Gough.

Clug, Samuel: (See Klug).

Cluverius, ———: Minister, York-Hampton Parish, York County, 1644.

Cocke, John: in Matthews County, 1780.

Cole, Roscow: Minister, Warwick Parish, Warwick County, 1754.

Cole, Samuel: Minister of Pianketank and Lancaster Parishes (later Christ Church Parish), Lancaster (later Middlesex) County, 1657.

Coles, William: licensed for Virginia, 2 February 1746.

Collier, Peter: Minister of Hungar's Parish, Northampton County, 1702-03.

Collins

Collings, Henry: Minster, St. Peter's Parish, New Kent County, 1722-25.

Collinson, Joseph: licensed for Virginia, 23 December 1759.

Collinson, Richard: licensed for Virginia, 28 December 1762.

Coney, Peregrine: Chaplain to Governor Nicholson, 1704.

Cordell, John: Chaplain of 11th Virginia Regiment during Revolution.

Cotton, William: Minister, Hungar's Parish, Northampton County, 1632-45.

Coutts, William: Minister, Martin's Brandon Parish, Prince George County, 1773-76.

Cowper, John: King's bounty to Virginia, 16 April 1716.

Cox, James: in Charles City County, 1723.

Craig, James: Minister of Cumberland Parish, Lunenburg County, 1759-95; officiated in Halifax County.

(Crague).

Craig, James: officiated in St. Stephen's Parish, Northumberland County, 1758; Minister of Hamilton Parish, Fauquier County, 1774.

Craigh, William: in Charlotte County, 1755.

Cruden, Alexander: Minister of South Farnham Parish, Essex County, 1752-74.

Currie, David: Minister of Christ Church and St. Mary's White Chapel Parishes, Lancaster County.

D

Dacres, Charles: vestry of Yeocomico (i.e. Wicomico) Parish, Northumberland County, 1683;

Daide

Dade, Townsend: first Minister, Fairfax Parish, Fairfax County, 1765-77.

Davenport, Joseph: Minister, Charles Parish, York County, 1757-85.

Davies, Charles (Davis): Minister, Farnham Parish, (Old) Rappahannock County, and Wicomico Parish, Northumberland County, 1680.

Davies, Price: Minister of Blissland Parish, New Kent and James City Counties, 1763-86.

Davies, William: Minister, Hanover Parish, King George County, 1773-76.

Davis, Jonathan: Minister of Pocoson Parish, 1680.

Davis, Peter: Minister, Southwark Parish, Surry County, 1754-58.

Davis, Superior: in Christ Church Parish, Middlesex County, 1682 and 1683.

Davis, Thomas: Minister, Warwick Parish, Warwick County, 1758.

Davis, Thomas: Minister of Elizabeth River Parish, Norfolk County, 1773-76 and 1806-08; Chaplain of 1st Continental Dragoons during Revolution; Minister of St. Stephen's Parish, Northumberland County, 1779-92; officiated in North Farnham, 1792-1806; officiated at Washington's funeral; Minister of Hungar's Parish, Northampton County, 1808; possibly son of William (below).

Davis, William: Minister of Hanover Parish, King George County, 1751-58; baptized James Madison, 31 March 1751; Minister of Westover Parish, Charles City County, 1758-73.

Dawson, Musgrave (Musgrove): Minister of St. Mary's Parish, Caroline County, 1751-58.

Dawson, Thomas, A.M.: Rector, Bruton Church, 1743-59; President, William and Mary College, 1755-61; brother of William (below).

Dawson, William: President, William and Mary College, 1743-52.

DeButts, Lawrence: Minister, Washington Parish, Westmoreland County, 1720-28;

officiated in Northumberland County and in North Farnham Parish, Richmond County; officiated in St. Mark's Parish, Culpeper, 1731-33; officiated in Truro Parish, Fairfax County, 1733-34.

DeJoux, Benjamin: first Minister of King William Parish, Henrico (later Powhatan) County, 1700-04.

Dell, Thomas: Minister of Hungar's Parish, Northampton County, 1721-29.

Deter, ———: officiated at baptism in King William Parish, (now) Powhatan County, 1728-29.

Dick, Archibald: Minister, St. Margaret's Parish, Caroline County, 1773-99; in Drysdale Parish, 1764.

Dickie, Adam: King's bounty to Virginina, 12 April 1731.

Dixon

Dickson, Robert: Minister, Lynnhaven Parish, Princess Anne County, 1748-76.

Dixon, John (Dixson): Minister, Kingston Parish, Gloucester County, 1754-70; officiated in Stratton Major Parish, King and Queen County, 1773.

Doggett, Benjamin: Minister of Christ Church and St. Mary's White Chapel Parishes, Lancaster County, 1670.

Doughty, Francis: Minister in Northampton County, 1655-60; Minister of Sittenburne Parish, (Old) Rappahannock County, 1668.

Douglass, William: Minster, St. James Northam Parish, Goochland County, 1750-77.

Doyley

D'Oyley, Cope: Minister of Elizabeth City Parish, Elizabeth City County, 1687; Minister of Denbigh Parish, Warwick County, 1688-96; Minister of Bruton Parish, James City County, 1697-1702; Chaplain of General Assembly, 1696.

Dudley, Samuel: Minister, Sittenburne Parish, Rappahannock County, 1680.

Dun, ———: Minister of Hungar's Parish, Northampton County, 1710.

Dunbar, Hancock: Minister of St. Stephen's Parish, King and Queen County, 1754-58.

Dunbar, John: Minister of Westover Parish, Charles City County, 1786.

Dunlop, William: Minister of Stratton-Major Parish, King and Queen County, 1768-79; Minister of St. Paul's Parish, Hanover County, 1779.

Dunster, Robert: in Isle of Wight County, 1656.

Durand, William (Durant): Minister of Elizabeth River Parish, Norfolk County, 1648.

E

Eaton, Nathaniel: Assistant in Hungar's Parish, Northampton County, 1645.

Eburne, Samuel: Minister of Bruton Parish, James City County, 1688-95; Chaplain of General Assembly.

Edwards, Thomas: Minister of St. Anne's Parish, Essex County, 1712-16.

Edzard, Esdras Theodore: Minister of Hanover Parish, King George County, 1727.

Elebeck, Henry: Minister of Southwark Parish, Surry County, 1747.

Emmerson, Arthur Sr.: Minister of Accomac Parish, Accomac County, 1754-55.

Emerson

Emmerson, Arthur Jr.: Minister of Meherrin Parish, Brunswick (now Greenville) County, 1773-76; Minister of Suffolk Parish, Nansemond County, 1785; Minister of Portsmouth Parish, Norfolk County, 1785-1801.

Evans, Archibald: in Matthews County (i.e. Kingston Parish), 1777.

Evans, Jonathan: ordained for Virginia, 27 May 1707.

Evans, Owen: King's bounty to Virginia, 14 March 1706-07.

F

Faber, Tanaquill: ordained for Virginia, 19 June 1709.

Falconer, James: Minister, Hungar's Parish, Northampton County, 1719; Minister, Elizabeth River Parish, Norfolk County, 1720; Minister, Elizabeth City Parish, Elizabeth City County, 1720-24; Minister, Charles Parish, York County, 1725-27.

Falconer, Patrick: Minister of Hungar's Parish, Northampton County, 1710-18.

Falkner, Thomas: Minister of Isle of Wight County, 1642.

Fanning, William.

Farnifold, John: Minister of Old Fairfield Parish, Northumberland County, 1672-1702, and of Boutracey Parish, 1690.

Faux, ———: King's bounty to Virginia, 10 October 1695.

Fenton, ———: died in Elizabeth City County, 1624.

Ferguson, Robert: Minister of Bristol Parish, Dinwiddie County, 1740-48.

Fielde

Field, Thomas: Minister, Kingston Parish, Gloucester County, 1774-78.

Fife: (See Fyfe).

Finney, Alexander: Minister, Martin's Brandon Parish, Prince George County,

1724-70.

Finney, Thomas: Minister of Charles Parish, York County, prior to 1686.

Finnie, ———: ordained for Virginia, 29 October 1709; possibly William (below).

Finney, William, M.A.: Minister of Henrico Parish, 1714-27; officiated in King William Parish, 1718.

Floyd, Thomas: licensed for Virginia, 19 May 1766; same as Thomas F. Lloyd.

Folliott, Edward: Minister of York Parish, York County, until 1690.

Fontaine, Francis: Minister, St. Margaret's Parish, Caroline County, 1721-22; Minister, York-Hampton Parish, York County, 1722; ministered in King William Parish, Henrico County, 1722-24.

Fontaine, James Maury: Minister of Petsworth Parish, Gloucester County, 1762-64, and of Ware Parish, 1764-95; officiated in Abingdon and Petsworth Parishes.

Fontaine, Peter: officiated in Martin's Brandon Parish and at Jamestown; ministered in Martin's Brandon, Wallingford, and Weyanoke Parishes, Charles City County, until 1720 (when Wallingford and Weynoke Parishes combined to make Westover Parish); Minister of Westover Parish, Charles City County, 1720-57; Chaplain to Colonel Byrd's commission to survey the Virginia-North Carolina dividing line, 1728-29; preached at the Huguenot Parish of King William, Henrico County, 1719-20.

Forbes, Alexander: Minister, Upper Parish, Isle of Wight County, 1710-27; Minister, "Warwick Creek" Parish, 1714.

Ford, Edward: master of grammar school, William and Mary College, 1737-39; perhaps Minister, Petsworth Parish.

Fordyce, Francis.

Fouace, Stephen: Minister of York-Hampton Parish, York County, 1690-1702; ministered in Martin's Hundred Parish, James City County, 1702.

Fowlis

Foulis, James (Foules): Minister of Antrim Parish, Halifax County, 1753-59.

Fox, John: Minister of Ware Parish, Gloucester County, 1737-64.

Frazier

Fraser, George: in Overwharton Parish, Stafford County; Minister of Dale Parish, Chesterfield County, 1738-58.

Fraser, John (Frazier): Minister, Overwharton Parish, Stafford (now King George) County, 1702, and of St. Paul's Parish, 1702.

Fyfe, William (Fife): Minister of

Elizabeth City Parish, Elizabeth City County, 1731-55.

G

Gamill

Gemurill, John (Gemmill): Minister, Upper Parish, Isle of Wight County, 1729-44.

Garden, James: Minister of St. Patrick's Parish, Prince Edward County, 1755-73.

Gardner, Robert: King's bounty to Virginia, 23 September 1735.

Garzia, John (Garcia): Minister, Elizabeth River Parish, Norfolk County, 1724.

Gavin, Anthony: Minister, Henrico Parish, Henrico County, 1735-36; Minister, St. James' Parish, Goochland County, 1736-44; preached to Huguenots in King William Parish, Manakintown, 1736 and 1739-44.

Gemmill: (See Gamill).

Giberne, Isaac William: Minister, Lunenburg Parish, Richmond County, 1762-95.

Glover, Nicholas: came to Virginia, 1611.

Godwin, Morgan: Minister, Marston Parish, York County.

Goldie, George: Rector, Hanover Parish, King George County, 1779-80.

Goodwin, Benjamin: officiated in St. Peter's Parish, New Kent County, 1709-10; applied for Bruton Parish, James City County, 1710; Chaplain of General Assembly, 1714; probably Minister of York-Hampton Parish, York County, 1714.

Goodwin, John: Minister of St. Stephen's Parish, King and Queen County, 1724.

Gordon, Alexander: Minister of Antrim Parish, Halifax County, 1763.

Gordon, John (Gourdon): Minister of Wilmington Parish, James City County, 1695 and 1702.

Gordon, John: Minister of Frederick Parish, Frederick County, 1765.

Gordon, William: licensed for Virginia, 11 June 1775.

Gorsuch, John: first Minister, Lancaster County, 1654-57.

Gough

Gouge, John (Gooch): Minister of Jamestown, 1676.

Grace, Isaac: invited to officiate in Bruton Parish, 1704.

Graham, Richard: Professor, William and Mary College, 1749-58 and 1761-70.

Graine

Graeme, Rowland

Grayne, Rouland.

Gray, Stephen.

Gray, Samuel: Minister of Christ Church

Parish, Middlesex County, 1698; Minister of Cople Parish, Westmoreland County, 1698; Minister, St. Peter's Parish, New Kent County, 1708-09; Chaplain of Grayson's Continental Regiment.

Grayson, Spence: Minister of Cameron Parish, Loudoun County, 1773-76; Minister of Dettingen Parish, Prince William County, 1784-87.

Green, Charles, M.D.: Minister of Truro Parish, Fairfax County, 1737-64.

Green, John: appointed by General Assembly of 1656 to examine and certify to the ability of ministers seeking exemption from public levies.

Green, Roger: Minister, Nansemond County, 1653; probably officiated at Jamestown.

Gregg, Stephen: Minister, Abingdon Parish, Gloucester County, 1695.

Gregory, John: Minister of Upper Parish, Nansemond County, 1680.

Griffin, Charles: taught Indian school at Fort Christanna, Brunswick County, 1714-18, and at William and Mary College, 1718-20.

Griffith, David, D.D.: Minister of Shelburne Parish, Loudoun County, 1771-76; Chaplain of 3d Virginia Regiment during Revolution; Minister of Fairfax Parish, Fairfax County, 1780-89; first Bishop-elect of Virginia, 1786.

Grymes, Charles: Minister of York Parish, York County, 1644.

Grundy, Charles: Minister of New Poquoson Parish, York County, 1645-48.

Guilliam, Lewis: Minister, Camden Parish, Pittsylvania County, 1771-77.

Gurley, George (Gurey): Minister of St. Luke's Parish, Southampton County, 1773-92.

Gwatkin, Thomas: master of grammar school, William and Mary College, 1773-74, and professor, 1770-73.

Gwynn, John: Minister of Ware Parish, Gloucester County, 1672-74; Minister of Abingdon Parish, Gloucester County, 1674-88.

H

Hall, Thomas: Minister of Trinity Parish, Louisa County, 1775-76; Minister of St. James' Northam Parish, Goochland County, 1781.

Halyburton, William: licensed for Virginia, 28 August 1766.

Hamilton, Arthur: Minister of Petsworth Parish, Gloucester County, 1768-77; Chaplain to the Governor, 1769; applied for Kingston Parish, 1775; officiated in

Stratton Major Parish, King and Queen County, 1778.

Hammond, John: in Isle of Wight County, prior to 1656.

Hampton, Thomas: Minister in Jamestown, 1640-45; Minister in York County, Hampton Parish, 1646; Minister of Wallingford Parish, Charles City County, and Wilmington Parish, James City County, 1680.

Hannah

Hanna, William: licensed for Virginia (Culpeper County), 11 June 1772.

Harlaw, Andrew: King's bounty to Virginia, 29 January 1721-22.

Harris, William (Matthew): in Virginia, 1753.

Harrison, Thomas, D.D.: Minister, Lower Norfolk County, 1640-48; Chaplain to Governor Berkeley; probably officiated at Jamestown.

Harrison, William: Minister of Bristol Parish, Petersburg, 1762-80.

Hartwell, Richard (Hartwol): Deacon; chosen Minister of Bristol Parish, 1739, but immediately rejected.

Hassell, Thomas: Minister of Chuckatuck Parish, Nansemond County, 1709.

Hatton, Thomas: Usher, William and Mary College, 1758-60.

Henderson, Jacob: King's bounty to Virginia, 1 July 1710.

Henderson, James: Professor, William and Mary College, 1792; probably same as below.

Henderson, ———: in York County, 1773.

Henley, Samuel: officiated in Bruton Parish.

Henry, Patrick: Minister, St. George's Parish, Spotsylvania County, 1733-34; Minister, St. Paul's Parish, Hanover County, 1737-77.

Herdman, James: Minister, Bromfield Parish, (now) Madison and Rappahannock Counties, 1774.

Hewitt, Richard: Minister, Hungar's Parish, Northampton County, 1761-74.

Higby

Higley, Willis (Hely): Minister on Mulberry Island, Warwick County, 1635.

Higby

Higley, Thomas: Minister of Hungar's Parish, Northampton County, 1651-56.

Hindman, John: first Minister of August Parish, Augusta County, 1747.

Holbroke, John: Minister of Hungar's Parish, Northampton County, 1729-47.

Holt, John White: Minister of Russell Parish, Bedford County, 1787.

Holt, Joseph: Minister of Stratton Major Parish, King and Queen County, and officiated in Petsworth Parish, Gloucester County, 1696-1700.

Holt, William: licensed for Virginia (Amelia County), 11 June 1772.

Hooe, Rice: (see Hove, Rice).

Hopkins, George: died in York County, 1645.

Hopkinson, Thomas: in Kingston Parish, Matthews County, 1784.

Horner, Hezekiah: performed baptism, 1665.

Horrocks, James: President, William and Mary College, 1764-71; Rector, Bruton Parish, 1764-71.

Hotchkis, ———: Minister of Southwark Parish, Surry County, 1754.

Housden, William: Minister of Lower Parish, Isle of Wight County, and Chuckatuck Parish, Nansemond County, 1680.

Hove, Rice: licensed for Virginia, 21 December 1756.

Hubard, William: Minister of Warwick Parish, Warwick County, 1773-76; Minister of Newport Parish, Isle of Wight County, until 1802.

Hudson, Edward: ordained for Virginia, 19 July 1709.

Hudson, George: died in Williamsburg, 1696.

Hughes, Thomas: Minister, Upper Parish, Nansemond County, 1716-19; Minister, Abingdon Parish, Gloucester County, 1719-44.

Hunt, Brian: King's bounty to Virginia, 8 May 1722.

Hunt, John: King's bounty to Virginia, 18 January 1775.

Hunt, Robert, M.A.: first Anglican Minister in Virginia; Minister at Jamestown, 1607-08.

Hurt, John: in Jefferson County, 1775; Chaplain of 6th Virginia Regiment in Revolution.

I

Inglis, Mungo, M.A.: master of grammar school, William and Mary College, 1694 and 1716.

Innes, Robert (Innis): Minister of Drysdale Parish, King and Queen and Caroline Counties, 1754-58.

J

Jackson, Andrew: in Lancaster County; died 1710.

Jacob, Henry: ministered in Isle of Wight County, until 1624.

James, Richard: Minister at Kent Island (now in Maryland), 1632.

Jameson, John: ordained for Virginia, 7 February 1709-10.

Jameson, Walter: licensed for Virginia, 29 June 1764.

Jarrett, Devereux: Minister of Bath Parish, Dinwiddie County, 1763-1801.

Johnson, Edward: died in York County, 1665.

Johnson, Josiah: master of grammar school, William and Mary College, 1767-72.

Johnson, Thomas: Minister of Cornwall Parish, Charlotte County, 1773-87.

Jones, Edward: Minister of St. Mark's Parish, Culpeper County, 1773-80; Minister of North Farnham Parish, Richmond County, 1786-87.

Jones, ———. King's bounty to Virginia, 8 September 1699.

Jones, ———. King's bounty to Virginia, 24 March 1700-01.

Jones, ———. King's bounty to Virginia, 7 June 1700.

Jones, Emanuel Sr.: Minister of Petsworth Parish, Gloucester County, 1700-39.

Jones, Emanuel Jr.: master of Indian school, William and Mary College, 1755-77.

Jones, Emanuel: Minister, St. Bride's Parish, Norfolk County, 1776; had a parish (probably St. David's) in King William County, until 1787; grandson of Emanuel Sr. and nephew of Emanuel Jr.

Jones, Hugh: preached at Jamestown; Chaplain to General Assembly; Minister of St. Stephen's Parish, King and Queen County, until 1726.

Jones, John: second Minister of Augusta Parish, Augusta County, 1750-73.

Jones, Nicholas: officiated in Lynnhaven Parish, Princess Anne County, 1726-28.

Jones, Owen: Minister, St. Mary's Parish, Essex (later Caroline) County, 1704-24.

Jones, Richard: in Martin's Brandon Parish, Charles City (now Prince George) County, 1650.

Jones, Rowland: Minister of Bruton Parish, 1674-88; Minister of Jamestown and Martin's Hundred, 1680.

Jones, Samuel: Minister at Jamestown, 1671.

Jones, Walter: Minister, Westmoreland County, 1724; may have been Minister of Cople Parish.

Judin, James: King's bounty to Virginia, 30 November 1732.

K

Kay, William: Minister of Lunenburg Parish, Richmond County, 1745-50; Minister, Cumberland Parish, Lunenburg County, 1751-55.

Keith, George: Minister of Kiskiack (Cheskiack) Parish, York County, 1634.

Keith, George: preached in Virginia, 1703-04.

Keith, James: Minister, Henrico Parish, Henrico County, 1730-33; Minister of Hamilton Parish, Prince William (later Faquier) County, 1736-57.

Kellsall, Roger: Minister, Elizabeth River Parish; died 1708-09.

Kenner, Rodham Sr.: Minister of St. George's Parish, Spotsylvania County, 1729-30, and officiated, until 1732.

Kenner, Rodham Jr.: Minister, Hanover Parish, King George County, 1780-85.

Kerneguy: (See Carnegie).

Key, Isaac: Minister, Hungar's Parish, Northampton County, 1676.

Kippax, Peter: Minister of North Farnham Parish, Richmond County, 1702; Minister of Sittenbourne and North Farnham Parishes, 1714.

Clug.

Kleig

Klug, Samuel: Minister of Christ Church Parish, Middlesex County, 1767-95.

King, John: in Middlesex County, 1767.

Kynaston

Kymaston, John: licensed for Virginia, 29 August 1770.

L

Lendrum

Landrum, Thomas: Minister of Hanover Parish, King George County, until 1771.

Lang, John: Minister, St. Peter's Parish, New Kent County, 1725-27.

Lake, Thomas: in Surry County, 1655.

Lansdale, Peter: invited to preach at Jamestown before General Assembly, 1660.

Latane, Lewis: Minister, South Farnham Parish, Essex County, 1701-37.

Lawrence, John (Larwence): Minister of Denbigh and Mulberry Island Parishes, Warwick County, 1680.

Leake

Leate, William (Leete): in Virginia, 1622.

Lecharcey, ———: preached in St. Stephen's Parish, Northumberland County, 1724.

Leigh, William: Minister of Manchester Parish, Chesterfield County, 1774-76; Minister of Dale Parish, Chesterfield County, 1775-86.

Leland, John Sr.: Minister of Wicomico Parish, Northumberland County, 1754-74.

Leland, John Jr.: Minister of Wicomico Parish, Northumberland County, 1775-91.

Le Neve, William: Minister of James City Parish, 1737; had church on Mulberry Island, Warwick County, 1723.

Lesley, Robert: performed baptism, Charles City, 1654.

Lewis, Roger: ordained for Virginia, 20 April 1709.

Lidford, Matthew: Minister of Christ Church Parish, Middlesex County, 1691-92.

Lindsay, David (Lindsey), D.D.: officiated in Lancaster County, 1658.

Lloyd, Thomas F.: King's bounty to Virginia, 13 May 1766.

Lloyd, ———: in Drysdale Parish, 1758.

Locke, John: officiated in Kingston Parish, Gloucester (now Matthews) County, 1750.

Locke, Richard: licensed for Virginia, 13 May 1749.

Lonsdale, Peter: preached before General Assembly; same as Lansdale.

Lowe, John: Rector, Hanover Parish, King George County, 1786-87 and 1794-96.

Lunen

Lunan, Alexander: licensed for Virginia, 24 December 1769.

Lunen

Lunan, Patrick: ministered in St. Andrew's Parish, Brunswick County, 1760; Minister of Upper Parish, Nansemond County, 1760-74.

Lundie, Thomas: Minister of St. Andrew's Parish, Brunswick County, 1769-87.

Lyford, John: Minister of Martin's Hundred Parish, James City County, 1628-29.

Lyon, John: Minister of St. George's Parish, Accomac County, 1774.

Lyth, John: licensed for Virginia, 10 October 1763.

M

Macartney

Mccartney, James: Minister of St. Patrick's Parish, Prince Edward County, 1773-74.

Maccallum, Nevil: King's bounty to Virginia, 11 September 1735.

McClaurine: (See McLaurin).

McClean, John: King's bounty to Virginia, 12 August 1773.

McCoy: (See McKay).

McCreary, ———: in Amelia County, 1759.

McCroskey, Samuel Smith (McCoskey): Minister of Hungar's Parish, Northampton County, 1774-1803.

Maccullock, Roderick: King's bounty to Virginia, 20 October 1730.

McDaniel, ———: proposed for St.

Mark's Parish, Culpeper County, 1739.

McDonald, Daniel: Minister, Brunswick Parish, King George County, 1732-62.

MacKae, Christopher: (See MacRae).

Mackay

McKay, William (Maccoy, MacKay): Minister of Hanover Parish, King George County, 1737-47; Minister of North Farnham Parish, Richmond County, 1754-74.

MacGowan, Walter: licensed for Virginia, 24 June 1768.

McKensie, ———: preached in Isle of Wight County, 1746; Minister of Suffolk Parish, Nansemond County, until 1753-54.

Mackenzey, Kennith: King's bounty to Virginia, 12 September 1711.

McKenzie, William: licensed for Virginia, 6 June 1773.

McClaurine

McLaurin, Robert: Minister of St. James' Southam Parish, Cumberland County, 1751-72.

McClean.

Mclean, John: licensed for Virginia (Botetourt Parish), 1 August 1773.

Mcmorran, James: recommended by Governor Spotswood to "Norfolk Parish," 1710.

McNoe, Robert: ordained for Virginia, 19 June 1709.

Mackae

Macrae, Christopher: ministered in Surry County; Minister of Littleton Parish, Cumberland County, 1773-87.

McRobert, Arch.

McRoberts, Archibald: Minister, Dale Parish, Chesterfield County, 1773-75; Minister, St. Patrick's Parish, Prince Edward County, 1776-79.

Madison, James: President, William and Mary College, 1777; first bishop of Virginia, 19 September 1790; last Rector of Jamestown Parish; Chaplain of Virginia House of Delegates, 1777.

Magowan, Walter: (See Macgowan).

Mallory, Philip: Minister of Lynnhaven Parish, Norfolk (later Princess Anne) County, 1657; Chaplain of General Assembly, 1658-59; probably Minister in Jamestown and York Counties.

Manley, George: Chaplain in Navy, 1725-28.

Manning, Nathaniel: Minister of Hampshire Parish, Hampshire County, 1772-74; given a parish by Governor Gooch, 1727.

Marsden, Richard.

Marsden, John: officiated in Lynnhaven Parish, Princess Anne County, 1728-29.

Marshall, Mungo: Minister of St. Thomas'

Parish, Orange County, 1745-58.

Martin, Lazarus: 1628.

Martin, Thomas: Minister, St. Thomas' Parish, Orange County, 1768-69.

Mayre

Mayre, James Sr.: Minister of James' Parish, Goochland County, and of King William Parish, Manakintown, 1730-32; Minister of St. George's Parish, Spotsylvania County, 1735-67.

Marye, James Jr.: Minister of St. Thomas' Parish, Orange County, 1761-68; Minister of St. George's Parish, Spotsylvania County, 1768-80.

Massamm

Massarum, ———: Minister, King William Parish, Powhatan County, 1729.

Massey, Lee: Minister of Truro Parish, Fairfax County, 1767-1814.

Matthews, John: Minister of St. Anne's Parish, Essex County, 1774-87; Rector of St. Bride's Parish, Norfolk County, 1799.

Maury, James: Minister of Fredericksville Parish, Louisa and Albemarle Counties, 1754-70; it was his case in which Patrick Henry made his speech, "Parson's Cause."

Maury, James: licensed for Virginia, 27 December 1755.

Maury, Matthew: Minister of Fredericksville Parish, Albemarle and Louisa Counties, 1770-1808; son of James (above).

Maury, Walker: Minister of Elizabeth River Parish, Norfolk County, 1786; son of James (above).

May, John: ordained for Virginia, 4 January 1709-10.

Maycock

Macocke, Samuel: came to Virginia, 1618.

Mease, William (Mays, Meese): Minister, Kecoughtan.

Mechlonberg, ———: King's bounty to Virginia, 7 May 1772.

Meiklejohn, George: in Mecklenburg County, 1776.

Meldrum, William: Minister of Frederick Parish, Frederick County, prior to 1765.

Menzies, Adam: Minister of Bromfield Parish, Culpeper (now Madison and Rappahannock) County, 1750-55; Minister of St. Stephen's Parish, Northumberland County, 1758-67.

Messenger, Joseph: licensed for Virginia (Stafford County), 7 May 1772.

Milne, Francis (Mylne): in Kingston Parish, 1714.

Milner, John: Minister of Upper Parish, Isle of Wight County, 1766-70.

Minge, James: came to Virginia, 1650.

Mitton, Roger: King's bounty to Virginia,

27 April 1692.

Moncure, John: Minister of Overwharton Parish, Stafford County, 1738-64.

Monro.

Monroe, Andrew: Minister of Newport Parish, Isle of Wight County, 1700-19.

Munro, John Sr.: Minister of "Pamonkie," Stratton Major (?), 1650.

Munro, John Jr.: Minister of Hungar's Parish, Northampton County, 1692; Minister of St. John's Parish, King William County, 1695-1723.

Moreau, Nicholas: Minister of St. Peter's Parish, New Kent County, 1696-97.

Morton

Moreton, Andrew: Minister of Drysdale Parish, King and Queen and Caroline Counties, 1774.

Morris, Richard: Minister of parishes in Middlesex County, 1663-66.

Morrison, James: King's bounty to Virginia, 1 May 1776.

Morrison, John: King's bounty to Virginia, 8 September 1699.

Mortland, David (Morthland): Minister of Lunenburg Parish, Richmond County, prior to 1745; Minister of St. Stephen's Parish, Northumberland County, until 1754.

Mossom, David: Minister of St. Peter's Parish, New Kent County, 1727-67; officiated at marriage of George Washington.

Muhlenburg, Peter: Minister of Beckford Parish, Shenandoah County, 1772-75; General during Revolution; Member of House of Burgesses and Virginia Convention.

Munro (Munroe): (See Monro).

Murdaugh, William (Murdock): Minister of St. James' Parish, Goochland County, 1725-27; Minister, King William Parish, Manakintown, 1727.

Moray

Murray, Alexander: Minister of Ware Parish, Gloucester County, 1665.

Mynnard, ———: Minister of Martin's Hundred Parish, prior to 1628.

N

Nivison, John

Navison, John (Nevison): Minister of Meherrin Parish, Greensville County, 1754-58.

Nearn, ——— (Nierne, Nearne): Minister of King William Parish, Manakintown (now Powhatan County), 1727-28; Minister of Varina (Henrico) Parish, Henrico County, 1727-28.

Nedin, ———: (See Judin).

Nelson, William: in King William County, 1724.

Nern, ———: (See Wern).

Nixon, William: elected in Elizabeth City Parish, Elizabeth City County, 1783.

Nugent, Theophilus: Minister, St. George's Parish, Accomac County, 1787.

O

O'Brien, Christopher: ordained for Virginia, 2 May 1707.

Ogle, Henry: ordained for Virginia, 5 April 1705.

Oglevie

Ogilvie, James: Minister of Westover Parish, Charles City County, 1776.

Otis

Osier, ———: Minister in Isle of Wight County.

Owen, Goronwy (Gronovius): Minister, St. Andrew's Parish, Brunswick County, 1760-69.

P

Page, John: Minister of Elizabeth City Parish, Elizabeth City County, 1677-87; Minister of St. Peter's Parish, New Kent County, 1687-88.

Palmer, Samuel: in Hungar's Parish, Northampton County, 1695.

Palmer, Thomas: in Hungar's Parish, Northampton County, 1647-48.

Panton, Anthony: Minister of "York and Chiskiack" Parishes, York County, 1639-40.

Parke, Robert: Minister of Upper Parish, Isle of Wight County, 1680.

Parker

Parkes, Henry: Minister of Accomac Parish, Accomac County, 1680.

Pasteur, Charles: King's bounty to Virginia, 19 March 1735-36.

Pasteur, James: Minister of Bath Parish, Dinwiddie County, 1755-56; Minister of St. Bride's Parish, Norfolk County, 1773-74; probably brother of Charles.

Patton, Thomas: King's bounty to Virginia, 5 May 1710.

Paulett, Robert (Pawlett): at Martin's Hundred; Preacher at Berkeley Hundred, 1621.

Paxton, Zechariah: invited to officiate in Bruton Parish, 1710.

Pead, Duell: Minister of Christ Church Parish, Middlesex County, 1683-90.

Peador, Thomas: Minister of Elizabeth City Parish, Elizabeth City County, 1727-31.

Peart, Francis: officiated in St. George's Parish, Spotsylvania County, 1730, and in St. Mark's Parish, Culpeper County, 1732;

Minister, St. Stephen's Parish, Northumberland County, 1731-42.

Peasley, William: Minister of Tillotson Parish, Buckingham County, 1773-87.

Pedier, ———: Minister, Isle of Wight County, 1770.

Pedin, James: Minister of Nottoway Parish, Amelia (now Nottoway) County, until 1742.

Pemberton, ———: came to Virginia, 1622.

Pender, Edzard: King's bounty to Virginia, 12 July 1726.

Pendleton, Nathaniel: came to Virginia, 1674.

Perkins, Thomas: died in Rappahannock County, 1684.

Pettigrew, Charles: chosen Minister of Lynnhaven Parish, Princess Anne County, 1783.

Phillipe, Mr.: same as Phillippe de Richebourg.

Phillips, Thomas: in "Parish of Potomac River," 1716 (possibly Overwharton or St. Paul's Parish, Stafford County).

Phillips, William: Minister of South Farnham Parish, Essex County, 1739-44.

Phipps, John: officiated a baptism in Overwharton Parish, Stafford County, 1747.

Poole

Powell, ———: preached at Jamestown, 19 May 1611.

Pooley, Greville: ministered at Fleur de Hundred.

Porter, James: Minister of Lynnhaven Parish, Lower Norfolk (later Princess Anne) County, 1678-83.

Portlock, Edward: Minister of Stratton Major Parish, King and Queen County, 1702-05.

Poultenay, Francis: King's bounty to Virginia, 8 January 1735-36.

Pow, William: Minister of St. Andrew's Parish, Brunswick County, 1750; Minister of Bath Parish, Dinwiddie County, prior to 1754.

Powis, Robert: Minister of Lynnhaven Parish, Lower Norfolk (later Princess Anne) County, 1645-52.

Pownall, Benjamin: in Virginia, 1719-21.

Preston, William: Minister at Jamestown, 1755.

Price, Thomas: Minister, Abingdon Parish, Gloucester County, 1773-78; ministered in Petsworth Parish, 1782; Preacher before Virginia Convention, 1774-75, and Chaplin, 1775.

Prichard, ———.

Preade, Robert: King's bounty to Virginia,

12 April 1758.

Pretty, Henry.

Prince, John: Minister of Hanover Parish, King George County, until 1723.

Proctor, William: Minister of Nottoway Parish, Amelia (now Nottoway) County, 1754.

Pruit: (See Peart).

Purdie, George: Minister of Cumberland Parish, Lunenburg County, 1750; Minister of St. Andrew's Parish, Brunswick County, 1751-60.

R

Rannford

Rainsford, Giles: ministered in Surry County, 1713-14; Minister of Lower Parish, Nansemond County, 1714; Minister of St. Anne's Parish, Essex County, 1717; held a parish in Culpeper County.

Ramsay

Ramsey, John: Minister of St. Anne's Parish, Albemarle County, 1754.

Read, Duell: (See Pead).

Reade, John: Minister of Stratton Major Parish, King and Queen County, 1736-43.

Read, Robert: Minister of Kinston Parish, Gloucester (now Matthews) County, 1778; called to Petsworth Parish, Gloucester County, 1762.

Reid, John: Minister of Newport Parish, Isle of Wight County, 1746-55.

Renney

Renny, Robert: licensed for Virginia, 1 July 1764.

Rhonnald

Rhonald, Alexander: Minister of Elizabeth River Parish, Norfolk County, 1762.

Richards, John: Minister of Ware Parish, Gloucester County, 1724-35.

Richardson, ———: King's bounty to Virginia, 12 July 1700.

Richardson, Daniel: ministered in Hungar's Parish, Northampton County, prior to 1676.

Richebourge, Phillipe de: Minister to the Huguenots of King William Parish, Manakintown, Henrico County, 1704-07.

Roberts, John: dismissed from his parish, 1740.

Robertson, Eleazar: Minister of Bristol Parish, Dinwiddie County, 1748-53.

Robertson, George: Chaplain of man-of-war, 1692; Minister of Bristol Parish, Dinwiddie County, 1693-1739.

Robertson, James: King's bounty to Virginia, 15 January 1717-18.

Robertson, John: Minister, St. James' Southam Parish, Powhatan County, 1746-51; Minister, St. John's Parish, King William County, 1752-56.

Robertson, Moses: Minister, St. Stephen's Parish, Northumberland County, 1743.

Robinson, Francis: Clerk.

Robinson, George: probably same as George Robertson.

Robinson, Thomas: master of grammar school, William and Mary College, 1742-58.

Robinson, William: Minister of Stratton Major Parish, King and Queen County, 1744-68.

Rodgers, John: in Northampton County, 1664; perhaps Minister of Nassawadox Parish.

Rose, Charles: Minister, Cople Parish, Westmoreland County, 1754-55; brother of Robert (below).

Rose, Robert: Minister, St. Anne's Parish, Essex County, 1725-46; Minister, St. Anne's Parish, Albemarle County, 1746-51.

Rosier, John (Rosyer, Rozier): Minister of Cheskiack and York Parishes, York County, 1640; Minister of Hungar's Parish, Northampton County, 1644.

Rowan, John: in Virginia, 1754.

Rowe, Jacob: perhaps Chaplain in Navy, 1756.

Rudd, William: Minister of Elizabeth River Parish, Norfolk County, 1702; Minister of Chuckatuck Parish, Nansemond County, 1703.

S

Sandford, Samuel: may have been Minister of Accomac or St. George's Parish, Accomac County, 1694-1702.

Sandys, George (David) (Sands, Saunders): Minister on Hog Island, Surry County.

Saunders, Jonathan: Minister of Lynnhaven Parish, Princess Anne County, 1695.

Saunders, John: ordained for Virginia, 24 October 1699.

Saunders, John Hyde: Minister of St. James' Southam Parish, Cumberland (now Powhatan) County, 1773-1801.

Sax, Thomas: Minister, Lancaster County, prior to 1654.

Sclater, James: officiated in Bruton Parish, 1688; Minister of Charles Parish, York County, 1686-1724; Minister of Mulberry Island, Warwick County, 1714.

Scott, Alexander, M.A.: Minister of Overwharton Parish, Stafford County, 1711-38; possibly Minister of St. Paul's Parish, Stafford County, 1714.

Scott, James: first Minister of Dettingen Parish, Prince William County, 1745-82; son of Alexander (above).

Scott, John: Minister of Dettingen Parish, Prince William County, 1782-83; son of James (above).

Scrimgour, William (Scrimington): Minister of Cople Parish, Westmoreland County, 1680.

Seagood, George: Rector of Sittenburne Parish, Richmond and King George Counties, until 1724.

Sebastain, Benjamin: Minister of Frederick Parish, Frederick County, 1766-67; Minister of St. Stephen's Parish, Northumberland County, 1767-77.

Selden, Miles: Minister of Henrico Parish, Henrico County, 1756-85; Chaplain at Convention of 1775 and House of Delegates.

Selden, William: Minister of Elizabeth City Parish, Elizabeth City County, 1771-83.

Sellick

Sellake, William: Minister of St. Peter's Parish, New Kent County, 1680-82.

Semple, William.

Sharpe, Thomas: Minister, Warwisqueake Parish, Isle of Wight County, 1702; Minister, St. Paul's Parish, Hanover County, 1708-20; officiated in St. Peter's Parish, New Kent County, 1720.

Sheppard

Shephard, John (Shepherd): Minister of Christ Church Parish, Middlesex County, 1668-82.

Shepheard.

Shepeard, Richard: ordained for Virginia, February 1706-07.

Sheild

Shield, Samuel: Minister of Drysdale Parish, King and Queen and Caroline Counties, 1776; Minister of St. Asaph's Parish, Caroline County, 1785; Minister of York-Hampton Parish, York County, 1786-90; Minister of Charles Parish, 1791-92.

Shorthose, Henry: King's bounty to Virginia, 27 February 1732-33.

Shropshire, Saint John: held a parish in lower Virginia, 1704; Minister, Washington Parish, Westmoreland County, 1714.

Simpson, James: Minister of Lynnhaven Parish, Princess Anne County, 1785-87.

Simpson, Joseph: may have been Minister of Hanover Parish, King George County, 1747-51; Minister of Lunenburg Parish, Richmond County, 1754-55.

Skaife, John: Minister of Stratton Major Parish, King and Queen County, 1710-36.

Skelton, William: Clerk.

Skyring
Skyren, Henry: Minister of St. John's Parish, King William County, 1773-87; Minister of Elizabeth City Parish, Elizabeth City County, 1787-95.
Slater: (See Sclater).
Smelt, John: Minister of St. Anne's Parish, Essex County, 1749-58.
Smith, Adam: Curate, Augusta Parish, Augusta County, 1772; Minister of Botetourt Parish, Botetourt County, 1774-76.
Smith, Charles: Minister, Elizabeth River Parish, Norfolk County, 1743-61; parished divided in 1761, and he retained Portsmouth Parish, until 1773.
Smith, Guy: Minister of Abingdon Parish, Gloucester County, 1702-19.
Smith, James: King's bounty to Virginia, 12 January 1702-03.
Smith, John: performed baptism in Surry County (?), 1742.
Smith, Joseph: King's bounty to Virginia, 21 September 1727.
Smith, Patrick: Minister of Southwark Parish, Surry County, 1690.
Smith, Thomas: Minister of St. Stephen's Parish, Northumberland County, 1753-58; Minister of Cople Parish, Westmoreland County, 1773-89.
Smith, William: King's bounty to Virginia, 24 September 1729.
Span, John (Spann): Minister of St. Stephen's Parish, Northumberland County, 1712-22.
Spencer, Archibald: licensed for Virginia, 30 August 1749.
Solomon, D.: in Virginia, 1702.
Squire, Richard: Minister of St. Peter's Parish, New Kent County, 1703-07.
Staige, Theodosius: Minister of St. George's Parish, Spotsylvania County, 1726-28; Minister of Charles Parish, York County, 1728-47.
Standard, Thomas: King's bounty to Virginia, 7 May 1723.
Stannard, William (Staynard): in Virginia, 1705.
Staples, Robert: probably in Virginia, 1622.
Stevenson
Stephenson, James: Minister, Camden Parish, Pittsylvania County, 1769; Minister, Berkeley Parish, Spotsylvania County, 1769-80; Minister, St. Mark's Parish, Culpeper County, 1780-94; Minister, St. George's Parish, Spotsylvania County, 1794-1805.
Stith, William: Minister of Henrico Parish, Henrico County, 1736-51; President, William and Mary College,

1752-55.
Stockton, Jonas: Minister, Henrico and Elizabeth City Parishes, 1627.
Strahan, David: King's bounty to Virginia, 18 October 1715.
Stritchley, John: tomb at St. Mary's Whitechapel, Lancaster County.
Stuart, David: Minister of St. Paul's Parish, Stafford (now King George) County, 1722-49.
Stuart, James: licensed for Virginia, 21 September 1766.
Stuart, William: Minister of St. Paul's Parish, Stafford (now King George) County, 1749-90; son of David (above).
Sturges, Daniel: Minister of Norborne Parish, Berkeley County (now West Virginia), 1771-86.
Swift, William: sent by Governor Gooch to St. Martin's Parish, Hanover County, 1728; officiated in King William Parish, Manakintown, 1728-29.
Swynfen, Henry: King's bounty to Virginia, 20 December 1720.
Superios: (See Zyperios).

T
Taylor, Daniel Sr.: Minister of Blissland Parish, New Kent and James City Counties, 1704-29; officiated in St. Peter's Parish, 1708; invited to officiate in Bruton Parish, 1710.
Taylor, Daniel Jr.: Minister of St. John's Parish, King William County, 1729-42.
Taylor, James: Minister, St. Asaph's Parish, Caroline County, 1786.
Taylor, Jeremiah: Minister, Elizabeth City Parish, Elizabeth City County, 1667.
Taylor, Thomas: Minister of Blissland Parish, New Kent and James City Counties, 1680.
Teakle, Thomas: Minister of Nassawadox Parish, Northampton County, and of St. George's Parish, Accomac County, 1662-94; Minister of Hungar's and Northampton Parishes, Northampton County, 1680.
Temple, Peter: Resident of Temple Farm, York County, prior to 1686; probably same as below.
Temple, ———.
Tennant, James: Minister of Lynnhaven Parish, Princess Anne County, 1714-26.
Thacker, Chicheley: Minister of Blissland Parish, New Kent and James City Counties, 1729-63.
Theodore, Esdras: King's bounty to Virginia, 12 July 1726.
Thomson
Thompson, Andrew: Minister of Elizabeth City Parish, Elizabeth City County,

1712-19.
Thompson, George: King's bounty to Virginia, 20 June 1726.
Thompson, James: Minister of Leeds Parish, Fauquier County, 1769-1812.
Thompson, John: Minister of St. Mark's Parish, Orange (later Culpeper) County, 1740-72.
Thompson, Thomas: Minister of Antrim Parish, Halifax County, 1762.
Thompson, William: Minister, Southwark and Lawne's Creek Parishes, Surry County, 1662-75; Minister of Washington Parish, Westmoreland County, 1690.
Thompson, William: came on appeal from Virginia to Boston for ministers, 1642.
Thornton, Thomas: Minister of Brunswick Parish, King George and Stafford Counties, 1785-87; Minister, St. George's Parish, Spotsylvania County, 1788-91; Minister, Dettingen Parish (Quantico Church, Dumfries), Prince William County.
Thurston
Thruston, Charles Mynn: Minister of Petsworth Parish, Gloucester County, prior to 1768; Minister of Frederick Parish, Frederick County, 1768-77.
Tillard
Tyliard
Tillyard, Arthur: invited to officiate in Bruton Parish, 1710.
Tinney, William: King's bounty to Virginia, 10 October 1709.
Todd, Christopher: officiated baptism, Drysdale Parish (?), 1777.
Townsend, Jacob: in Virginia, 1754.
Typerios: (See Zyperios).

U
Urmstone
Urnstons, John (Urmstons): King's bounty to Virginia, 29 June 1722.
Urqhart, John: Minister of Wicomico Parish, Northumberland County, 1702.

V
Veasy, ———: Minister of Norborne Parish, Berkeley County, 1786; in Frederick Parish, 1781.
Vere, William: Minister of Accomac Parish, Accomac County, 1774.
Vicars
Vicaris, Thomas (Viccaris): Minister of Petsworth Parish, Gloucester County, 1677-97.

W
Wadding, James: Minister at Jamestown,

1672; Minister of Petsworth Parish, Gloucester County.

Wagener

Waggener, Peter (Waggoner): in Virginia, 1705.

Walker, Alexander: Minister of Southwark Parish, Surry County, 1702.

Wallace, James: Minister of Elizabeth City Parish, Elizabeth City County, 1691-1712; invited to officiate in Bruton Parish, 1710.

Wallis, Samuel: in Chuckatuck Parish, Nansemond County, 1714.

Worden, John

Worden, Samuel

Warden, James: all three same man; officiated at Jamestown, 1712; Minister of Weyanoke and Martin's Brandon Parishes, Charles City and Prince George Counties; Minister of Lawne's Creek Parish, Isle of Wight County, 1717-25.

Ware, Jacob: Minister of St. Peter's Parish, New Kent County, 1690-95; Minister of Henrico Parish, Henrico County, 1695-1709.

Warrington, Thomas (John): Minister of Charles Parish, York County, 1749-56; Minister of Elizabeth City Parish, Elizabeth City County, 1756-70.

Watson, Leonard: licensed for Virginia, 10 March 1762.

Watson, Ralph: died in York County, 1645.

Watts, Richard: King's bounty to Virginia, 10 May 1727.

Waugh, Abner: Minister of St. Mary's Parish, Caroline County, 1773-1806; Minister of St. George's Parish, Spotsylvania County, 1806; Chaplain of a Continental regiment and Virginia Convention of 1788.

Waugh, John: Minister of Potomac Parish, Stafford County, 1667; parish divided into Overwharton and Choatanck (later St. Paul's) Parishes, and he continued in charge of both, until 1700.

Wayre: (See Woyre).

Webb, William: Minister of Upper Parish, Nansemond County, 1747-60.

Wern, William (Nern): Minister of Elizabeth River Parish, Norfolk County, 1680.

West, William: Minister of Fairfax Parish, Fairfax County, 1778-79.

Weyre, ——— (Wayre): (See Woyre).

Wheatley, Solomon (Whately): Minister of Lynnhaven Parish, Princess Anne County, 1702; Minister of Bruton Parish, Williamsburg, 1702-10; Chaplain of House of Burgesses, 1705.

White, Alexander: Minister of St. David's Parish, King William County, 1754-75.

White, George: in Denbigh Parish, Warwick County, 1635.

White, Thomas: came to Virginia, 1622.

White, William: Minister of York Parish, York County, 1658.

Whittaker, Alexander, M.A.: first Minister of Herico Parish, Henrico County, 1611; religious instructor of Pochontas; "The Apostle of Virginia."

Wickham, William: Minister of Henricopolis, 1616, as curate to Alexander Whittaker (above).

Wilkerson, William (Wilkinson): in Lynnhaven Parish (?), 1635.

Wilkinson, Thomas: Minister of Bristol Parish, Dinwiddie County, 1753-62; Minister of Nottoway Parish, Amelia County, 1773-76.

Williams, Paul: Minister of Weyanoke and Martin's Brandon Parishes, Charles City and Prince George Counties, 1680.

Williams, William: Minister of St. Stephen's Parish, King and Queen County, 1680; officiated in St. Peter's Parish, New Kent County, 1689-90.

Willie, William: Minister of Albemarle Parish, Sussex County, 1753-76.

Wilson, Francis: Minister of Washington Parish, Westmoreland County, 1782-87.

Wilson, James: in Elizabeth River Parish, Norfolk County, 1658.

Wilson, John: Minister of Elizabeth River Parish, Lower Norfolk County, 1637-40.

Wingate, John: Minister of St. Thomas' Parish, Orange County, 1774.

Wishart, John: Minister of Brunswick Parish, King George County, until 1774.

Wood, John: Minister of Lower Parish, Nansemond County, 1680.

Woodmason, Charles: elected to Bromfield Parish, Culpeper County, 1771.

Woodside, Frederick: King's bounty to Virginia, 21 April 1708.

Worden: (See Warden).

Worthen, ———: in Virginia, 1723.

Woyre

Wayre, John (Weyre): Minister of Lawne's Creek Parish, Surry County, 1680.

Wright, John: Minister of "New Towson" (Pocoson) Parish, York County, 1680.

Wright, John: sent by Governor Gooch to parish in Northern Neck.

Wyatt, Hawte (Wiatt) (Haute): Minister at Jamestown, until 1626.

Wyatt, John: in Virginia, 1705.

Wyatt, Richard: in Virginia, 1705.

Wye, William: in Northumberland County, 1727.

Y

Yancey, Robert: Minister of Trinity Parish, Louisa County, 1774.

Yates, Bartholomew Sr.: Minister of Sittenburne Parish, and north side of St. Mary's Parish, Richmond County, 1702; Minister of Kingston Parish, Gloucester (now Matthews) County, prior to 1703; Minister of Christ Church Parish, Middlesex County, 1703.

Yates, Bartholomew Jr.: Minister of Christ Church Parish, Middlesex County, 1736-67.

Yates, Robert Sr.: Minister of Christ Church Parish, Middlesex County, 1699-1703; brother of Bartholomew (above).

Yates, Robert Jr.: Minister of Petsworth Parish, Gloucester County, 1741-61.

Yates, William: Minister of Abingdon Parish, Gloucester County, 1750-59; Rector of Bruton Parish, James City County, 1759-64; President, William and Mary College, 1761-64.

Young, George: Minister of Petsworth Parish, Gloucester County, 1699-1700.

Young, W. George: in Westmoreland County, 1776; Rector of Lunenburg Parish, Richmond County, 1800-02.

Z

Zyperios, Michael: Minister of Kingston Parish, Gloucester (now Matthews) County, 1680.

Zyperne, Michael: same as above; Minister of Kingston Parish, Gloucester (now Matthews) County, 1680-87.

COLONIAL CHURCHES CONTACT INFORMATION

Abingdon Episcopal Church
P.O. Box 82
White Marsh, Virginia 23183
(804) 693-3035
www.abingdonchurch.org

Aquia Episcopal Church
P.O. Box 275
2938 Jefferson Davis Highway
Stafford, Virginia 22555
(540) 659-4007
www.aquiachurch.com

Augusta Stone Presbyterian Church
P.O. Box 118
28 Old Stone Church Lane
Fort Defiance, Virginia 24437
(540) 248-2634
www.augusta.stone.org

Blandford Church
111 Rochelle Lane
Petersburg, Virginia
(804) 733-2396

Bruton Parish Church
P.O. Box 3520
Williamsburg, Virginia 23187-3520
(757) 229-2891
www.brutonparish.org

Buck Mountain Episcopal Church
P.O. Box 83
Earlysville, Virginia 22936
(434) 973-2054
www.us.net/edov/15/bmc

Christ Church, Lancaster County
Foundation for Historic Christ Church
P.O. Box 24
Irvington, Virginia 22480
www.christchurch1735.org

Christ Episcopal Church
118 N. Washington Street
Alexandria, Virginia 22314
(703) 549-1450
www.historicchristchurch.org

Chuckatuck Church, now St. John's
    Episcopal Church
828 King's Highway
Chuckatuck, Virginia 23432
(757) 255-4168
www.stjohnschuckatuck.org

Deep Run Baptist Church
10907 Three Chopt Road
Richmond, Virginia 23233
(804) 270-3831
www.deeprun.org

The Falls Church (Episcopal)
115 E. Fairfax Street
Falls Church, Virginia 22046
(703) 532-7600
www.thefallschurch.org

Fincastle Presbyterian Church
96 Valleydale Street
Double Gate
Bluefield, Virginia 24605
(540) 322-3032

Glebe Episcopal Church
P.O. Box 5042
4400 Nansemond Parkway
Suffolk, Virginia 23435
(757) 538-8842

Grace Episcopal Church
111 Church Street
Yorktown, Virginia 23690
(757) 898-3261
www.gracechurchyorktown.org

Hickory Neck Episcopal Church
8300 Richmond Road
Toano, Virginia 23168
(757) 566-0276
www.hickoryneck.org

Hungars Episcopal Church
Bayside Road
Bridgetown, Virginia
parish house: (757) 678-5486

Little Fork Episcopal Church
Little Fork Church Road
Rixeyville, Virginia 22737
(540) 937-4306
www.us.net/edov/1/littlefork

Lower United Methodist Church
P.O. Box 98
Hartfield, Virginia 23071
(804) 776-6250
www.oasisonline.com/lower/

Mangohick Baptist Church
Hanover, Virginia 23069
(804) 994-5400

Mauck Meeting House
Contact: Page County Heritage
    Association
P.O. Box 627
Luray, Virginia 22835
(540) 743-3915

Merchants Hope Church
11500 Merchant Hope Road
Hopewell, Virginia 23860
(804) 458-1356

North Farnham Episcopal Church
231 North Farnham Church Road
Farnham, Virginia 22450
(804) 394-4107

Old Donation Episcopal Church
4449 North Witch Duck Road
Virginia Beach, Virginia 23455
(757) 497-0563
www.olddonation.org

The Old Presbyterian Meeting House
office: 316 S. Royal Street
sanctuary: 321 S. Fairfax Street
Alexandria, Virginia 22314-3719
(703) 549-6670
www.opmh.org

Pohick Episcopal Church
9301 Richmond Highway
Lorton, Virginia 22079
(703) 339-6572
www.pohick.org

Providence Presbyterian Church
3388 Three Chopt Road
Gum Spring, Virginia 23065
(804) 556-6327

Slash Christian Church
11353 Mount Hermon Road
Ashland, Virginia 23005
(804) 798-4520
www.slashcc.org

St. George's Episcopal Church
P.O. Box 540
Accomac, Virginia 23301
Saint George Circle
Pungoteague, Virginia 23422

St. John's Episcopal Church
100 West Queens Way
Hampton, Virginia
(757) 722-2567

St. John's Episcopal Church (King William
County)
122201 Richmond Street
P.O. Box 3886
Chester, Virginia 23831-8471
www.stjohnschester.com

St. Luke's Church
14477 Benn's Church Boulevard
Smithfield, Virginia 23430
(757) 357-3367
www.historicstlukes.org

St. Paul's Episcopal Church
201 Saint Paul's Boulevard
Norfolk, Virginia 23510-2701
(757) 627-4353

St. Peter's Parish Church
8400 Saint Peters Lane
New Kent, Virginia 23124-2718
www.geocities.com/stpeterstc

Timber Ridge Presbyterian Church
166 Timber Ridge Road
Lexington, Virginia 24450-9850
(540) 463-6939

Vauter's Church
(804) 443-4788

Ware Episcopal Church
P.O. Box 616
7825 John Clayton Memorial Highway
Gloucester, Virginia 23061
www.warechurch.org

Wren Chapel
The Chapel of the Sir Christopher Wren
Building
The College of William & Mary
P.O. Box 8795
Williamsburg, Virginia 23187-8795
(757) 221-1540
www.wm.edu/about/wren/wrenchapel/

Yeocomico Episcopal Church
Contact: Cople Parish
P.O. Box 110
72 Coles Point Road
Hague, Virginia 22469
(804) 472-2593
home.us.net/~Cople/yeocomico.html

BIBLIOGRAPHY

Addison, James Thayer. *The Episcopal Church in the United States, 1789-1931.* 1951.

Bassett, John Spencer. *Writings of Colonel William Byrd.* New York, 1901.

Brock, Dr. R. A. *The vestry book of Henrico Parish, Virginia, 1730-1773.* From the original manuscript.

Brydon, Dr. G. MacLaren. *Highlights Along the Road of the Anglican Church.*

Buckingham Baptist Church: A Brief Review of 200 Years.

Caldwell, Hellen. *Fincastle Presbyterian Church History,* n.d.

Cheshire, Joseph Blount. *The Church in the Confederate States.* 1912.

Chorley, Pres. Kenneth. *Colonial Williamsburg.* An address delivered at the College of William and Mary on Charter Day, 8 February 1945.

Chumbley, George Lewis. *Colonial Justice in Virginia.* Dietz Press, 1938.

Cocke, Charles Frances. *Parish Lines Diocese of Southern Virginia.* 1964.

———. *Parish Lines Diocese of Virginia.* The Virginia State Library, 1967.

Colonial Churches in the original colony of Virginia. Second edition. Richmond, 1908.

Cumbia, Rev. Philip, ex officio. *The History of Deep Run Church.* 1967.

The Daily Progress, Charlottesville,

Virginia. 20 January 1966, 29 April 1971.

Davis, Vernon, and Rawlings, James. *Colonial Churches in Virginia, North Carolina, and Maryland.* 1985.

Dover Association Minutes, 1792-1930.

Ferm, Vergilius, ed. *The American Church of the Protestant Heritage.* 1953.

Foote, Rev. William Henry. *Sketches of Virginia: Historical and Biographical.* 1850.

Goodwin, Rev. Edward Lewis. *The Colonial Church in Virginia.* Morehouse Publishing Co., 1927.

Harris, Malcolm H. *History of Louisa County, Virginia.* 1936.

Hileman, Charles S. *Historical sketch and year book of Timber Ridge Presbyterian Church.* 1931.

The History of the College of William and Mary, from its foundation, 1693-1870. Baltimore: John Murphy & Co., 1870.

Huddle, Rev. W. P. *History of the Hebron Lutheran Church, Madison County, Virginia, from 1717-1907.* 1908.

Hughes, Charles Randolph. *Old Chapel.* Clarke County, Virginia. The Blue Ridge Press, 1906.

Hundley, William Thomas. *History of Mattaponi Baptist Church, King and Queen County, Virginia.* 1928.

Johns, John. *A memoir of the life of Right Rev. William Meade, D.D.* Baltimore, 1867.

Jones, Dianne A. and Elizabeth L. Miller. *Slash Christian Church*

(Disciples of Christ): The History of Slash, July 17, 1729—October 4, 1998.

Maloney, Eugene A. *A History of Buckingham County.* 1976.

Mason, George Carrington. *Colonial Churches of Tidewater Virginia.* 1945.

Massey, Don W. *The Episcopal Churches in the Diocese of Virginia.* Keswick, Virginia: Diocese Church Histories, 1989.

McCartney, Martha W. *Hickory Neck Church in Blisland Parish, Toano, Virginia.* Hickory Neck Church Historical Committee, 1992.

McConnell, S. D. *History of the American Episcopal Church from the planting of the colonies to the end of the Civil War.* 1980.

Meade, William. *Old Churches, Ministers, and Families of Virginia.* 2 vols. Philadelphia, 1872.

Moore, J. Staunton. *History of Henrico Parish, 1611-1904.*

Morton, Oren F. *A History of Rockbridge County, Virginia.* 1920.

Niederer, Francis J. *The Town of Fincastle.* 1965.

Norris, Walter Biscoe, ed. *Westmoreland County, Virginia, 1653-1983.*

Pennington, Edgar Legare. *The Church in England in Colonial Virginia.* 1937.

Peyton, J. Lewis. *History of Augusta County, Virginia.* 1953.

The Pilgrimage to Jamestown, VA of the Bishops and deputies of the general convention of the Protestant

Episcopal Church in the United States of America. Saturday, October 15, 1898.

Powell, Mary G. *The History of Old Alexandria, Virginia. From July 13, 1749 to May 24, 1861.* 1928.

Rawlings, James Scott. *Virginia's Colonial Churches: An Architectural Guide.* Richmond, 1963.

Rose, Harold Wickliffe. *The Colonial Houses of Worship in America.* New York, 1964.

Ryland, John A. *King and Queen County, Virginia: Its Churches and Religious Life, 1691-1791.* West Point, Virginia, 1967?

Slaughter, Philip. *The History of Truro Parish in Virginia.* Philadelphia: George W. Jacobs, & Co., 1908.

Smith, Margaret Vowell. *Virginia, 1492-1892. A brief review of the discovery of the continent of North America with a history of the executives of the colony and the Commonwealth of Virginia.* 1893.

St. Paul's Church, 1832. Original the Borough Church, 1739, Elizabeth River Parish. Norfolk, Virginia, 1934.

Tyler, Lyon Gardiner. *The Cradle of the Republic: Jamestown and James River.* The Hermitage Press, Inc., Richmond, Virginia, 1906.

Up from Independence. The Episcopal Church in Virginia. 1976.

Virginia Historical Magazine, 24: 22.

Yonge, Samuel H. *The Site of Old "James Towne," 1607-1698.*

INDEX

French, Daniel, 155, 175, 176
Fry-Jefferson Map of 1751, 148
Fulton, Rev. John M., 161

G
Gaines, Francis, 57
Gamble, Rev. Cary, 95
Gammill, Rev. John, 13
Garden Club of Virginia, 38
Gardner, William, 155
Garrick, Rev. Samuel, 143
Garrisonville, Virginia, 144
Garver, George, 35
Garzia, Reverend, 98
Gates, Sir Thomas, 18
General Assembly of Virginia, 23, 30, 32, 38, 44, 50, 57, 60, 63, 71, 77, 93, 112, 116, 130, 132, 149, 168, 183
General Association of the Separate Baptists in Virginia, 148
General (Baptist) Association, 126
George I, King of Enland, Duke of Hanover, 55, 69
George II, King of England, 69, 116, 122
George III, King of England, 41, 120, 148
Georgetown, 171
George Washington's Burgess Route to Williamsburg, 75
Germanna Colonies, 101, 179
Germanna Road, Culpeper County, 179
Germany, 55, 102, 104, 122
Gibson, Rev. William, 171
Giffin, Thomas, 102
Giles: Governor, 160; Martha Peyton, 160
Gilliam, Paul R., 149
Glasgow, W. A., 160
Glebe (Episcopal) Church, 89-91, **89, 91,** 139
Gloucester Circuit of Methodist Churches, 58
Gloucester County: 25, 26, 44, 47, 57, 58, 71, 75, 87, 134, 135; Courthouse, 25
Godspeed, 16
Gooch: Gov. Sir William, 122, 179; Lady, 41; Maj. William, 29
Goochland County, 123
Good Hope Church, 143
Goodin, Rev. Benjamin, 33
Goodrich, Dr. Charles, 48
Goodwin: Dr. W. A. R., 41; Mary, 157; Rev. F. D., 87
Gordon: Rev. John B., 118; Thomas, 116
Goshen (Baptist) Association, 148
Governor's Council of the Virginia Colony, 171
Grace (Episcopal) Church, Yorktown, 28-30, **28, 30**
Grace Episcopal Church, Kilmarnock, 67

Graham, Rev. William, 143
Grant, Andrew, 152
Grasty, Rev. John S., 161
Graves, Alexander, 38
Gray: Rev. Arthur P. Jr., 75; Rev. Daniel, 33; Rev. Samuel, 35, 160; Samuel, 33
Great Awakening, 126, 141
Great Fork Church, 179
Greenbriar County, 159
Green: Rev. Charles, 175; Robert, 179
"Greenway," 66
Gregory, Roger, 57
Griffin, Billy E., 149
Griffith, Dr. David, 154, 164
Grigg, Milton, 48
Grymes: Benjamin, 152; John, 38, 122
Gryms family, 81
Gum Spring, Virginia, 121, 122
Gum Tree, Virginia, 80
Gunn, Bishop George, 169
Gunnell, Henry, 154
Gunston Hall, 146, 175
Gwaltney, L. L., 128
Gwynn, Rev. John, 26

H
Hague, Virginia, 35
Hamburg, Virginia, 103
Hamilton Parish, 154, 176
Hammond, J., 87
Hampden-Sydney College, 123
Hampton Creek, 53
Hampton Parish, 29, 30, 50. *See also* York-Hampton Parish; Elizabeth City Parish
Hampton, Rev. Thomas, 30
Hampton, Virginia, 49, 50, 51, 52, 75
Hancock, John, 99
Handy, Dr. I. W. K., 118
Hankins family, 169
Hanover County: 32, 54, 55, 71, 80, 81, 120, 122, 123, 167; Courthouse, 55
Hanover, Germany, 55
Hanover Parish, 151, 157
Hardin, John, 183
Harper: Capt. John, 173; Edward, 173
Harper family, 173
Harrell, Ira S., 128
Harrison: Benjamin, 65; Benjamin (speaker of the House of Burgesses), 65; Benjamin (signer of the Declaration of Independence), 65; Dr. Elias, 171, 172, 173; E., 128; Elizabeth Burwell, 65; Pres. William, 65; Pres. Benjamin, 65; Reverend, 90; Rev. Jeptha, 161; William, 77
Harrison family, 66
Harris, Rev. William, 51
Hartfield, Virginia, 43

Hartford, Connecticut, 32
Harvard College, 23
Harvard, John, 23
Harvey: Gov. Sir John, 18, 29; Patsey, 160
Hastewood, John, 39
Hatch, Rev. Frederich, 120
Hawkston, England, 55
Hay, John, 128
Hays, Patrick, 116
Hayter, Rev. J. T. Jr., 161
Hazel River, 179
Heartease Creek, 71
Hebron (Israel), 101, 102
Hebron (Lutheran) Church, 100-102, **100, 102**
Hedges, Reverend, 13
Heffelfinger, Jacob, 50
Heiston, Abraham, 104
Henderson: Alexander, 155, 175; W. T., 149
Henley, James, 126
"Henning's Statutes at Large," 68
"Henrico Church on Richmond Hill." *See* St. John's Church, Richmond
Henrico County, 108, 109, 125
Henrico Parish, 109, 125, 126
Henricopolis, 109
Henrico, Virginia, 16, 18, 50, 125
Henry family, 81
Henry: John, 81; Patrick, 41, 55, 80, 81, 108, 109, 123; Rev. Patrick, 55
Henry, Prince, 125
Henshall, Mr., 168
Hepburn family, 173
Hepburn: Katherine, 80, 81; Parson S. S., 80, 81
Herring Creek, 65
Herrin, Woodrow W., 128
Heshaminy River, 141
Hewitt, Rev. Richard, 114
Hickman, Henry, 57
Hickory Neck Academy, 168
Hickory Neck (Episcopal) Church, 166-69, **166, 169**
Hickory Neck Historical Committee, 167
Hickory Neck School Society, 168
Higby, Rev. Thomas, 113
Higgenbotham, Fannie, 127
Hildebrandt, Rev. R. E., 118
Hindman, Rev. John, 116
Hipkins: John, 38; Samuel, 87
History of Henrico Parish, 126
History of Virginia from the First Settlement to the Dissolution of the London Company, 109
Hite: Isaac Jr., 183; Jacob, 183
Hoge, Rev. Moses, 143
Holdcroft, Mrs., 167
Holladay, Rev. J. M., 161
Holland, 101
Hollowing Creek Church, 81
Holt, Michael, 101

Holbrooke, Rev. John, 114
Holder, Richard, 35
Holker: John, 181; Maria, 181
Holladay, Anthony and Esther, 138
Holladay's Point Plantation, 138
Hooe: John, 152; Rice W., 152
Hoover, Pres. Herbert, 102
Hopewell, Virginia, 23
Houseman, Peter, 145
House, Michael, 101
House of Burgesses, 41, 68, 69, 74, 75, 97, 145
House of Delegates, 126
Houston: John, 143; Rev. R. R., 161; Sam, 143
Hovland, Rev. James M., 118
Howard: Gov. Francis, Baron of Effingham, 97; M. C., 112
Hubardto, Rev. William, 13
Huddle: Rev. and Mrs. William P., 102; Ruth Elizabeth, 102
Hudsdan, Rev. William, 13
Huffard, Robert, 132
Hughes: Rev. Thomas, 26; Will, 32
Hungars Neck, 112
Hungars Parish, 112, 113, 154
Hungars (Episcopal) Parish Church, 111-14, **111, 113, 114**
Hungry Church. *See* Deep Run Church
Hunter family, 173
Hunter: Hon. James, 48; P. S., 47
Hunting Creek, 93
Huntley, Francis, 179
Hunt: Rev. James, 122; Rev. Robert, 16, **19, 20,** 21
Huston, Robert, 142
Hutton, Malcolm M., 128

I
Ireland: 123; County Antrim, 116; Dublin, 116; Ulster, 141
Irvington, Virginia, 67, 68
Irwin, Rev. D. C., 143
Isle of Wight County, 12, 13
Issac Watts's Child's Catechism, 171
Ivy Hill Cemetery, 172

J
Jackson: Rev. Andrew, 106; Thomas, 32
Jacobs, Norman F., 149
James City County, Virginia: 16, 17, 18, 32, 41, 132, 166, 168; School Board, 168
James City, Virginia, 16, 17, 18, 32, 50
James, Duke of York, 30
James I, King of England, 16, 50, 125, 141
James II, King of England, 97
James River, 13, 16, 17, 23, 50, 53, 65, 77, 83, 90, 97, 109, 125, 132, 138, 148
James River Association, 149
James River Bridge, 147